SEASON OF THE WITCH

ALSO BY PETER BEBERGAL

The Faith Between Us (coauthored with Scott Korb)

Too Much to Dream: A Psychedelic American Boyhood

JEREMY P. TARCHER/PENGUIN

a member of Penguin Group (USA)

New York

SEASON OF THE WITCH

HOW THE OCCULT SAVED
ROCK AND ROLL

PETER BEBERGAL

JEREMY P. TARCHER/PENGUIN
Published by the Penguin Group
Penguin Group (USA) LLC
375 Hudson Street
New York, New York 10014

USA · Canada · UK · Ireland · Australia
New Zealand · India · South Africa · China

penguin.com
A Penguin Random House Company

Most Tarcher/Penguin books are available at special quantity discounts for bulk
purchase for sales promotions, premiums, fund-raising, and educational needs.
Special books or book excerpts also can be created to fit specific needs.
For details, write: Special.Markets@us.penguingroup.com.

Library of Congress Cataloging-in-Publication Data

Bebergal, Peter.
Season of the witch : how the occult saved rock and roll / by Peter Bebergal.
    p.   cm.
Includes bibliographical references and index.
ISBN 978-0-399-16766-9
1. Rock music—History and criticism.   2. Music and occultism.   3. Mysticism in
music.   4. Music—Philosophy and aesthetics.   I. Title.
    ML3534.B38   2014   2014027012
                781.66—dc23

Printed in the United States of America
1   3   5   7   9   10   8   6   4   2

Book design by Lauren Kolm

For my father, my captain, my friend, Byron Leon Bebergal
(1928–2014)

CONTENTS

My hair is holy. I grow it long for the God.

—EURIPIDES, *The Bacchae*

WE ARE ALL INITIATES NOW

I

In 1978 my older brother had just joined the air force, leaving me access to the mysteries of his room. The suburbs of southern Florida were row after row of single-level ranch houses and manicured lawns. I was eleven, filled with restless, inexplicable feelings. It was just before the dawn of puberty. Except for what I could glean from my brother's dirty magazines, sex was still an abstraction. Some other secret thing was beckoning. I had caught glimpses when I heard the music coming from his room, so different from my own small collection of Bay City Rollers and Bee Gees 45s. One by one, I began to play his records, holding the sleeves in my lap, trying to learn the grammar of this new musical language. I was not quite prepared for what I found. His music made me feel hot and cold at the same time, a small fire starting in my belly while shivers ran up my spine. Here was a seductive and impenetrable catalogue of arcane and occult symbols, of magic and mystical pursuits, of strange rituals involving sex, spaceships, and faeries. I went into his room looking to hear some real rock and roll. I came out spellbound and hypnotized by the spectacle.

The record collection was a lexicon of the gods: the Beatles, Led Zeppelin, David Bowie, Arthur Brown, King Crimson, Hawkwind, Yes, Black Sabbath, and Pink Floyd. Already immersed in the arcana of the 1970s by way of J. R. R. Tolkien reprints, Dungeons & Dragons—almost universally known as D&D—*Heavy Metal* magazine, horror comics, and the animated films of Ralph Bakshi, I sat in long hours of deep listening, studying the lyrics, the album cover art, and even the hidden messages etched into the inner ring of the vinyl. I searched for the clues to Paul McCartney's rumored death and felt the chill of ghosts staring out from the cover of *Abbey Road*, the barefoot Beatle unwittingly symbolizing his own demise through some terrible necromancy. I held the vinyl of *Led Zeppelin III* up to the light so I could search for the fabled occult missive carved into the record's inner ring: "Do what thou wilt." I stared in nervous fascination at the various characters inhabited by David Bowie and tried to crack the mystery of his lyrics that told of aliens, Aleister Crowley, and supergods who are "guardians of a loveless isle." Black Sabbath was formed by sorcerers, working their dark art through heavy doom-laden riffs. Arthur Brown admitted he was the "god of hellfire."

The music became a fixture of my psyche. I thought I alone had uncovered a well of arcane truth, like the paperback *Necronomicon* that sat on my bookshelf. There was something both transcendent and abysmal lurking within the grooves of these records and the fantastic lives of the characters inhabiting them. Roger Dean's artwork on Yes albums were landscapes once populated by ancient races, their arcane wisdom lost, sunken like Atlantis. At the other end of the spectrum was the Beatles' impenetrable and terrifying penultimate song on the *White Album*, "Revolution 9," a spoken-word, feedback-infused collage of hidden occult messages suggesting a palpable violence. These often opposing qualities nonetheless shared a common thread: they referenced a reality beyond normal perception, a vast metaverse inhabited by demons and angels, aliens and ancient sorcerers, all of which could be accessed by potentially dangerous methods such as magic, drugs, and maybe even sex. But I also sensed the peril in reading too deeply into these songs and albums. The film *Helter Skelter*, often shown on the UHF channels' late-night movie programs, taught me that fixating on a band's life and work can sometimes take a fanatical turn. In this instance, an album helped to precipitate a murderous call to arms when Charles Manson believed the Beatles were sending him secret, violent messages through their music. Although the connection between the music and the murders was overblown, my adolescent self couldn't shake the feeling there *was something* to the Beatles' songs that made this kind of interpretation possible. And sure, it was crazy to think so and everyone knew it wasn't true, but maybe, just maybe . . . Paul really was dead.

Despite my ambivalence about my teenage fantasies, my brother's albums really were a glimpse into the sometimes explicit, sometimes hidden occult language of rock, a window into the pervasive influence of magic and mysticism on the most essential and influential art form of the twentieth century. Within a single collection representing a microcosm of rock history and styles was another hidden story, of how rock—its songs and its staging, its lyrics and its pyrotechnics—have been shaped by magical and mystical symbols, ideas, and practices.

Like many teenagers in those days, I wondered if magic really did exist outside the lists of spells in the D&D *Player's Handbook*. I bought books on white magic and lit candles, making sure the window was open so as to not alert my mother, who was ever on the lookout for the danger of an open flame. My friends and I dimmed the lights and hovered our fingers over the plastic planchette of my Ouija board. Nothing seemed to manifest. I could not pull out of thin air the potent feelings that came from those records. There was magic here, but it was even bigger than I could have imagined. From between the gatefold covers, from the vinyl tucked snugly into the sleeves, an enchantment had been woven that bewitched all of popular culture.

I didn't know it then, but I was a participant in a vast cultural phenomenon. The Beatles had already converted an entire generation of listeners whose ideas about spirituality would be shaped by LSD, tarot cards, and free copies of the Bhagavad Gita handed out by young Hare Krishna devotees. As I listened to *Houses of the Holy* in my brother's room, Led Zeppelin had already shaped rock's imagination about the power of the magical arts. And only a few years earlier, progressive rock bands had fashioned dreams of inner and outer space, offering otherworldly hope at the closing of the Aquarian dream.

Rock had used a cloak of glamour in the original use of the word: an enchantment. *Glamour* is even related to the word *grammar*, which was sometimes used to denote occult language, the verbal weaving of a spell, and eventually became *grimoire,* a book of magic. Just as in stage magic, where the audience allows itself to be tricked, to be seduced by the illusion, rock and roll has fed off a similar instinct. A person's willingness to be tricked is how the palm reader plies the trade, the shaman hypnotizes the tribe, and why I listened to those songs and gazed at those album covers in wonder and excitement, certain I was unlocking a chamber where a magical artifact was hidden.

Those days sitting cross-legged on my brother's floor were an initiation into a mystery cult, where I would become a disciple of rock and roll. Throughout my teenage years, rock was the musical narrative of my inner life. There was always an album that spoke perfectly to whatever inscrutable feelings I was negotiating at the time. Rock's often sphinxlike truths were the key to not only my own inner life; they could open the door into other mysterious realms. Eventually I stopped searching for esoteric riddles on album covers and in song lyrics, but I never ceased being aware of where the occult imagination was at play. It's a plot I've been following ever since I first opened the gatefold cover to David Bowie's *Diamond Dogs* album to the grotesquely erotic painting of a caninesque Bowie, half man, half dog. I came to realize that magic cannot exist without a conduit, a means of expression. And even if it can, I am not interested in the metaphysics of the occult. I believe in those horned gods only when I hear them speaking from out of the grooves in the vinyl, the shiny surface of a CD, and even in the sonic reduction of the MP3. And in those moments they are as real as the music itself. I don't need the magic to be anywhere else. It exists as the most potent spell in the awesome spectacle of rock and roll.

II

At pivotal moments in its development, rock musicians and their audiences together made an almost unconscious pact to expand their consciousness and push beyond the restraints of traditional American music and its underlying spiritual identity. The occult became rock's very salvation then, taking possession of the imagination of rock musicians and their fans, and redefining popular music and culture. Moreover, the occult imagination saved rock and roll from sugary teenybopper purgatory and urged musicians, engineers, and producers to look beyond the conventional toward the possibility of raising the collective spiritual consciousness into the astral planes. The occult imbued rock with an immortal soul that continues to resonate in Western culture, and musicians and their audiences continue to feed off one another, looking for deeper meaning as a way to make sense of the primal and ancient urges that rock and roll has always evoked.

Rock is the sound of both spiritual and musical rebellion, and for the long and continuing history of this most indispensable of musical forms, these two things have become inseparable. What is it about rock, more than any other art form of the modern age, that makes it such a perfect vehicle for this ancient and often unconscious drive to penetrate the veil between the phenomenal world and the numinous realm of the spirit? Why have so many musicians staged their rock concerts to appear as moments of shamanic and religious rites and created personas simulating magicians, demons, the gods Pan and Dionysus, even appearing as people possessed by gods or devils or worse? Why have they covered their album covers with images of the occult, conjured their lyrics out of the stuff of legend and myth, and even in their personal lives sought their own mystical and magical experiences? Why have they performed shows in front of ancient relics?

Rock's spiritual affinity with occultism is due in large part to the nature of the occult itself. The occult—the popular term for a wide range of spiritual beliefs and activities concerned with supernatural, Gnostic, magical, and mystical ideas—operates within an unorthodox, nonconformist, and sometimes heretical temple, worshipping in ways at odds with the traditional and established religious order. These practices are an attempt by the individual or group to take a more active role in their own spiritual destiny, to commune with the divine through some form of intercession. Spirits, divination, amulets, charms, and even the worship of other deities feel direct and experiential.

This purposeful drive toward a divine encounter has surfaced in various manifestations throughout history and all over the world: in the Jewish mystics of medieval Europe, in the American Pentecostal Christians, and in the American appropriation of Buddhism and yoga. Christianity would often see this impulse as the work of the devil, even within its own ranks. Renaissance magicians and alchemists such as Giordano Bruno were called heretics, and later Lutheran and other American Christian sects would look on snake handlers and those who spoke in tongues as liars at best, devil worshippers at worst. In many cases, it was Christianity that perpetuated a belief in a pagan lineage through laws against magic and more active and often false accusations such as the infamous witch trials. The use of occult fears for political gains only prolonged superstitions and the other beliefs that religious authorities claimed to be trying to eradicate. Christianity would seal the pagan chamber completely, even as it defined itself by appropriating pagan myths such as the solstice and a resurrecting god. As the instinct for ecstatic experience continued to bubble up, it became by definition heterodox. The original intention of this kind of authentic practice, once organized around communities with rituals bordering on the theatrical and the hypnotic, was mostly lost.

Until rock and roll.

The phenomenon is modern, but rock's soul was burnished in the fires of ancient mystery cults, when myth and initiation were fused in a potent mix of dance, intoxication, and other forms of ecstatic revelry. But despite the spectacle of this kind of worship, it's still a simple human need being played out in theatrical ways: it's the desire for community, for myth and ritual, and for direct communion with the divine.

It's best to imagine the occult roots of rock as an estuary. While early rock and roll can be traced directly to the blues, gospel, and folk, rock's overall development was also shaped by jazz, experimental and early electronic music, and even classical strains. In each of these influences the occult is also present, often exhibiting the same characteristic: artists looking for ways to revolt against convention by using the occult as both an inspiration and a vehicle for their ideas. While rock is essentially a recent phenomenon, it does not exist in a vacuum of modern human experience. Rock is an aspect of the ancient impulse to hammer out sounds on whatever tools are available, to express what it means to be human. For millennia, making music has been inseparable from religious activity. Rock and roll's origins are in the blues and folk—forms of music deeply engrained with Christian traditions and values, but whose own roots grew in the soil where other gods were worshipped. As popular music developed, it struggled with this tension between Puritanism and the shadow of other non-Christian traditions that were just as much a part of American music.

Just as religious traditions have always sought to make sense of their own pagan origins—usually by prohibiting and de-monizing the old gods—ministers, parents, and record-burning mobs saw in rock the threat of sex and chaos. Rock's response was its true salvation: musicians pushed out further, conjuring spirits with power chords. When rock was finding its electric sound and its hormonal teenage audience, it chose sex as its expression of agitation. This was its first claim to autonomy, a wriggle of the hips in the face of the religious hierarchy. As rock critic Dan Graham explains: "Rock turned the values of traditional religion on their head. To rock 'n' roll meant to have sex . . . NOW." Because the mainstream church often saw sex as a symptom of ungodliness and the influence of evil spirits, rock musicians felt the good burn of rebellion as they plugged in their amps, calling out to a greater salvation than Christian redemption: "When the chimes ring five, six, and seven, / We'll be right in seventh heaven."

Rock's erotic tension gave it the label of devil's music, its very soul seen as having been burnished in the fires of one of the first sins: human sexual awareness. Rock's first words were sexual, drawn from deeply explicit blues lyrics and the very physicality of its rhythms, themselves arising out of ancient soil. As the American slaves were developing their own form of Christianity that used song as the essential form of worship, they tread carefully even as they incorporated African tribal music and movement. Slaves would shuffle around in a circle, calling out and shaking in the throes of religious ecstasy, but their feet had to remain on the floor, lest they be accused of turning their precise religious devotion into the most profane pastime: dancing. Unless it is glorifying God, music is profane and solicits dancing, one of the most sexually charged pastimes. And where sex is, the devil is winking nearby.

Fear is a funny thing, though. It often titillates and strengthens the rumors and stories that engender it. We want to feel afraid, and the supernatural and the occult have long provided a tempting morsel, particularly with people and things that defy convention or place themselves outside the mainstream. People have long believed music contained some enchanted attributes, something that could electrify the listener as well as the player. Rumors of the occult, particularly stories of deals with the devil, both attract and repel. The famed early nineteenth-century violinist Paganini was believed by peasants to be possessed by the devil for his masterful and ecstatic playing of Satan's favorite instrument. During a concert in Vienna, one audience member was said to have seen the devil actually standing next to Paganini, guiding his fingers along the strings. Rumors of Paganini selling his soul to the devil did not keep devout Italian Catholics away from his music. While it a took a mental toll on the musician, who wanted to be recognized for his own talent, it added to his reputation and increased the size of audiences at his concerts.

There was also a deeply racist subtext in Christian leaders' reign of fire against rock music. Rock's earliest manifestations drew directly from the blues, gospel, and even African American spirituals, all of these seen as incarnations of the perceived barbarism and ungodliness of black Americans, many of whom it was believed had sinister intentions regarding the white daughters of America.

Rock musicians had still not given it an explicit name, using sex as a means of spiritual transgression until the planets aligned in the 1960s and sexual liberation, antiwar protests, and other social movements collided. In this climate, musicians and fans alike would blow their music and their minds with LSD, opening up a cultural third eye exposing them to alternative religious and occult practice. It was a shot heard round the world in song, such as the spirituality of the Beatles' "Tomorrow Never Knows," one the first great mystical moments in popular music. By the 1970s the word *occult* had become fairly well attached to the then burgeoning New Age movement, which attempted to draw, from various beliefs and practices, an all-inclusive spiritual tool kit for the masses. "Take what you need and leave the rest" was the note attached to the inner lid of Pandora's box, in which you could find mantras, crystals, tarot cards, a smattering of magic by way of the Kabbalah and Wicca, quantum physics, ancient aliens, all wrapped in a cloth of cosmic mysticism. New Age and the occult became mostly synonymous in popular culture. Until the word *occult* was dropped, New Age often summoned up a darker spirit, such as Satan worshippers, strange sex rituals, and black magic. Now the term "New Age" invokes images of angelic messengers and the piano pecking of George Winston.

All the essential rock genres, from heavy metal to progressive, from glam to goth, gathered their wool from the occult's harvest. Magic and mysticism gave rock its sure footing even as it took the greatest leap of faith and plunged into the abyss. It could have gone another way and become merely a fusion of American blues and folk without its own real identity. Instead, the biggest names in popular music willingly participated in this spiritual rebellion and in so doing crafted rock's mythic soul. The Beatles, Led Zeppelin, David Bowie, King Crimson, Black Sabbath, Yes, and even the Rolling Stones, among many others, not only transformed rock with their musical innovations, but saved rock from becoming a series of radio-friendly 45s spinning out endless redundant chords.

These bands transmitted an ancient echo that is an essential part of human culture and expression, an imperative to reach beyond convention and strain to hear the music of the spheres. All of popular culture was triggered. Even producers and DJs were forced to rethink what was sellable, and soon found a willing audience pouring money into the music industry. And even when the musicians themselves insisted it was all just a marketing game, they helped carve out a pop culture mythology.

To describe how the occult imagination is the vital force of rock and rock culture, I will engage in a series of narratives. The true conversion didn't happen overnight. There is no single album or performance that serves as a lodestar. There have been many musicians who perfectly possess the spirit of the old gods, but are not necessarily representative of the occult current being traced here. Jim Morrison was called an "electric shaman" by the media and his fans. Morrison's stage performances were hypnotic, and at points he seemed to be inhabited by the spirit of a Native American shaman. In the 1970s, Patti Smith would take on the mantle when her friend William Burroughs said Smith is "a shaman . . . someone in touch with other levels of reality." Other examples abound, and while they help cast a wide net over the subject, they are blips, shiny objects leading into Alice's rabbit hole. In a photograph taken by his then bandmate Andy Summers, Sting is lying with his arm draped over his forehead, looking into the hidden distance, a paperback copy of an unnamed Aleister Crowley book tucked under his other hand. The black-and-white photo is compelling, a glimpse into the offstage interests of a musician. The photo was published in a collection titled *Throb*, in 1983, just as the Police were coming out of the storm of their chart-topping album *Ghost in the Machine* and releasing *Synchronicity*. The pop darling Daryl Hall insisted on recording *Sacred Songs*, an album inspired by Aleister Crowley—particularly the book *Magick Without Tears*—a musical release that would almost cost Hall a label contract as well as his professional and personal relationship with his partner, John Oates. The progressive rock band Tool has incorporated ritual magic, sacred geometry, and other esoteric practices into their recording sessions and live shows. These are all effective illustrations, and they are also a clue as to how vast a subject rock and roll and the occult really is.

It would be futile to list every album employing a penta-gram, a devil's visage, a sigil, or some other mystical or occult symbol; to name every song that references wizards and war-locks, devils and demons, tarot cards and fortune-tellers, karma, past lives, alien saviors, or Aleister Crowley; to examine every musician that has ever dabbled in the occult. What I have opted for instead is a narrative history, drawing on key moments in the development of rock and roll, from its origins in African American slave songs up until the ascendancy of electronic in-struments in the 1980s. Along the way, some well-known names will make an appearance, and among them some lesser-known ones will rear their heads. The hope is by focusing on particular musicians and bands at certain moments in time, a larger narra-tive will emerge. My aim is not to upend or challenge the ac-cepted history of rock (in all its various permutations) but to show that weaving in and out of the most important moments of rock's development is the occult, the central thread that, if pulled out, would unravel the whole intricate design.

I also hope to reveal that these musicians are human after all and their magical and mystical aspirations are a microcosm of a greater American spiritual hunger. But there is dark paradox here. Many artists saw their lives turned upside down by fame and excess. The occult provided a grammar through which to make sense of their almost inexplicable lives. These are the tales of musicians and magicians, rock fans and rock's detractors, the light shining from a creative spiritual quest and the darkness finding its way in when mixed with drugs and fame. These stories serve as a window exposing how without the occult imagination there would be no rock as we know it.

III

There is no satisfactory definition of the occult, especially since the term carries so much baggage. Believers in certain occult ideas will often claim there is a direct transmission from the ancients in the way of coded writings, mediums, and even aliens. The *Corpus Hermeticum*, for example, is an Egyptian collection of texts dating to around the second or third century, a synthesis of Gnostic Christianity, Neoplatonism, and Greek and Roman cultic myths. The texts contain alchemical, magical, and astrological teachings, but at their heart, they describe a universe where human beings are divine and unity with God is the true destiny of creation. The *Corpus* has found its way into any number of occult and magical teachings, such as the popular idea often expressed as "so above, so below." During the Renaissance it was attributed to a named figure, Hermes Trismegistus. It's likely the character was an invented, albeit brilliantly conceived, combination of the Greek god Hermes and the Egyptian deity Thoth, both messenger gods who enjoy writing and magic.

Nevertheless, many modern-day adherents of the *Corpus* claim, despite all the evidence to the contrary, that these texts were written by one sage belonging to a single ancient-Egyptian mystery cult. Others have tried to prove witchcraft was part of an actual religious lineage that began in the ancient world and spread through Europe, eventually landing in modern-day Wiccan and neo-pagan communities. Unfortunately, there is no direct path for the occult as a belief. It twisted and turned through the ages, seemingly disappearing entirely, only to spring up when people once again sought something—some meaning or experience—that the Church or other religious authorities could not provide.

On the other side are the detractors who claim the occult is not to be taken seriously, especially in an age when science and reason have all but made religion, and any beliefs in the supernatural, irrelevant. Particularly for those who think religion is something with no value, the occult has even less, being something more akin to superstition: an irrational, silly trend. Religion at least has shaped civilizations and culture. The religious imagination bore the music of Bach, the Sistine Chapel, and even *The Lion, the Witch and the Wardrobe*. For good or ill, it's something to be reckoned with. But the occult is a distraction for dreamy-eyed New Agers and stoned teenage metal heads. The occult is even more of a fool's game than religion.

A more balanced definition is one that takes into account the remarkable influence occult beliefs have had on culture while also recognizing that these beliefs are themselves a conglomerate of bits of mythology, religion, and actual experience, which often take the form of mystical or other states of altered consciousness. Despite its darker connotation, the occult is merely a set of practices and beliefs—some stretching back to antiquity, others of a more recent vintage—that attempt to understand reality (spiritual or otherwise) in a way traditional religious practice cannot or chooses not to explore. More often than not, occult practices are in direct response to traditional religious practice and derive their language and beliefs from those practices. In this respect then, the occult is a spectrum of beliefs and actions seeking to understand God, nature, or the cosmos in a way at odds with normative or mainstream religious communities. These practices attempt to place some measure of control into human hands. The gods are too fickle, and evil too ever present. A charm over a door to ward off malevolent spirits might work even better than a prayer. Even mainstream religious communities used occult methods, even as they sought to outlaw them. The gargoyles of Notre Dame and other cathedrals, for example, are wards, willful attempts to trick devils into believing these locations are already occupied by their kind and to go looking for some other place to infest.

The occult has also found expression in art, music, and literature. I would argue that these things, more than any magical ceremony in a lodge or grove, are the surest and possibly most authentic expressions. Occult and esoteric religious ideas have long held the fascination of artists. In the late 1800s there was what is called the Occult Revival when a number of artists, society people, and intellectuals were joining magical fraternities (the poet W. B. Yeats and the Welsh writer Arthur Machen were both members of the Hermetic Order of the Golden Dawn). The Symbolist art movement of that time was deeply inspired by occult symbolism such as the Renaissance-period alchemical emblems used by magicians to meditate on occult ideas through a complex system of signs they believed activated the spiritual center of the magus. The early twentieth-century artist Austin Osman Spare would go on to become an influential magician, having devised his own system of what is known as sigil magic, an extension of his artwork. It was composers and musicians, however, who defied convention by seeking nontraditional (often non-Christian) spiritual ideas and experiences that aligned with their musical innovations. The composer friends Erik Satie and Claude Debussy both joined the Kabbalistic Order of the Rose-Cross, a mystical fraternity. This would extend into the mid-century, particularly with experimental composers. Pierre Schaeffer, the father of musique concrète, was a devotee of the Russian mystic George Ivanovitch Gurdjieff. The electronic music vanguard Karlheinz Stockhausen studied Eastern mysticism and once claimed he received his musical education in the Sirius star system.

It makes more sense, then, to talk about the occult imagination rather than the occult purely as a belief system. The occult imagination may express itself as magical ritual, but it is just as likely to express itself as symbolic elements in art. Moreover, the occult imagination is at work when something is perceived as being driven by supernatural purpose, as in the case of a Christian televangelist finding devilish intent in a rock band's lyrics. The ground on which intention and perception get conflated is where culture is created. Rock and roll is the fertile soil where this landscape has flowered and grown in remarkable ways. And it is here the occult becomes a metaphor for resisting customs, for challenging the status quo, and for staking a claim for individuals taking control of their own destinies, often in the face of extreme cultural homogenization. If the occult is a current needing a river to take it to the oceans of the world, then rock is the raging waterway that made it possible. And rock found in the occult imagination a sure spiritual partner that could help it defy convention.

What is needed, then, is a grand story, the story that represents the archetypes that rock so beautifully encapsulates.

Having a story act as an overarching metaphor also helps to steer this examination toward myth and away from metaphysics. While I will need to discuss things like gods and demons, divination and devils, magic and UFOs, I make no claims about the reality of these things, only that they are powerful ideas that persist, and, for reasons I hope to establish, have found a particularly potent mode of expression in rock music. So to guide my hand away from any kind of claim for or against the occult, I will keep one of the great myths close by.

IV

The last thing you want to do is anger the god of madness, but this is exactly what the prince of Thebes had done. Dionysus had come to the great city with his female entourage, the maenads. The charismatic god of wine and ecstasy was in Thebes to avenge the reputation of his mother, Semele, as well as the dismissal of his own divine origins. Dionysus is called the "god who arrives." No matter how you might try to avoid, ignore, or otherwise banish him, he will appear in your midst eventually. Many years before, Zeus—ever on the lookout for mortals to bed—took Semele as his lover. Semele gossiped with her sisters about her energetic lovemaking with Zeus. If he really was a god, they teased, he should prove it. Semele, embarrassed and maybe a little doubtful herself, begged Zeus to reveal his true nature. He refused, saying that she could not withstand being in the presence of an unclothed divine being. So Semele put off his advances until the frustrated god gave her what she asked. She was incinerated on the spot. But Semele was pregnant, and at the moment of her immolation, Zeus plucked the baby from her womb and sewed it into his thigh to one day be born as Dionysus.

Semele's family came to live in Thebes where her sister Agave's son Pentheus was king. When Dionysus entered the city, he quickly possessed his aunt Agave and her sisters, turning them into bacchante, wild women who fled from the city into the hills to dance with the maenads, satyrs, and Dionysus himself. The king rebuked them and outlawed the worship of Dionysus. The god himself, disguised as one of his own priests, was promptly arrested. Pentheus mocked him, but over the course of their conversation, the cracks began to show. Pentheus appeared to be obsessed with the orgiastic rites of the maenads and the bacchante even as he spat on their beliefs. Dionysus advised Pentheus to spy on the women to learn their secret rituals and better know his enemy; the deity also suggested that the king dress as a woman to mingle among the maenads and the bacchante. Pentheus was stirred into a flurry of excitement; he dressed in drag and made his way outside the city to where the women were dancing. But they saw him for who he was and tore him apart, his own mother taking his head, believing it to be a lion, the final curse on the house of Semele's family.

This telling of the Dionysus myth is largely taken from the ancient Greek play *The Bacchae* by Euripides, a piece of literature often used to demonstrate the relationship between religious ritual and theater. And what is rock if not theater, particularly in the moments that reshaped and ultimately solidified the mythos of popular music. Theater is where gender easily becomes fluid, and like Pentheus, who eagerly masquerades in drag to witness the god's beautiful frenzy, rock musicians warped and weaved their sexuality. It can be seen in Robert Plant's masculine gracefulness, David Bowie's hermaphroditic aliens, Mick Jagger's tumescent lips, and Patti Smith's binary swagger.

Rock also taps into the Dionysian principle in its tragic forms. Pentheus secretly wants to participate in the secret rites, but he is not properly initiated. He wants the thrill without the sacrifice, but the god demands it, and so Pentheus is destroyed. This is rock's perpetual misfortune, where the lure of the ecstatic—often by way of intoxication—resulted in various forms of tragedy, including madness and death.

It's in the Dionysian intoxicating madness that the human drive for creative freedom was born and where rock would one day derive its essential vitality. The archetype of Dionysus reveals that the earliest roots of rock and roll's spirit are pagan at its core. Rock channels, through some mechanism of the unconscious (or maybe it really is magic after all), the faces of the old gods—of Dionysus and even others such as Pan and Hecate—of the mystery cults, where libation and dance are the vehicles through which one worships and experiences transcendence. So it is Dionysus haunting these proceedings—not a god one chooses to worship lightly. He is a god who will demand that you twist and shout your way across the hills, banging on your drum or whatever instrument is at hand. Don't worry if the music is any good or not. All it has to be is loud enough to annoy the neighbors. They might even peek out their windows to see what all the noise is about, and maybe even let their hair grow long and join the revelry.

CHAPTER 1

(YOU MAKE ME WANNA) SHOUT

I

If you want to learn to play guitar, find a crossroads and wait there at midnight. If you are patient, "a large black man" will emerge from the gloom. It could be Papa Legba, a Haitian deity whose strange origins lie in the religion known as vodou. Legba is the guardian of the spirit world, and you must first treat him with respect if you expect to gain any favor from the *orisha*, the spirits who are expressions of the creator god. It could also be Eshu, a West African Yoruba god who is a messenger, trickster, and the guardian of pathways. He will take your guitar and tune it in such a way so when you play it, you will be gifted with a preternatural power to play the blues. If you tell someone about it, they will surely think you unwittingly sold your soul to the devil, for who else would seemingly bestow you with such a momentous gift without actually asking for anything in return? When your time comes, they will tell you, you must answer to

Old Scratch himself. But they would be wrong. It's not the devil who waits at the crossroads. In their long journey from Africa to the southern United States, Legba and Eshu slowly transformed into something sinister, warping the dark trickster gods at the spiritual source of the blues and later fighting for their rightful place as rock and roll looked to them for its own wild designs.

The legend of musicians selling their souls at the crossroads has become the creation myth for the popular association of rock with the occult. It is typically attributed to the life and legend of one young man; the poor, black Robert Johnson, whose influence on rock and roll is unsurpassed, was said to have made the deal that would give him uncanny proficiency on the guitar but would also doom him to a death at the age of twenty-seven. The story of Johnson meeting the devil has become popular music's stock parable for a Faustian bargain that ultimately ends in disaster. Curiously, the original story was likely not about Robert Johnson at all, but about the Mississippi blues singer Tommy Johnson. He sang in a ghostly falsetto that suggested otherworldliness, and he fostered this by putting out the rumor that he'd received his vocal gift from the devil at a crossroads, a story perpetuated by his brother LeDell and pulled deep into the history and mythology of the blues.

The crossroads legend, despite its pervasiveness, is merely symptomatic of a deeper occult strain swimming in the undercurrent of rock and roll. Despite the story not originating with Robert Johnson, the legendary guitarist was still wading in a bayou of voodoo and Christianity. One of Johnson's most well-known songs, "Cross Road Blues," makes no mention of the devil, but it was believed to be his confessional that something happened to him at the devil's favored location. Most scholars and critics now agree that the song is about something just as common as the devil: riding the rail in search of better luck and a less baleful fate. Nevertheless, Johnson was still part of a culture knee-deep in a swamp of superstition.

The devil is often a stand-in for any non-Christian deity that might pose a threat to the conventional Judeo-Christian narrative, and it was no different in the American South in the hundred years or so leading up to the time of Robert Johnson and the blues. It began in 1820 when a Yoruban by the name of Ajayi was captured by the Fulani people, who had come to dominate much of West Africa in the nineteenth century. It was common practice for Africans to sell other tribal people into slavery, and Ajayi was only thirteen years old when he found himself bound in chains on a ship heading to Portugal. A ship belonging to a British antislave group stopped the Portuguese vessel and was able to secure the rescue of the captured Africans on board, who were then taken to Sierra Leone, where antislavery Christians had begun to gather and settle. There, the young man was exposed to a Christian missionary and soon converted. He was mentored in the church by Samuel Crowther (whose name he adopted as his own), ordained in 1843, and later became a missionary himself. And what better place to begin than in his homeland, where he knew the people, the customs, and the language?

To make sure his message would be well received, Samuel Ajayi Crowther began work on a translation of the Bible into the Yoruban tongue. But there were challenges. Crowther wanted the new Bible to feel Yoruban. Afraid it might appear as an alien text, he made sure it embraced the authentic culture of the Yoruban people. To this end, Crowther also borrowed from the Yoruban religion and in so doing shaped the culture of American music and preserved something he had hoped to eliminate. For the Yoruban people, there was no word corresponding to the biblical word for Satan or the devil. So Crowther chose the name for the Yoruban deity who had similar characteristics, at least from a nineteenth-century Christian viewpoint: it would be Eshu, the trickster god of the crossroads.

The consequences of Crowther's shell game were immense. Given that the beliefs of African religion were transmitted orally, it would be impossible to trace exactly what route this new Eshu-in-devil's-clothing would take in the journey across the Atlantic, but if we follow the religion's beliefs overall, eventually we are sure to find him waiting at the crossroads somewhere in the American South. By the time we get there, though, Satan has taken his place.

Eshu first appears outside of Africa as the *orisha* known as Legba in Haiti. Here, the African slaves practiced vodou, a tradition blending the religion of the Fon people of West Africa known as vodun with the French Catholicism of their masters. Vodun and the Yoruba religion share some essential features, not the least of which is the figure of this trickster deity that acts as an intermediary between this world and the spirits. As for Catholicism, this brand of Christianity made perfect sense to a people who saw their own spirits performing the same function as saints; intercessors who could be prayed to for various human needs, such as curing illness, changing the course of luck gone bad, or even exorcising other ill-tempered entities. And like the *orisha*, Catholic saints each have their own symbol, often a plant, animal, or something akin to a charm or amulet. In fact, saints were combined with various African spirits based on the similarities of their symbolic objects.

During the thirteen-year-long Haitian revolution of French slaves from 1791 to 1804, vodou was the spiritual heart of the revolt, and many believed the magic of their homeland would empower them. Numerous freed blacks, slaves, and slave owners fled to Louisiana and helped to increase the already swelling black population. The complex aspects of vodou intermingled with the stew of other beliefs and practices, including Evangelical Christianity, occult practices molded out of the Yoruba religion, and European superstitions. Together these elements would come to be popularly known as voodoo.

Even before the slaves brought vodun to Louisiana, the African deities had already begun their decline as important intermediaries with the transcendent creator god in Yoruba (known as Olorun) to devils and even Satan himself. The Western view of African religion was filtered through fear and racism. Even those who considered themselves scientists viewed their subjects as though studying a strange nonhuman creature. In 1849, David Christy, a member of the American Colonization Society, gave a lecture to the Ohio House of Representatives titled "A Lecture on African Colonization," in which he argues against the slave trade and proposes instead to "civilize and Christianize Africa." Whenever the chance arises, Christy refers to their beliefs as superstitious and barbaric, in need of Christian cleansing. Between the subtle psychological conflation of the African trickster god with the Christian devil, as well as the deliberate attempt to paint African religion as backward, it is no surprise that for African Americans there was a troubled negotiation between their newly adopted Christianity and stories and folktales that survived from Africa. Music became the location where the lines were clearly drawn. Inside the church is the music of a promised salvation; outside the church the devil lurks. In the American South, it was difficult to separate the devil from those traditions that had been passed along, so while certain occult practices continued, the real magic was spread through whispers and gossip. Like all occult phenomena, tracing what was actually practiced as opposed to what was rumored can be difficult.

In the American South, people spoke in hushed tones about conjurers, spells, and gris-gris—small bags containing objects such as pubic hair or bone that served as talismans—and they may even have paid someone to cast a luck charm or to help ward off evil. Their Christianity did not preclude people from accepting there was power in another kind of belief, even though such practices would be intolerable within the actual church community. Voodoo also offered a direct and unmediated way to try and change one's conditions. In his masterful book *Slave Religion*, Albert J. Raboteau explains why conjure (magic) was so attractive to the slave despite, for example, the Christian prohibition against it: "Not only was conjure a theory for explaining the mystery of evil, but it was also a practice for doing something about it." The post–Civil War South continued to see voodoo practices, but it is likely many African Americans didn't call it by name. Folk beliefs become so familiar, and so habitual, they can seem mundane, just parts of living requiring attending to.

For the Christian South, distrustful of anything that did not conform to the church and suspicious of secular music in general, the blues was a perfect storm, a tempest challenging the idea that an American black identity had to be bound up in the church. From its earliest days, the blues were seen as the devil's music, a secular pastime bumping up directly against the sacred music of the church, which by this time was mostly gospel. The blues were not about salvation, faith, or redemption but about worldly things. While borrowing much of its musical rudiments from slave spirituals, the blues were psychologically in tune to the songs sung in the fields and on the rail. Work was not the stuff of church and, particularly post–Civil War, did not have theological implications as it had when blacks were slaves and their labor would be rewarded with heavenly salvation. Work songs for the freed blacks were honest in the way the work was honest, pure labor under the hot sun: "Oh, I b'lieve I git religion an' jine de church / I'll be a black-jack preacher, an' not have to work."

As the blues developed, ever more liberated from the church, sex and relationships became the preferred topic. Some of the more explicit songs were performed by women artists, which only highlighted how much the blues were also about personal agency and didn't need to conform to Christian ideals about the place of the sexes. The Delta blues singer Lucille Bogan's 1935 song "Shave 'em Dry," for example, not only placed the power of sex with the woman, but drew a clear line in the sand: the blues might be the music of black folk, but it is not black church music: "I got nipples on my titties, big as the end of my thumb, / I got somethin' between my legs'll make a dead man come." Most blues songs are not this sexually explicit, but they are emotionally explicit, dealing plainly with love's gains and loss. As the late writer and poet LeRoi Jones (later known as Amiri Baraka) explains, the blues humanized the slave songs by making the hopes and suffering more earthbound and not simply a part of a great cosmic drama. And while the blues often suggest that the trouble is merely bad luck that befalls you, there was something you could do about it, if only to locate the source of misfortune: hoodoo inserted agency and will into the black spiritual identity. Personal agency, however, was often in opposition to the will of God. For example, if you didn't have much talent for playing the guitar, well, this was just the hand God dealt you. It wasn't for you to make any kind of deal behind his back.

If you are heartsick over a lover who has run away, Jesus can't help, but a "gipsy woman" might, as in a song by Joshua Johnson: "Well I went to the gipsy an' I laid my money on the line, / I said, 'Bring back my baby, or please taker her off my mind.'" If your mate is cheating, don't ask God to change your lover's ways. The root of a certain orchid resembling a withered hand— known as a mojo hand—will help you in a way frowned upon by your Christian fellows: "I'm going to Louisiana, to get myself a mojo hand / 'Cause these backbiting women are trying to take my man." Freedom, even if it was by the hand of God, didn't necessarily mean life would be easy. Work was still hard to find. Manual labor for little money meant that gambling became more than a pastime. It was a hope that things could get better. And hoodoo could shake up the odds in your favor: "He give me some good luck tea and said, 'Drink it before it gets cold' / He give me some good luck tea and said, 'Drink it before it gets cold' / He said, 'Drink it all day, doggone your bad luck soul.'"

Sometimes, however, hoodoo was the reason for luck gone bad: "I believe, somebody's / done hoodoo'd poor me / I believe, somebody's done hoodoo'd poor me / Every card I pick's the first one that falls, / Dice won't do nothing but two, twelves, and three." And hoodoo won't help you with a cheating lover if it's hoodoo luring her away: "Now, when your woman start actin' funny, and begin to run aroun', / You better get you somebody, 'cause she's fittin' to put you down, / Better let her go, man, just as quick as you can, / Because that hoodoo girl is going to hoodoo the hoodoo man." As the blues made its way out of the South and into the northern cities, the superstitions and occult beliefs were cast off like old clothes in the hope for better things to come. Where there was industry there was likely more work. And this meant less time to be concerned with the curses spat out by an old conjurer.

It's the legend of Robert Johnson that remains, however, even though the consensus among music critics and historians is that for Johnson himself, the devil was not part of his self-identity. As the blues historian Elijah Wald explains, "There is no suggestions from any of his friends or acquaintances that the hellish or demon-harried aspects of his work were of particular importance to him, or that they were even noticed by the people that crowded around on the streets of Friar's Point." The fact the legend persists is valuable in and of itself: Robert Johnson meeting the devil is a cultural crossroad: the place where all the avenues of occult meet and a point where the occult will continue to reveal itself in the music and culture of rock. The music itself is a product of a synthesis consisting mainly of those rhythms and vocal expressions coming directly out of the religious practices of Africa, practices that involve precisely what we now term the occult. These include spirit possession, divination, and sympathetic magic, all of which are in opposition to Christian norms.

Most important is the belief that the occult's power lies in what is imposed on those who are on the margins or who defy convention held fast. By virtue of not being the music of the church, the blues were believed to raise the devil in their midst. But Johnson's popularity gave a face and a name to the complex relationship between African American music, outsider musicianship, and actual occult beliefs in the form of voodoo.

The legend of Robert Johnson still has the power to ring spiritually true; when you are playing with unseen forces, no matter your intentions, the devil is always close by, maybe even more present than Christ Himself. The devil is so at hand that one could chance to meet him at a highway crossroads on a moonless night and darkly trade one's soul for a gift. It was as if the spirit of Papa Legba knew it was about to be lost forever, and so embraced its new identity as Satan, if only to ensure it would continue to find expression in rock and roll. Better to be accused of being the devil than to be forgotten completely.

II

When Elvis Presley appeared on *The Ed Sullivan Show* in 1956, the cameramen worked overtime to position the angles of the shots so as to not emphasize his crotch and gyrating hips. But it wasn't merely Presley's display of lustiness that was a concern. American Pentecostalism, the source for much of the early polemic against rock and roll, sees any hint of aberrant sexuality as an invitation to demonic influence. Ironically, it was the Assemblies of God Church, an offshoot of Pentecostalism, where Elvis was raised. The Pentecostal Church insisted on its congregants striving for a direct connection to God through music, dance, and speaking in tongues. The example was taken directly from the African American churches. While viewed with a deep skepticism by white Christians, the black congregations had a method of worship, which, while infernal in its origins, could be used to holy purpose. One leader of the early Pentecostal Church was heard to have pronounced: "The devil should not be allowed to keep all this good rhythm." White churches saw the remnants of pagan Africa in the black churches, black churches saw the devil in the blues, and everyone saw the Pentecostals as possessed by the devil. Rock and roll would become the one thing they could all agree was evil by design. From the very beginning, rock would be associated with devilish intent. Throughout its history it would both embrace and challenge this suggestion. Even the churchgoing Elvis would push back.

Elvis was not shy in pointing out these contradictions. In interviews with his longtime friend Larry Geller, Elvis fondly remembered the energy and ecstasy of the hellfire preaching and the congregation that would "jump up and down, stomp their feet, and get themselves worked up to a frenzy." The very same church would call out Elvis for sidling up to Satan and corrupting the youth of America: "They said I was 'controversial.' And there were some preachers who actually said that my music was dirty, and I was leading the kids to hell. They even had a bonfire and burned my records and albums. Can you imagine that? Hell, all I did was what came naturally—what I learned when I was a little kid in church, movin' my body to the music." What Christians were able to perceive—unconsciously to be sure—were the deep non-Christian influences of Elvis's music. On the one hand was the carnal music of the blues and roots music, via voodoo-charmed swamps of the bayous. On the other was an influence even more deeply non-Christian, and it could be heard and felt in the music and worship of their own church. It was the sound of the shout, born in the spirit-conjuring circle chants of Africa, and an early link in the chain of rock and roll's occult origins.

To retain their own heritage, one in which the old gods and their rituals provided a tie, slaves found ways to blend African religious practice with their already malleable Christianity. In the religion of African tribes, gods and spirits permeated every aspect of life. Theirs was an animistic tradition, in which every tree, stone, and river was not merely imbued with spirit but was the spirit's true manifestation. For many Africans, this supreme deity was transcendent, incapable of answering prayers, responding to entreaties, healing or otherwise interacting with human beings at all. The gods and spirits are intermediaries, often chaotic, invoked and tamed through complex rituals involving spirit possession, the sacrifice of animals, and divination. African forms of worship have been described as "danced religions" because all the beliefs are expressed through ritual, with music as the force driving them.

Slaves practiced a form of ring dancing and singing, often in the seclusion of the secret gatherings in the woods or other private outdoor areas known as "hush harbors." Whites were mostly opposed to this practice and in order for it to remain secret, slaves would either fill a large bucket of water to catch the sound, or, when indoors, hang a basin from the ceiling to act as a dampener. To worship outside the prescribed time and ways of the church was suspect, but the shout was particularly suspicious. The shout was akin to some devilish African rite that should have been cleansed from the slave's consciousness by Christianity. And if it hadn't been scrubbed away, it meant the masters and the ministers were not doing a good enough job. As one witness to a shout recounted: "What in the name of religion, can countenance or tolerate such gross perversions of true religion! But the evil is only occasionally condemned."

For the slave, the ring shout presented the most important symbolic moment, a relationship to God unmediated by the master, by the white church, or by any interpretation of the Bible. God can appear anywhere, even in the midst of a plantation, and the shout is the sound of a voice saying what it wants; the dance is the movement of feet unchained.

The ring shout has its own internal constraint, in which the feet shuffle alongside each other very closely, barely leaving the ground. It is in the body, arms, hands, and head where the joyful ecstasy is released. The hands clap and wave, and the eyes look up to heaven. But despite the energy rising out and sustained by the movement of the feet, it was imperative that the feet never cross. If it looked like dancing, the devil's own feet might join. This fear of dancing was part of a much deeper current in which the slave folk song—contrary to the spiritual song—was slowly eradicated by forces both inside and outside the slave community.

In the early years of slavery, masters often allowed their slaves to socialize, and this by definition included music and dance. But this was not always met comfortably by the whites. Many slave owners banned drums and other percussive instruments, believing them to be a call to rebellion. For the white Evangelical Christian community, dance was not only a mirror of sexual desire, it was too much like the slave's African pagan past. As early as 1665, the minister Morgan Godwin of Virginia was appalled by what he witnessed. The dance of slaves was "barbarous and contrary to Christianity."

Slaves with powerful conversion experiences or even those raised in the Church began to internalize these ideas. Once, Africans and African Americans had made no distinction between secular and sacred dance, but by the mid-1800s the pressure from the Christian authority was beginning to exert real influence. In an 1848 report for the "Religious Instruction of the Negroes in Liberty County, Georgia," it was abundantly clear what the Church thought of slaves and dancing: "Their dances are not only protracted to unseasonable hours, but too frequently become the resort of the most dissolute and abandoned, and for the vilest purposes." Christian slaves began to adopt this opinion and many even went so far as to disavow the use of the fiddle, a popular accompanying dance instrument slaves played for themselves and for their masters.

The fiddle itself had already been considered an instrument most useful to the devil, particularly as it was favored for dance, a recreation already suspect. But for many slaves, the fiddle offered opportunities that others could never even hope for. As one slave remarked, fiddling "relieved me of many days' labor in the fields." It also provided slaves with the ability to travel and gain some basic conveniences such as shoes and tobacco. As such, for a fiddle player to give up their instrument so as to not offend God represents a great psychic rupture, and furthered the division between secular and sacred music.

The pull of Christianity for some slaves was strong, and as one slave remarked: "When I joined the church, I burned my fiddle up." Destroying the fiddle was a deeply symbolic act. Dancing, fueled by the fiddle, was one of the truly African traditions kept alive by slaves. For many African traditions, the entire world turns on a spiritual axis and is imbued at every level with divine purpose. How can any part of life be separate from the spirits in every stone, animal, and plant? Nevertheless, the extreme violence that wrenched African people from their homelands and traditions created a vacuum filled easily by the white Christian myth equating slavery with God's will. Christianity was hope in a hopeless foreign land. Whether through whispers in a hush harbor or simply in the way in which culture is encoded in the memory of generations—even when the origin of the memory may be lost—being human, slaves found a way to retain their impulse to dance. The shout was a bridge between the two worlds.

While the gods and their names were abandoned or forgotten with each generation, the manner in which they were worshipped was etched deep into the slaves' spiritual DNA. It was the shout where the genetic marker was most pronounced. Listening to shouts today, the tension between the ancient tribal rhythms and the biblically themed lyrics is a powerful reminder of how the Christian training of the slave coalesced with the sounds and gestures of a religion finding expression in spirit possession, magic, and divination, the very things governing

15

whites, which the Church had hoped to drive from the slave to instill not only docility and obedience, but to ensure that the devil had not hitched a ride on the slave galleys. Yet something akin did come with the Africans, but it was not the devil. It was a spirit far older.

While the theology of the African dance and the ring shout of the Christian slave revealed different divine interactions with humans, the structure and rhythm of the shout are deeply African and reflect a vital non-Christian religious spirit. Significantly, the ring moves counterclockwise, a tradition likely drawn from an African cosmology where the spirit world moves in a circle, eternally. There is no final revelation, no second coming that wraps up human history in a heavenly bow. "Rather," as Jon Michael Spencer explains, "a person begins as this-worldly spirit and returns to the world of the spirits for continued life after death." This cycle never ends. The slave shout is a way for the slave to be obedient to God through self-agency regarding the work of their own souls. The master does not determine their fate; the slave follows the eternal shape of the universe, a force no white man can stop or control.

The power of the spirit world is most dramatically revealed in the African traditions that allowed the faithful to be overtaken—possessed—by the gods. Percussion and dance are the means by which the spirit reveals itself, and since each spirit had its own name and personality, the style of dance is a clue as to which spirit had manifested. The shouting and dancing are a result of the worshipper being "mounted by the god." When the deity inhabits the person, his or her own identity is subsumed.

In the American South, drums were banned, so the slaves

relied on hand clapping and feet stomping. For the Christian slave, it was the Holy Spirit who took hold, but only to make itself known. It was not the voice of gods or of God, but the voice of praise, unrestrained and utterly free. But just as in the African tradition, worship in the slave community was communal, an attribute that extended into every form of popular music its influence reached, most especially rock and roll.

The other essential aspect of the ring shout is call-and-response, a method of song used not only in religious ritual but in work songs chanted in the fields. It was a means through which the group agrees on what is taking place and through agreement are bound by a common truth, one that might even be communicated via the shout and the back-and-forth rhythm. Working on the plantation, one slave would begin a song and then the verse would be repeated by the others; like the spiritual, it could be used to communicate more subversive ideas, such as a hope for worldly freedom beyond a heavenly salvation. In the ring shout, call-and-response functioned to bind song; responsive repetitions served as the moral of the parable, the nugget of meaning transcending the particular of the story.

In the wildly moving shout song "Adam in the Garden," the leader calls out, "Oh Eve, where is Adam?" and the responders sing, "Picking up leaves!"—a telling of the original story explaining humorously why God could not find Adam, as he ashamedly knew he was naked after the fateful bite of the forbidden fruit. As they move around the ring, the responders bend down as if to scoop leaves from the floor. The shout does not emphasize or even remark on the shame or the sin. While this aspect of the story is inherent in the shout, what the ring dancers are communicating is something larger about being human, about the everyday task of having to perform the most basic functions to keep your dignity. The shout even reflects on the work of slaves, the constant bending down in the fields. God knows where Adam is, just as God knows where the slave is. He is hunched over in a plantation, singing under his breath to keep the vital connection going. Herein lies the subtle form of spiritual rebellion. The slave shout uses a story of the Bible, told through an ancient and non-Christian form of religious worship, to say that no one needs to be ashamed to do what you have to do to survive. It's easy to hear the fetal heartbeat of rock in this shout, the rhythms circling round and round, punctuated by calls of defiance for a spiritual identity not dictated by authority, with time kept by a drumbeat.

While enacted by Africans adopting Christian behaviors, these ancient songs and musical signatures, rituals to connect with the gods, are pre-Christian in their very expression because they endeavor to employ methods of magic—trance, divination, spirit possession, dance—in order to have a direct encounter with the deities. This is the oldest form of religious worship, when magic and religion were inseparable, where myth was communicated through a colorful and often wild blending of costume, song, and dance. This type of yearning for freedom and self-expression is our first and earliest glimmer of the spirit of rock and roll, a primeval and communal method to transmit a truth, to celebrate, to mourn, to sacrifice something to the gods. And to do it together.

Out of the work songs sung in the fields and in the ring shout of the church came the spiritual, a form of music that would become one the most influential in American music. From the spiritual came gospel, and gospel itself would soon become a staple not only of African American churches but of white churches as well. With each successive generation, whatever was deliberately African about the shout and spiritual was eventually lost. But the rhythms and stylistic forms remained. More important, the spiritual rebellion inherent in the music would continually find its expression in every form of African American music. Soon it would begin its snakelike climb into the branches of American popular music, from gospel to the blues and eventually to rock, where it would provide popular music with a means to lift it out of the ordinary, to challenge ideas of what music could and should be, and what it could mean.

Pentecostalism brought together the music and worship style of the African American churches. Once thought to promote the devil, shouting and other ecstatic practices were claimed by Pentecostalism as an authentic response to being filled with the spirit of God. But mainstream churches did not approve of such behavior as an expression of worship, even if it was white folks doing the shouting. Within mainstream Christian sects, the Pentecostal movement was believed to be the devil's secret congregation.

For white America, including the church he was raised in, Elvis brought to bear much of what they were afraid of: sex by way of the devil's own infinite lust. This fear was also deeply racist. Many believed that what was most potent and dangerous about rock was its roots in African American music: rock music was tribal, pagan at its core, and would seduce white teenagers like the serpent seduced Eve. Rock is sex. In the 1957 book *Close*

That Bedroom Door! by Lambert and Patricia Schuyler, the authors claim a conspiracy among black men, aided by the government, to have sex with white women. The conspiracy runs deep. With their "jungle music," blacks have taken to inculcating the youth into loving rock and roll, merely a means to a nefarious end: "[Teenagers] have been taught to love it and never does it cross their minds that this incessant emphasis upon the Negro with his repulsive love songs and vulgar rhythms is but the psychological preliminary to close body contact between the races."

Fears of popular music were bubbling up long before Elvis, however. The post–Civil War African American churches saw the devil everywhere. Secular music and dancing were particularly questionable. But in an effort to keep the devil at bay, congregations still used the methods of worship adopted as slaves, what the historian Eileen Southern calls "the hand clapping, foot stomping, call-and-response performance, rhythmic complexities, persistent beat, melodic improvisation, heterophonic textures, percussive accompaniments, and ring shouts." The great irony of these young churches is that such musical elements were once employed to call upon the spirits, heal the sick, and divine the future. The even deeper irony is how these also became staples of white churches, where the devil was once seen as having to be worked and beat out of the slaves.

Little Richard embodied the basic conflict within rock's relationship with church music, with those very same churches calling it the devil's music. Little Richard (born Richard Wayne Penniman) was raised a Seventh-day Adventist, a congregation with an apocalyptic theology that sees any form of secular music as opposed to the teaching of Jesus. He grew up playing and singing gospel, and by the time he left home to make a mark for himself, he was already drawn to the blues, his first act of rebellion. Gradually he incorporated rock into his songs, not always successfully, but in 1955 he turned "Tutti Frutti," originally a sexually explicit blues song, into a vehicle for his own flamboyant style of musicianship. Richard played standing up, banging away on the piano, and looking over his shoulder at the audience with a mischievous gleam in his eye. He knew what his family church thought of his music and his gregarious sexual lifestyle, but Little Richard was playing the music that was in his heart. In a 1970 interview with *Rolling Stone*, he explained the origins of his rock and roll interpretation of an old blues song: "Well, you know I used to play piano for the church. You know that spiritual, 'Give Me That Old Time Religion,' most churches just say, *[sings]* 'Give me that old time religion' but I did, *[sings]* 'Give me that old time, talkin' 'bout religion,' you know I put that little *thing* in it you know, I always did have that *thing* but I didn't know what to do with the *thing* I had." That "thing," of course, is the shout, perhaps transformed as it became part of the mainstream church, but remaining as the lifeblood of American religious music, its tribal pagan past invisible, its rebellious instinct snaking its way into rock and roll. Little Richard, however, could possibly feel the old gods calling to him, but like many Christians, called those feelings of rebellion the devil. In 1957, Little Richard had a vision of a coming apocalypse. During what *Rolling Stone* calls the "height of his success," Little Richard left rock and roll and returned to the church. During the following years he denounced rock music:

"My work is for the Lord and I have dedicated myself to Him. I renounced all things associated with my past life such as songs of the devil, women, carousing all night and other evils associated with rock 'n' roll." Little Richard eventually returned to rock, and brought his religiosity with him. Maybe rock was the real salvation after all: "I think that rock and roll is getting ready to shake the world again. That rock and roll, with them wild names and that thing that makes you dance yourself to glory, I think that's what's getting ready to happen to the music."

III

In a 1956 article for the *Washington Post*, the reporter Phyllis Battelle interviewed psychiatrist Jules Wasserman to help explain why teenagers are so drawn to rock and roll. Battelle wrote, "[Wasserman] compares it to the 'dionysian revels in Greece, where the god of sex (Priapus) and the god of drink (Bacchus) were feted in the same two-beat rhythms.'" Rock's detractors were even more sensitive to the music's occult wellspring than the young fans. A perfect example of the occult imagination at play in the history of rock, this outside characterization of rock as a pagan rite would become part of the internal identity of rock and would shape the music and its presentation for decades to come. If parents and ministers hadn't imposed their own fears of paganism and tribal religion on rock and roll, the occult imagination might not have been sparked in the same way. As a result, intentions to stop the music in its tracks instead started a conflagration that has never gone out.

No matter the outrage from parents and religious leaders,

even Catholic youth discovered that rock offered a means to worship that felt crucial, filled with vitality. The rebellious spirit of rock was not unlike the one Jesus brought to the money changers at the temple, a raucous response to authority that had all but given in and given up. But even when put toward Christian worship, adults were hesitant to accept rock as anything more than a pagan virus. In 1957, the then Roman Catholic archbishop of Chicago, Cardinal Samuel Stritch, spoke against even allowing rock and roll to be played at Catholic youth centers, especially because it promoted dancing, hips and all. In a letter to his flock, he wrote, "Some new manners of dancing and a throwback to tribalism in recreation centers cannot be tolerated for Catholic youths. . . . Too much familiarity between the adolescent girl and the adolescent boy is dangerous and sinful." Notwithstanding the subtle racism, the association of what was deemed tribal with sexuality, manifest in the music and rhythms of rock and roll, was exactly right.

Eventually it was all too much, even for the record labels and DJs. Rock and roll was a force sweeping up the nation's youth in a way parents, church leaders, and even radio music executives could not have foreseen. The only solution would be to exorcise the demon entirely, a black demon to be sure. The answer came in the form of a white Christian, Pat Boone, who sang of chaste love and never even lifted a foot off the ground, never mind pulse anything below the waist. But the attacks didn't cease, and many suggested the fad called "rock 'n' roll" would soon fall out of popular favor.

In response to a 1957 article in the *Chicago Tribune* titled "Rock 'n' Roll's On Way Down, Say 3 Experts," one letter writer was thrilled at the prospect and was glad to see that, in the wake of rock's demise, "a trend towards sentiment, love, and romance is becoming apparent." The subtext here is that the demon of sex, conjured by those barbaric tribal rhythms, had lost what little power it had regained and became, like many parts of the pagan world, enfolded into the dominant white Christian mainstream. The soul of American youth might have been saved, but the soul of rock had become a pale, flaccid thing.

In coffeehouses and bars in New York City and San Francisco, writers and poets were creating their own brand of agitation. The public first took notice in 1957 when *Life* magazine covered the obscenity trial of the 112-line free-verse poem "Howl." The publisher, Lawrence Ferlinghetti, owner of City Lights, was accused of the intent to "willfully and lewdly print, publish and sell obscene and indecent writings, papers and books, to wit: 'Howl and Other Poems.'" The poet Allen Ginsberg first read his poem in 1955 to an astonished audience. "Howl" was perfectly timed to speak to a growing unrest among young adults; they realized that the post–World War II idealism of American preeminence was a pipe dream, consistently undermined by poverty, racial strife, and a conformist streak that covered the suburbs in a gloom of dullness. "Howl" called for a celebration of sexual and religious ecstasy, drugs, and a recognition that the "bum's as holy as the seraphim!" "Howl" was also an attack on the dehumanization caused by the corporate machine, one that stole human souls to sacrifice to the insatiable appetite of Moloch, "whose factories dream and croak in the fog!" The judge, Clayton W. Horn, found in favor of the publisher, and concluded that the poem "does have some redeeming social importance." The result of the trial wouldn't have mattered, though. A movement had already begun to challenge the social and religious status quo by way of literature, poetry, and music.

Ray Smith, the narrator of Jack Kerouac's 1958 novel, *The Dharma Bums*, introduces the rugged and humble poet Japhy Ryder. Ryder is well versed in Eastern mysticism and philosophy and believes that bodhisattvas—enlightened masters who become teachers—can be found among ordinary people. The two writers share their interest in various saints, in particular Avalokiteshvara, a bodhisattva so compassionate that, in seeing so much suffering, he literally blew up in despair. Kerouac based the working-class Buddha-like Ryder on Gary Snyder, a poet whose work shows a deep association with Buddhist meditation, as well as a sympathetic—and spiritual—affinity with ancient religions and their emphasis on the natural world as a divine expression. Snyder's interest in Buddhism, particularly by way of Zen, exposed many other writers to the possibility of a spiritual identity far removed from what many perceived as the crushing homogeneity of mainstream Christianity. In a later conversation with the conservative writer John Lofton, Ginsberg tries to explain his use of the word *madness* in his poem "Howl": "In Zen Buddhism there is wild wisdom, or crazy wisdom, crazy in the sense of wild, unlimited, unbounded."

As Eastern religion and occultism were becoming important tools of inspiration to what is commonly known as the Beat Generation (a term originally coined by Kerouac), these writers were inspiring others looking to understand the spiritual nature of the unconscious that Freud had failed to fully explain. Novels such as *Siddhartha* by Hermann Hesse were being read on college campuses, and the Beat writers themselves were citing visionary artists such as Charles Baudelaire and William Blake as kindred souls.

Bebop provided the soundtrack. Jazz musicians had been looking for a way to challenge what they believed were the limitations of swing and big band music. Musicians began improvising, playing off of each other instead of the sheet music. Standard songs became playgrounds for experimentation. As the scholar Christopher Gair explains, bebop showed how technical prowess and spontaneity could be combined to great result. Bebop also "[e]xposed [the Beats] to an African American culture and language that would have a profound . . . effect on their own work." The Beats would record bebop's complex rhythms onto their own prose and verse, what they heard as a reflection of their existential and psychic angst. What better way to express the longing for a spiritual experience that was immediate and unmediated than the language of bebop. But soon the 1950s counterculture would come across a faint echo from America's rural locations, the sounds of ghosts strumming their guitars, singing murder ballads, spirituals, hillbilly tunes, and blues songs.

The filmmaker and artist Harry Smith, a regular of New York's infamous Chelsea Hotel, had been collecting recordings of folk songs on 78s since the 1940s. The bulk of his collection was commercial records produced between 1927 and 1932. The names of the singers and musicians were all but forgotten by the time Smith was finding the recordings. His collection came to the attention of Moses Asch, the founder of the Folkways record label, who suggested to Smith he cull the best of what he had so that Asch could release them as a set. 1952 saw the Folkways release of the *Anthology of American Folk Music*, a three-volume set, personally curated by Smith, and packaged with extensive notes, collages, and, inexplicably, occult symbols. The cover of the anthology is a reproduction of *The Celestial Monochord*, a seventeenth-century print by the astrologer and mathematician Robert Fludd. He used the monochord—an instrument using a single string to demonstrate how octaves can be understood mathematically—to imagine that the universe was a perfectly tuned manifestation of God, whose string reaches through the heavenly realm into nature. As a result, certain magical formulas can function to vibrate those parts of heaven that have a corresponding element in nature. This would become the basis of a magical practice based on the idea of "like as to like." For Smith, this image made perfect sense. Smith was an occultist and student of the Kabbalah, magic, and peyote mysticism. The music of the anthology—social music, songs, and ballads—was separated into three sections coded by the colors red, blue, and green, corresponding to the elements of fire, water, and air. For Smith, the anthology represented a deeply human microcosm of the music of the spheres, where love, pain, joy, and death correspond to a divine property. Smith believed it was on the margins of America where an authentic way of life dwelled—free from the gaping maw of Moloch, as Ginsberg might have said.

Many of the songs in the anthology are echoes of the music played and sung in the shadows of the Appalachian Mountains, an area settled as early as the 1700s by British, Welsh, and Scottish immigrants, who brought with them their own folk music. Many of these songs came to be known as Child Ballads, named after the nineteenth-century Harvard University folklorist Francis Child, who was the first to compile them in a rigorous way. The anthology would become the creation myth for the mid-twentieth-century generation of folk musicians, such as Bob Dylan, many of whom would go on to influence rock and roll. The critic Luc Sante called the anthology "a treasure map of a now hidden America." Smith's anthology linked folk music to a past where the spirits of old could manifest themselves in song.

Plutarch, in his *Moralia*, reports that, during the reign of the emperor Tiberius Caesar Augustus, a messenger brought the news that Pan had died—the last of the old gods to survive the quickly spreading new religion called Christianity. But if the gods are merely aspects of us, then Pan could never stay dead. His spirit hitched a ride on the slave ships under a different cover: the god Eshu, believed to be the devil by some. What was left of the old African religion was stripped bare to its fundamental core. All that was left were its methods of worship: song and shout, dance and drum. But the spiritual rebellion powering this music could not be buried. The ancient and all-too-human drive for a direct religious communion would find a way to present itself in every generation. Even when rock and roll was being exorcised of sex and rebellion in the late 1950s, a phantom was lurking on the edges of the mainstream. It was being driven by the fiery poetry and prose of the Beats as well as by experimental composers and artists. There was a wind coming in from the East, and it was bringing with it spiritual ideas that could bridge the dark pagan past and the milk-white Christian present. Gurus and bodhisattvas, some who seemed to possess their own special powers and others with a third eye open wide, came to teach the one essential truth the West badly needed. Heaven is on earth now. We had never been parted from it. There is no duality tearing apart the world, no devil trading musical secrets for souls. God is not in the starry heaven above, God is within you.

CHAPTER 2

RELAX AND FLOAT DOWNSTREAM

I

Syd Barrett's bandmates watched in sick astonishment as their lead singer and guitarist stood at the front of the stage. His face appeared to be melting. Barrett, the mind and soul behind Pink Floyd, looked out across the audience at the Cheetah Club in Venice, California, as he strummed a single chord on his mirror-covered Fender Telecaster. In 1967, an audience watching Pink Floyd was ready for anything. Pink Floyd revolutionized the live experience as they played long interstellar jams as movie projectors flashed images and smoke swirled around the ever-moving people lit up on acid. Usually the audience grooved to their individual rhythms as much as to the collective conscious-ness, and rode whatever wave the band was on. But like any mystical journey, there was the danger of being seduced by the ecstasy, of mistaking one's own hopes and expectations for the truer union and getting blasted across the universe as a result.

The audience might have thought the ghastly strobing visage of Barrett was part of the spectacle, but what they were really seeing was a young man at the peak of his powers imploding. They were also witnessing a kaleidoscopic fun house of mirrors: an ever-reflecting cascade of the occult's influence on rock and roll and, by extension, on all of pop culture.

Both Syd Barrett's music and his psyche were being swept up by a current that was finding new energy in England. American rock and roll had turned down its Pentecostal-like fire and dowsed its own sexual and spiritual rebellion—once the essential drive behind rock's restless spirit. By the early 1960s rock had become neutered. In garages around the United States, teenagers were plugging in their cheap electric guitars and banging on three-piece drum kits, trying to reignite the flame, but it was in England where bands found a formula for injecting a dose of adrenaline into the syrupy pop that had become the staple of radio play. Bands like the Beatles, the Who, and others of the British Invasion looked past Pat Boone to rock's original roots in the blues and reminded people what they loved about rock and roll in the first place. It was the LSD experience, however—held aloft by a fusion of Eastern mysticism, mythology, and occultism—that would utterly transfigure rock's sound and performance, in clothing and staging, and in its ability to convince fans it was a transmitter for a new spiritual truth. Barrett, especially through his steerage of Pink Floyd, willingly embraced being the messenger.

Through Pink Floyd, Barrett conjured a mystical dream for the audience to inhabit, drawn from his own drugged imagination, which was fueled by his interest in mysticism, as well as the popular fascinations of his era, such as the British pastoral fantasy of J. R. R. Tolkien's *Lord of the Rings* and the *I Ching*, the text outlining the ancient Chinese system of divination. Even more essential is what music critic Rob Young, in his essential *Electric Eden*, describes as Barrett being "strangely pushed and pulled between nostalgia for the secret garden of a child's imagination and the space-age futurism of interstellar overdrive." Barrett was channeling a spirit that was trying to pierce the veil between these worlds, and while this nostalgia and futurism, as Young puts it, seem opposed, they are actually two ideas at the heart of magic. The practice of magic is one requiring a link to the past and a vision of the future. Barrett added this directly to the lyrics of his songs and his live performances, experimenting with light and sound in an attempt to work the audience into a trance. The method is new, but the intention is ancient. On that November night in 1967, a dark magic was being worked by the young musician.

Backstage a few minutes earlier, Barrett had poured the contents of a bottle of hair gel mixed with crushed Quaaludes onto his head. Under the hot lights of the stage, the gel and pill mix slowly dripped down his face. This was no mere prank to freak out his audience. Something had gone terribly wrong. Barrett was in a trance of his own as he played the same monotone chord over and over again. Barrett's behavior had been getting more and more erratic, his almost maniacal LSD consumption inducing or at the very least aggravating some form of mental illness.

His bandmates were more than worried. They were afraid. Syd had become so unpredictable, they could never be sure what would happen next. Later that year, Barrett would walk out onto a stage, helped by his fellow musicians. Barrett stood still, the tension rising. June Bolan, a friend and business associate of Pink Floyd, remembered the moment as one when the tension never lifted: "Suddenly he put his hands on the guitar and we thought, 'Great, he's actually going to do it!' But he just stood there, he just stood there tripping out of his mind."

Acid and the pressure of fame are often blamed as the reason behind Syd Barrett's downfall, but his drug use was mixed into an explosive compound by his compulsion for spiritual awareness. It began in 1966 when Barrett became involved with a group that practiced Sant Mat, a strange synthesis of Sikhism, Hinduism, and Sufism. The Sant Mat philosophy requires initiation into its teachings, and Barrett was not considered spiritually fit. Sant Mat emphasizes chastity, abstinence from drugs and alcohol, and a commitment to meditation practice, not something a young up-and-coming rock and roll star in the mid-sixties was likely to find easy. Barrett was saddened by the esoteric order's rejection of him, but there were distractions to take his mind off it: Pink Floyd and LSD. Instead of a spiritual practice, Barrett tested the limitations of sound and lyrics, crafting songs about the *I Ching* and cosmic consciousness by way of space travel. Pink Floyd's first album, *The Piper at the Gates of Dawn*, is a *Wünderkammer*, a cabinet of curiosities containing the relics that littered Barrett's psychic landscape and a construct mirroring the counterculture's spiritual yearning.

The Piper at the Gates of Dawn is a direct reference to the chapter in Kenneth Grahame's 1908 book, *The Wind in the Willows*, where the animals unexpectedly find themselves in the presence of the god Pan. Rat and Mole are traveling in a boat along the riverbank. It is Rat who hears the piping first. Mole is skeptical. That is, until he comes across the god himself. In a moment not in any way related to the main plot of the book, Mole and Rat undergo a religious epiphany as they are seemingly initiated into the cult of Pan:

> Then suddenly the Mole felt a great Awe fall upon him, an awe that turned his muscles to water, bowed his head, and rooted his feet to the ground. It was no panic terror—indeed he felt wonderfully at peace and happy—but it was an awe that smote and held him and, without seeing, he knew it could only mean that some august Presence was very, very near. . . . Trembling he obeyed, and raised his humble head; and then, in that utter clearness of the imminent dawn, while Nature, flushed with fullness of incredible colour, seemed to hold her breath for the event, he looked in the very eyes of the Friend and Helper. . . .

The music of the 1960s would prove to be a grove in which to worship Pan. The hippies had much in common with the first real revival of the horned deity by way of the Romantic poets and writers, not only in their use of pagan and natural imagery, such as Percy Bysshe Shelley's "Hymn of Pan," wherein the god "sang of the dancing stars," but also in the suggestion that drugs could offer a window into Pan's ancient realm, as in Samuel Taylor Coleridge's opium-infused poem "Kubla Khan." Even more significantly, the 1960s counterculture revived the Romantic belief that reason and the age of industry were anathema to the natural world and the spirit of myth and poetry. This is the experience many young seekers in the 1960s were looking for, a direct, immediate communion with nature and by extension the universe. Art and music were the vessels for both the Romantics and the hippies. The piper at the gates of dawn was playing his panpipe for those who needed to hear. And the youth of the 1960s were pulled toward it like a siren song. There was no turning back. Rock culture was now inhabited by a Romantic soul that looked to the gods of the past. And like the Romantic poets who were their forebears, rock musicians crafted music that did more than tug at the heartstrings of teenagers. It was music that urged them toward transcendence, toward creating their own inner landscapes and exploring the antipodes of their minds.

The Piper at the Gates of Dawn shines forth from Syd Barrett's psyche as if he's a prism of the collective unconscious of the generation. The album opens with "Astronomy Domine," sometimes subtitled "An Astral Chant," referencing both cosmic awareness and Gregorian chants. The song is a stream-of-consciousness vision relating the tension between getting as far out as you can, all the while terrified of leaving the "blue" of the earth. Other songs make reference to a cat named Lucifer ("Lucifer Sam"), a gnome named Grimble Crumble ("The Gnome"), and a paganlike idyll echoing "Hymn of Pan" in its celebration of the joyful mystery of nature ("Flaming"). Then there is the literal "Chapter 24," taken almost word for word from the popular *I Ching* translation by Richard Wilhelm and Cary F. Baynes, first published in 1950. The twenty-fourth hexagram, *fu*, is eerily prescient as it "counsels turning away from the confusion of external things, turning back to one's inner light. There, in the depths of the soul, one sees the Divine, the One." Whether it was intentional or not, in "Chapter 24" Barrett expressed not only his own spiritual desires, but the yearning of an entire generation that was coming of age listening to Pink Floyd.

The Piper at the Gates of Dawn is filled with its own internal spiritual anxiety, mixing pagan folk images with Eastern mysticism. This would characterize much of the 1960s' otherworldly desire, which borrowed from everything that was even vaguely non-Christian and out of tune with mainstream religious mores. Nevertheless, there is a single spark in both pagan magic and Eastern theology with which the counterculture could build a fire that would burn for generations and would feed the New Age movement and almost every subsequent contemporary alternative religious community. Barrett's writing of "Chapter 24" was even more prophetic than he could have imagined. The twenty-fourth hexagram of the *I Ching*, *fu*, which inspired his song, is the hexagram of self-knowledge and individuality, of not giving in to the temptation of the crowd, but recognizing the unity of all things: "To know this One means to know oneself in relation to the cosmic forces." *The Piper at the Gates of Dawn* is the dream of one man, made audible through a group consciousness. And for much of the counterculture that identified with this dream, LSD was the method to attain it.

Barrett's own intense turn toward LSD as a path was congruent with the times. The table had been set for a mystical communion to be given on the tongue as a hit of acid. By 1967, mystical consciousness and psychedelic drugs had become synonymous. LSD and other hallucinogenic drug experiences seamlessly aligned with occult and Eastern religious imagery and ideas. The feeling of ego dissolution, for example, corresponds nicely to the Buddhist notion of ego transcendence. A sense of

unity or "becoming one with the universe"—a common phenomenon for those who have had a psychedelic experience—is
akin to pantheism, where God is believed to be in all things,
and all things are in God. None of this is to suggest that the
LSD trip somehow communicates special spiritual knowledge.
But the acid experience can be overwhelming, and Eastern
mysticism and occultism are well suited to make sense of an
otherwise inexplicable occurrence.

This sacred marriage between LSD and the East was beautifully, if not artificially, realized in the 1966 book and—as perfectly suited to the time—companion record, *The Psychedelic
Experience: A Manual Based on the Tibetan Book of the Dead*, by
Timothy Leary, Ralph Metzner, and Richard Alpert (later
known as Ram Dass). The authors had their work cut out for
them. They had to make two simultaneous, possibly opposing,
claims: first that the psychedelic experience is remarkably similar to the classical mystical experience as described by Eastern
traditions, and second that LSD can take the place of rigorous
religious discipline to achieve the mystical state of consciousness. This idea was first elevated to the popular consciousness by
Aldous Huxley in his 1954 book, *The Doors of Perception*, a ca-
nonical text during the 1960s. Huxley, who had once been a
devotee of the Hindu philosophical system known as Vedanta
and wrote forcefully against attempts to circumvent rigorous
spiritual discipline to attain a union with the divine, took a little
less than half a gram of mescaline—the psychoactive substance
found in the peyote cactus—and had a change of heart. Huxley
came to believe psychedelic drugs could bypass the need for any
religious exercises. The notion that a mystical experience could

exist independent of any religious community was radical indeed, and for a generation desperately seeking some divine connection without being pinned down to any kind of tradition or hierarchy, it was just the thing the hippies were after.

Nevertheless, Leary and company recognized that their audience of novice trippers would be well served by having a religious framework for what could be an unpredictable and sometimes terrifying journey, and *The Tibetan Book of the Dead*, which according to Leary was essentially a guidebook to the mystical journey, was exotic enough, but also could make sense of the LSD trip. But he would qualify the use of this deeply religious text so as not to scare off those who might be skeptical. Leary writes in the liner notes of the album: "Today psychedelic drugs such as LSD make it possible for anyone to propel himself out of his mind into unknown, uncharted neurological regions. The yogas and spiritual exercises of the past are no longer needed to escape the inertia of the symbolic mind. Exit is guaranteed."

This was it, then. The mystical experience could be untethered completely from religion. But despite this freedom given to the new consciousness explorers, occult and Eastern mystical imagery and ideas would still come to dominate the landscape. Not only did occultism and mysticism offer other ways of making sense of a world seemingly spinning out of control by way of war and racism, they put the fate of the individual in their own hands; no experience, no matter how transcendent, happens in a vacuum. There was an urgent need for the counterculture to have a spiritual basis. The Beats of the 1950s had grooved to Zen Buddhism, but it was not oriented toward either bliss or revolution and did not offer a cosmic vision that could contain the acid trip. The wave breaking on the shore of the counter-culture was too strong. It was not enough to change the social and political system. One had to change one's very being and relationship to the universe. Only a direct experience with the divine governed by the individual's desire would suffice.

This spiritual rebellion would need a soundtrack, and so two of the editors of the influential London underground magazine *International Times* (*IT*), Joe Boyd and John "Hoppy" Hopkins, ran the UFO Club on Tottenham Court Road from December 1966 to October 1967. During that short year, the UFO Club helped shape the look and feel of the new mysticism and revolutionized the rock concert by turning it into a spectacle through the use of film, lights, and the soon ubiquitous shape-morphing slides that were projected onto the walls. It was the show posters, however, that gave the counterculture an occult-laden aesthetic found even in the rock art poster of today, a potent alchemy of various nineteenth-century art movements, including Romanticism, Art Nouveau, and Symbolism, each of them underscored by a search for esoteric secrets.

The nineteenth century would, in many respects, be the last of a truly enchanted time for artists and musicians until the 1960s. In the late 1800s there was what is called the Occult Revival, when a number of artists, society people, and intellectuals were joining magical fraternities, and writers and thinkers like Arthur Conan Doyle and William James were interested in psychic research and spiritualism. Even Harry Houdini spent great time and effort in the hopes of finding a medium who could help him correspond with his beloved dead mother, only to become an expert in ferreting out frauds and charlatans. It was the artists,

however, who painted the nineteenth century in mystical symbolism, often hidden from plain view unless you knew where
to look. For the Symbolists, art was a method to transmit secret
meaning in an effort to undermine the realism and naturalism
that was coming to dominate modern art. The poet Jean Moréas
conceived of the Symbolist manifesto in 1886: "So, in this art,
the pictures of nature, the actions of human beings, all concrete
phenomena would not themselves know how to manifest themselves; these are presented as the sensitive appearance destined
to represent their esoteric affinity with primordial Ideas." Partly
a response to what Moréas saw as the failure of Romanticism to
usher in a new age, but more deeply a polemic against a purely
scientific worldview that was becoming increasingly in vogue,
the Symbolist ideal was easily folded into the occult interests of
the time. Many of the artists and musicians who associated with
Symbolism were members of various Rosicrucian orders, including Claude Debussy and Erik Satie. Joséphin Péladan, a novelist
and esoteric Christian, began a series of art and literary salons
presented as a Rosicrucian lodge, the Salon de la Rose + Croix.

The Decadent movement, closely linked to Symbolism, included an attack on the upper class and often incorporated more
explicit sexual and taboo elements into the work. The aquiline
illustrator Aubrey Beardsley, whose work belied his own shy and
internal moral tension, was most well-known for his drawings of
Oscar Wilde's play *Salomé* and for publishing an edition of Aris-
tophanes' *Lysistrata*, the latter of which is replete with grotesquely
large phalluses. Other drawings referred to pagan and mythological themes, many that were at the heart of occult ideas at the
time. Beardsley's drawing *The Mysterious Rose Garden*, found in

41

the literary journal *The Yellow Book* (edited by Beardsley), shows a nude young woman in a garden, listening to secrets from a wing-footed man, reminiscent of Hermes, the god who would become a core figure in the Hermetic doctrine that would shape nineteenth-century occult thought. The spiritual rebellion inherent in Beardsley's work would finally give way to Catholicism, and near the end of his short life he wanted most of his work destroyed.

This turn toward myth and occultism and the reaction against realism inspired artists to look toward their own unconscious, such as dreams, but even more dramatically to the visions of hashish and opium. These drugs would help to expand on the idea of individuality, of the value of inwardness, and the power of mythic archetypes often unfolding during drug intoxication. In Charles Baudelaire's *Les Fleurs du Mal* (*The Flowers of Evil*), the poet writes of the splendid "poison" of opium: "Opium magnifies that which is limitless, / Lengthens the unlimited, /Makes time deeper, hollows out voluptuousness, / And with dark, gloomy pleasures / Fills the soul beyond its capacity." This is a spiritual encounter not mediated by church or priest, by book or creed, but by the willful seeking of a direct encounter with the divine, and is eerily prophetic of the occult-infused LSD experience in the 1960s.

The more obvious influence on the UFO Club's posters comes by way of the Czech artist Alphonse Mucha, whose style would define the Art Nouveau style of the fin de siècle. A Freemason with a penchant for spiritualism, he was true to the spirit of his time. Mucha believed that the aim of art was to communicate hidden spiritual realities. His work *Le Pater*, a series of drawings related to the Lord's Prayer spoken by Jesus in the

Gospels of Matthew and Luke, is profoundly esoteric, filled with visionary figures, devils, and heavenly visitation. Mucha used the prayer to reflect on the divine evolution of humanity, and believed, like the hippies of the 1960s, that a new spiritual age was dawning. Even his poster art, often used for advertisements (which is what rock posters are, after all), illuminated this idea of spiritual perfection, most often in the form of a woman, usually surrounded by florally decorated halos, dressed in long, rapturous fabrics, and with a look of deep spiritual peace on her face. These elements would find their way into almost every poster for the UFO Club, and were a revival of the nineteenth-century ideal that art could change the spiritual condition of the world.

The bands of the UFO Club—the Soft Machine, the Crazy World of Arthur Brown, Pink Floyd—played against a backdrop of projection created by the art collective known as the Boyle Family (Mark Boyle and Joan Hills). In earlier performances, Boyle and Hills projected bodily fluids, including blood, sperm, and vomit, onto screens. During UFO shows, acid was poured onto zinc slides and the destruction was projected. Colored liquids were also used, and sometimes entire evenings would center around one color, with colored fabric, paint, and confetti thrown around during the performances. The writer David Thompson described Boyle's work as a kind of mysticism: "[Mysticism] is the only serious word that adequately covers the aim and the activity. The aim is not to 'create' something, to communicate, to demonstrate, to define or to discover. It is to isolate for examination." It is, according to Thompson, a romantic conception of art that is not interested in dividing up the world into categories but rather is seeking unity. Combining these projections with

43

the music, all of it fueled by copious amounts of LSD, pushed at the edges of culture, creating a counterculture that the mainstream would ultimately embrace, if only in a commercial sense.

It would be impossible to catalogue every instance of the rock poster art influence on British and American advertising, but there are standout examples that either cynically ripped off the most noncommercial art form next to graffiti or simply had to give over to a psychic transformation that was so powerful, the counterculture alone could not contain it. A 7UP television commercial by the artist Peter Max, whose work is reminiscent of the Beatles' *Yellow Submarine* film, features a flared-panted character walking on clouds, imagining prizes, each presented in a highly colorful quasi-mystical setting. There are even hints of the ubiquitous LSD "trails." A Brim commercial for its then new decaffeinated coffee suggests the drink contains another special ingredient. Each person who drinks it is shown going wide-eyed as colorful animated thoughts swirl from the top of their heads, as if their crown chakras have been awakened, revealing Mucha-like swirls and flowers, and there's even a figure vocalizing the word *Love* as it exits his throat on a rainbow. In the print advertising world, a 1969 Pepsi ad features the iconic bottle surrounded by floral mandalas and haloed by a rainbow-colored sun, as if a divine presence has descended into our midst.

Change was not only in the air, it was in the very look and sound of the time, but there was often tension about whether the revolution was social, political, or spiritual. Sometimes even other hippies found the effort to change one's mind, instead of the system, to be a dangerous and often futile effort, especially for the more politically motivated freaks. Even in *IT,* one nameless editor opens the 1967 issue with an angry stream-of-consciousness rant to not let the mystically inclined acidheads derail the true project of the revolution. American readers had been writing, asking where all the LSD-inspired mandalas were. The editors responded that they were worried a focus on drugs and other high weirdness would undermine their mission by not only making them more suspect in the eyes of the law, but causing the drug quest to become its own kind of fundamentalism: "This is the drag about LSD: it's a tease. We must not get hung up on some drug scene. Finally, the only scene is where you are with yourself 'spiritually.' The human soul, the inner-vision, call it what [sic] you like, transcends everything, including the psychedelic experience—which is not the only way nor necessarily the best to explore eternal/mystical/Zen/Schizoid states of consciousness." There was no irony here. Even in 1967 people were witnessing the sometimes dark consequences of mixing acid with occultism.

As Pink Floyd continued its upward momentum in 1967, Syd was accelerating downhill. The other members of Pink Floyd could no longer rely on Barrett being able to perform. He would detune his guitar, and stare blankly toward some inner vision, and his appearances on TV were unpredictable. While he had some ability to work in the studio, by 1968 the rest of the band agreed he had to be fired and replaced with David Gilmour, who would help usher in an entirely new direction for the band. Syd would soon be out of the music business entirely, but not before recording a few solo records with the production help of Gilmour. Sadly, it's the song "Opel" that does not appear on his masterful album *The Madcap Laughs* (it is included on later compilations) and is Barrett's spiritual confession, the most simple and lucid account of his desperate spiritual journey, as he sings, "I'm trying / I'm trying to find you!"

Syd would try one more time with the 1970 effort *Barrett*, an overly produced mess with only a smattering of brilliance. Soon after, he performed his last show in front of an audience, backed by Gilmour, at the Olympia Exhibition Hall, but fifteen minutes into his set Barrett suddenly, but gently, put down his guitar and walked offstage. This was the beginning of Barrett becoming a recluse. Then in 1975, a hollow-eyed, overweight Barrett showed up unexpectedly at the recording studio where the now world-famous Pink Floyd, having produced *The Dark Side of the Moon*, was working on its follow-up, *Wish You Were Here*. The band was recording "Shine On You Crazy Diamond," a suite of songs about Barrett, with lyrics prefiguring the man who came to visit them as well as capturing the brilliant musician they had once known: "Now there's a look in your eyes, like black holes in the sky. / Shine on you crazy diamond." But even more chilling is the remark about Barrett's esoteric spiritual quest, a warning offered to many people on the same journey: "You reached for the secret too soon, you cried for the moon."

Madness and the visionary experience are difficult to parse. What were once believed to be religious visions were later understood to be chemical imbalances. For the occult imagination, this distinction is meaningless. But for the psychedelic sixties, it wasn't going to suffice to simply be seized by visions over and over again. There would always be the danger, as the historian of religion and early psychedelic advocate Huston Smith said, of creating a religion of little more than religious experiences.

Syd Barrett was burdened by a consciousness always seeking occult connections, but all he found was an infinity of meaning with no single truth on the horizon. For a while, his music gave this perpetual state of being turned-on a creative outlet, and audiences quickly identified their own unique hallucinogenic experiences in the storybook occult fables of Barrett's music.

While Syd Barrett's mystical psychosis via Pink Floyd, as well as the other bands of swinging London, would channel a new spiritual movement through their music and the rock posters that announced their shows, it was across the Atlantic where an even greater wave of occult-inflected mysticism was turning into a tsunami. The hippies were in need of something more than a hit of acid, but where was wisdom to be found. They were always told it came with age, but the grown-ups were making a mess of things. Where were the adults who might actually have something to teach worth learning? Western culture had long romanticized the notion of the bearded teacher, a demigod who walked between heaven and earth, like the old man in William Blake's etching *The Ancient of Days* whose esoteric knowledge can measure the universe and bring order out of the chaos. Occultism would merge with Eastern mysticism, and young people would seek out gurus and other enlightened beings to show them how to turn their stoned insights into tools of the revolution.

II

George Harrison's starry-eyed mystic insights were infectious. He had been studying Transcendental Meditation (TM), and his wife, Pattie, had heard that the long-haired giggling guru who had been touring the world to teach his meditation technique was going to be appearing in London. Harrison wanted the Beatles to go and hear Maharishi Mahesh Yogi talk. It wasn't a hard sell. Paul McCartney recalls that the band was in psychic disarray. Being a Beatle only heightened their personal struggles. There was only so much the nervous system could take. So the group, already experiencing the shadow of the tensions that would ultimately split them apart, agreed to go. They needed something to calm the stormy waters. At 20 Grosvenor Park, Harrison, McCartney, and John Lennon, along with Pattie and McCartney's then girlfriend Jane Asher, listened to the maharishi speak on the benefits of TM. Any single moment during any single day can change the world, and this happened to be the one that would begin a shift in the spiritual aspirations of a generation.

The Maharishi Mahesh Yogi's Transcendental Meditation offered an easier, softer way to achieve enlightenment. After being interviewed by the maharishi or one of his disciples, you were given a personal mantra, usually a Sanskrit word, which was apparently tuned to your own vibration. The mantra was not cheap, but the promise of a life free from stress—one of serenity and fulfillment—seemed worth it. And it was even said that after a certain amount of time, some practitioners were able to levitate (which in reality looks to be more like hopping while in the lotus position, a feat almost as remarkable).

The imperative of the West to find a guru in the East originates in an idea that sprang out of the Occult Revival of the late nineteenth century. Helena Petrovna Blavatsky, known as Madame Blavatsky, was born in Russia and had traveled all over the Middle East and Europe before landing in New York City in 1875, where she founded the Theosophical Society. Her physical size was matched only by the weight of her charisma and her intellect. Blavatsky was an encyclopedia of occult lore, and claimed to have developed uncanny powers. But her most essential teaching, the one that would have the most lasting impact, was that all religions—no matter their superficialities—are just different representations of a single divine reality. The subtext here was that Christianity was not the one true path it had sold itself to be for millennia. In fact, it might even be a stopgap to greater spiritual wisdom. This secret teaching was given to Blavatsky by the Mahatmas, a group of ascended masters who dwell in the Himalayas. Blavatsky popularized the idea that true knowledge is found in the exotic East. The Vedanta movement brought the great Hindu teachers like Swami Vivekananda to the States around the turn of the century, and this became the religion of choice of many intellectuals and writers in the 1940s and 1950s, including Aldous Huxley and Christopher Isherwood. In the 1950s, Beats such as Jack Kerouac began grooving on Zen Buddhism, and the mystic hedonist Alan Watts turned Eastern mysticism into pop psychology with a psychedelic vibe through his books like *This Is It* and *Psychotherapy East and West*. But it was what the scholar Wouter J. Hanegraaff rightly describes as theosophy's "force of religious innovation" that infused the West with a fascination about the occult, one dependent on the idea of teachers from the East to give it form and function.

Mixing magic with LSD in the 1960s just about made everybody's head crack like Humpty Dumpty. There had to be someone who could put it all back together again. The day after the lecture in London, the maharishi met with the Beatles and invited them to a retreat in Bangor, North Wales. This time the whole Fab Four went along, with friends and girlfriends in tow. The scene at the train station belied the serene intentions of the trip. The media and fans mobbed the group as they tried to board the train, and while they eventually got to their destination, there was one casualty. Mistaken for a fan by police, Lennon's wife, Cynthia, was kept back and the train left without her. Less interested in the spiritual pretentions of the Beatles than the drama of their daily lives, the newspapers snapped photos of the distraught young woman and printed stories the next day that focused on her crisis, the short article in the *Times* of London being typical, "Beatle Wife Misses the Train," complete with a photograph of the distressed Mrs. Lennon.

Cynthia being stranded, however, is uncannily symbolic of the Beatles' spiritual journey: forever trying to cast aside the chains of celebrity as they explored altered states of religious and chemical consciousness, but having access to anything they wanted to explore, chant, or swallow by virtue of their stardom. The privilege that comes with status is part of why rock and the occult became wedded so quickly. Rock stars had money and cultural cachet, had access to ideas and people most others did not. Granted a private meeting with the maharishi and being invited to a retreat is only one such example, but it's certainly a glimpse into how certain cultural elites are able to safely break free of mainstream religious communities. Fans who did not have access but who were also seeking something different could use the Beatles as a guide. The infamous 1966 *London Evening Standard* article where Lennon was quoted as saying "We're more popular than Jesus" shared an observation more prescient than anybody could have imagined at the time. For many, the Beatles were precisely that, in softly theological terms: a mediator between heaven and earth, a bridge from the drudgery of middle-class culture to the dream of something greater: cosmic awareness, inner peace, and the eternal high. Similarly, during the Great Depression of the 1930s, Hollywood films about the rich and successful were hugely popular. People who had nothing to hope for flocked to movie theaters to watch Fred Astaire in tux and tails dance on the deck of a luxury ocean liner. Fame and fantasy were a glimpse into what was possible.

In the mid-1960s, however, the cultural anxiety was not one of money but of sex, war, race, and religion. And even though the public often looked to bands like the Beatles for a glimpse beyond the confusion, the chaos sown by their celebrity status was a strangely privileged microcosm of the chaos of the West. People wanted to know every detail of their lives, not only because of how wild and fun it all looked, but because the Beatles were also a cultural mirror. And in 1967, when Cynthia was left grief-stricken at the station, people witnessed the chaos inherent in the tension between spiritual desire and the demands of the world.

In Bangor, though, the Beatles themselves seemed to fall into the quiet meditative rhythm quite naturally. The Beatles, never shy of the press, were quick to speak about the benefits of TM. By the end of the first day they were ready to proselytize for the maharishi. At a press conference, McCartney told reporters: "I had given up drugs before becoming interested in the yogi's teachings. The only reason people take drugs is because they hear so much about experiences that can expand the mind. By meditating, this expansion can be done without drugs and without their ill effects. Mediation is a way of expanding the mind naturally." Only a few months earlier, he had admitted to using LSD, and lauded its benefits: "After I took it, it opened my eyes. We only use one-tenth of our brain. Just think what we could accomplish if we could only tap that hidden part. It would mean a whole new world."

An anti-LSD position was radical for a rock band in 1967, especially a group who had already shaped the LSD musical aesthetic with songs like "Tomorrow Never Knows" and "Within You Without You." But even as the Beatles denounced drugs, Harrison kept ashore of the new hippie ethos to be wary of being preached to. It would not do to trade the mainstream Christian proselytizing for another type of evangelization, even if it did come from the East: "We don't know how this will come out in the music. Don't expect to hear Transcendental Meditation all the time. We don't want this thing to come out like Cliff and Billy Graham."

As if fated to test their newfound state of peace, their trip was cut short when, after two days, they received devastating news. Their beloved manager and friend, Brian Epstein, was dead at the age of thirty-two from an overdose of barbiturates mixed with alcohol. Epstein was supposed to meet the band at the retreat and become initiated into the TM practice. He killed himself instead. As the Beatles were heading back to London, the media immediately bombarded them with ludicrous questions: What will you do now? What are your plans? They tried to answer as best they could. Grainy, almost inaudible, footage of the moment still clearly reveals their shocked and grief-stricken faces. But this trip to learn from the maharishi, this sudden commitment to a spiritual discipline in the midst of their inscrutably chaotic lives, had to mean something, especially now. Film from that time shows Harrison in shock, but he wouldn't let the blow derail him from what he hoped, needed even, to be the truth of the maharishi. So Harrison, who once had been reluctant, drew deep from the well and said to the press, "There's no real such thing as death anyway. I mean, it's death on a physical level, but life goes on everywhere . . . and you just keep going, really. The thing about the comfort is to know that he's OK."

The death of Epstein pushed the Beatles further toward the charismatic teachings of the maharishi. The ever-smiling guru was an island, a private retreat offshore from the fans, from the press, and from the tragic loss of their manager. But always ready to meet with the media, the Beatles could not withhold even their most private moments of introspection and mourning. Despite Harrison's promise that they were not the maharishi's missionaries, Transcendental Meditation had become too important, too life-changing, to keep to themselves. Of the practice, Lennon told the press a month after Brian's overdose, "This is the biggest thing in our lives at the moment, and it's come at a time when we need it. . . . We want to learn the meditation thing properly, so we can propagate it and sell the whole idea to everyone."

In the 1960s, the culture of rock and the lives of the musicians and the music they made were inseparable. There was too much at stake for a band like the Beatles to not become a perfect microcosm of those tumultuous years. Harrison became the spiritual face of the band; his interest in Hindu spirituality had been evolving. It began, Harrison once said, with hearing Indian music. Once he began his now-famous relationship with the late sitar player Ravi Shankar, Harrison saw that the music of the Beatles and spiritual intentions didn't have to exist in separate realms. Shankar described first meeting the eager young man who wanted to learn the sitar: "It is strange to see pop musicians with sitars . . . it had so little to do with our classical music. When George Harrison came to me, I didn't know what to think. I never thought our meeting would cause such an explosion, that Indian music would suddenly appear on the pop scene."

For three days in June 1967, at the Monterey County Fairgrounds in Monterey, California, a marriage of Eastern and Western spirituality came together in a stunning display of musical talent. Even more so than the Human Be-In, with its focus on the politics of consciousness, the Monterey Pop Festival oriented the counterculture toward music as a method for transcendence. The official logo announced the spirit of the festival with a blunt visual: a satyr playing the panpipe in a bed of flowers. The lineup is a who's who of 1960s music, and it's hard to imagine the shape popular music would have taken if even one of these performers had never existed: Jimi Hendrix, Janis Joplin, Otis Redding, Simon and Garfunkel, the Mamas and the Papas, the Who, and the Byrds, among others. Beyond including some of the most iconic performances in rock history (the Who destroying their instruments, Jimi Hendrix setting his guitar on fire), the atmosphere of the Monterey Pop Festival was both thick with pot smoke and a collective consciousness that tuned in to a singular spiritual vision. Eric Burdon, the lead singer of the Animals, said it simply: "To me, Monterey wasn't a pop music festival. It wasn't a music festival at all, really. It was a religious festival. It was a love festival."

Footage from the weekend shows stoned and tripping faces beaming as if illuminated from both within and without. Various reviews in the rock and popular press describe something akin to bearing witness to ancient rite. Writing for *Newsweek*, Michael Lydon describes Hendrix's guitar burning as a pagan religious sacrament: "And when he knelt before the guitar as if it were a victim to be sacrificed, sprayed it with lighter fluid, and ignited it, it was exactly a sacrifice: the offering of the perfect, most beloved thing, so its destruction could ennoble him further." It was the performance of Shankar, though, his first public appearance in America, that infused the festival with a sense that something special was taking place. Shankar played three hours of raga to an audience of thousands (whom he politely asked not to smoke during his performance, all of whom obliged).

While Shankar appreciated the reception at Monterey and respected Harrison and the passion the Beatles brought to his musical and spiritual devotion, he was skeptical about the hippie movement in general. In an interview not long after the festival, Shankar admitted to some ambivalence that his music was so loved by the hippies. In the top-forty magazine *KRLA Beat*, Shankar drew a line between the essential religious roots of his music and the drug culture: "We don't believe in the extra, or the other stimulus taken, and that's what I am trying my best to make the young people, without hurting them, of course, to understand."

Shankar had his fans, but alone he would not have the impact soon to come when sitar playing was woven into pop music. Not only were these songs presented to the youth culture by the Beatles, in the context of rock, and especially psychedelic rock, but the sound itself resonated deeply with them. The sitar clothed the LSD experience in something authentic, both culturally and musically. By this point it was impossible to divorce the mystical from the psychedelic, the magical from the drugs, as they lent themselves so perfectly to the ideal of consciousness revolution. And the sound of the sitar in the hands of George Harrison elevated pop music beyond anything that had come before. Through lyrics like those of "Tomorrow Never Knows" ("Lay down all thoughts, surrender to the void / It is shining, it is shining"), the popular consciousness was being transformed. It would spread, like all of rock's most important milestones, into commercial and marketing efforts of the most cynical kind, but more important, it would change rock's sound and reception forever. While Beatles fans were not the only ones to hang on to every word and every chord, the band's popularity set a precedent by which rock bands and musicians would be held up as avatars of a special sort, not as priests or apostles, but as tricksters who would show that the emperor had no clothes, that normative Christianity (and Judaism, as the case may be) was empty and without the kind of spiritual nourishment the next generation would need. Rock was a method to change the spiritual order of the world. The Beatles' explicit expression of mysticism would only supercharge the electrical connection between bands and their audiences.

While it certainly is true that much of it was mere copycat spirituality, Eastern mysticism soon became all the rage in the counterculture of the 1960s. If a Beatle believed in it, it must be true. This made many in the religious establishment wary. While other spiritual ideas might offer some hope, they are ultimately in opposition to Christian teachings. The beloved preacher of the Fifth Avenue Presbyterian Church in New York, Dr. John Sutherland Bonnell, said it is often "spiritually undeveloped people" who are drawn to mysticism and other occult activities. Bonnell used the Beatles as the example of the tragic turn away from the simple, perfect message of Christ: "I suppose an instance of this would be the Beatles, who supposedly found nothing acceptable in Christianity, but then journeyed to India to sit starry-eyed at the feet of Maharishi Mahesh Yogi, a Hindu mystic."

In February 1968, the Beatles, along with the musician Donovan and Mike Love of the Beach Boys, went to see the maharishi at his ashram in New Delhi. Boredom, and rumors that the long-haired, giggling yogi was making sexual advances toward the female guests, led the Beatles to fly back to London confused and angry.

The role of the guru in the 1960s counterculture might seem opposed to the magical-oriented stew of beliefs and practices. But the Western view at the time was that mysticism and the occult were mostly synonymous. Except for a few dedicated Buddhists and other intellectuals who were committed to a rigorous exploration of yoga and other Hindu practices centered around the philosophical tradition known as Vedanta, any alternative form of religious practice was kept in the public consciousness through artists and writers. Their fame and their genius, as well as their explicit public statements about spirituality and religion, all worked to inspire the idea that they must be hiding something, that either some unseen force worked to shape their life and music, or they were willing players in various (often believed to be dark) conspiracies that both benefited and cursed them in equal measure. Like many artists whose larger-than-middlebrow life made them suspect of infernal dealings, often thought to have sold their soul to the devil, the Beatles became mirrors for every kind of occult speculation.

The cover of *Abbey Road*, the now iconic image of the Beatles crossing the street, is the portrayal of a benign and banal activity, and was a departure from their previous two outlandish covers: *Sgt. Pepper's Lonely Hearts Club Band*, with its collage of celebrities, saints, and sinners, and *The Beatles*—better known as the *White Album*—which was just that, a white cover, a blank slate available to the pen and Magic Marker doodlings of thousands of adolescents. But *Abbey Road* became a template for secret messages.

The first believed case of this was supposedly discovered by a Detroit DJ, who responded to a caller's query about the rumored death of Paul McCartney by playing the avant-garde song off the *White Album*, "Revolution 9," backwards. The refrain "Turn me on, dead man . . ." could be heard (especially if you are listening for it) and was the first "clue" that there was a conspiracy to hide the news of the beloved Beatle's death. While the "Paul is dead" rumor did not involve occult elements, the obsessive looking for clues in Beatles album covers inspired what would become a regular part of the activity of listening to rock and roll: searching for hidden meaning in every album cover. The band always denied ever deliberately helping to perpetuate the myth, but the emblematic quality of some of their album covers are evocative of those mysterious Rosicrucian posters and other occult drawings of the eighteenth and nineteenth centuries. Originally conceived of in the Renaissance, emblems served as a visual allegory for some deeper, often esoteric truth. Meditating on the symbols could bring spiritual or psychological illumination. The album cover, however, is not in the context of a tradition. Many emblems were clearly meant to convey biblical or alchemical truths, but the album cover exists in a vast sea of culture. There is no telling exactly what all those people and items on the cover of *Sgt. Pepper* meant to the band, if anything at all. What makes the album covers occult is the same thing that gives any graphic form the power to function as an emblem. In the case of the 1960s, awash with LSD and mystical mottoes, the desire of the viewer and the spiritual rebellion at the heart of rock and roll came together. This is where the culture was created, in that special and powerful bond between the audience and the musician. The painter and graphic designer Paula Scher was once asked about her experience with *Sgt. Pepper* as an art student in 1967: "Everyone I knew stared at the cover for hours on end, unlocking special, secret clues to its meaning . . . and we debated our obscure findings forever. Nothing before or since affected me as strongly. I doubt anything ever will."

There is also a negative side to how rock inspires this kind of exegesis. Those with enough time and inclination could read the Beatles album covers as an occult terrorist's handbook, a step-by-inscrutable-step guide to helping Satan and his legions take over the world. Even today, the search continues. One contemporary blogger has gone to the trouble of compiling every esoteric connection that can be found, if the right lens is applied to the task. From the cover of *A Hard Day's Night*: "Eight

SEASON OF THE WITCH

eyes. 8=sun worship." From *Help!*: "H=8 (the sun worshipper's number), HE=13 (occult), ELP=33 (masonic degrees) . . . So 'HELP'=Masonic occult sun-worshipper's record." From *Yellow Submarine*: "John Lennon makes the 'devil's horns' ('corna') hand sign." And *Sgt. Pepper* is a veritable encyclopedia of hidden occult symbols:

> [A] hookah (drug bong), a purple velvet snake (serpent/satan/ phallic), Snow White (from mason Walt Disney), a Mexican Tree of Life (usually depicting the serpent satan offering Adam and Eve forbidden knowledge in the Garden of Eden), and a Saturn trophy (sun/satan) near the "L" (90 degree square).

It is almost too easy for those with a particular religious agenda to find in the Beatles all the evidence they need to claim a vast occult conspiracy working its subliminal messaging through the mass media. The Beatles' fame made them either willing participants or naive dupes under the control of a satanic master plan. The Beatles pushed every fundamentalist button. The band's history included a guru and an admission of drug use, and even the tragedy of Lennon's death was seen as a key to their infernal dealings. But this is more often than not the voice of someone preaching to other believers. It is a self-perpetuating delusion that only fuels itself. Unfortunately, this kind of confused occult interpretation can also take a darker turn.

When the police arrived at 3301 Waverly Drive, the home of Leno LaBianca and his wife, Rosemary, they were met not only by the atrocities of the way the couple had been killed, but with the graffiti on the walls, written in the blood of the victims.

One phrase was familiar: "Helter Skelter." The title of a Beatles song from the *White Album*, these words had become the murderous rallying cry of the charismatic cult leader Charles Manson. The night before killing the LaBiancas, the followers of Manson had slaughtered five people, including Sharon Tate, wife of the filmmaker Roman Polanski (and as some occult conspiracy theorists would point out, a year earlier Polanski had directed *Rosemary's Baby*, about a woman who is impregnated by the devil by way of upper-class Satanists). At his trial, Manson would describe how the Beatles' music was in fact specific instructions to incite a race war: "Helter Skelter is confusion. Confusion is coming down fast. If you don't see the confusion coming down fast, you can call it what you wish. It's not my conspiracy. It is not my music. I hear what it relates. It says 'Rise!' It says 'Kill!' Why blame it on me? I didn't write the music. I am not the person who projected it into your social consciousness." The Beatles were devastated that their music was interpreted in this way, and became increasingly sensitive to how they were being perceived by the public.

The Beatles had become a mirror of the 1960s, a decade that had been tempered with a deep and almost anxious need for spiritual meaning, for a religious experience that was not governed by Christianity. The Beatles were the perfect mediating principle between their audience and the tumultuous decade. They offered a way to measure the effects of every experiment, be it acid or Eastern mysticism. By the time it was all over, the Beatles had each gone their separate ways, musically and spiritually. Lennon would later pen his own personal response to what he saw as the failure of the 1960s, of the starry-eyed naiveté of their own "Love Is All You Need" absolutism: "I don't believe in magic . . . I don't believe in Tarot . . . I don't believe in mantra . . . I don't believe in yoga . . . the dream is over." In a 1971 interview with *Rolling Stone*, Lennon was even harsher. He was tired of having become a messianic figure of sorts, seen by many as a spiritual savior whose private life was nonexistent insofar as it could shed meaning on their own lives: "I'm sick of it," he said. "I'm sick of them, they frighten me, a lot of uptight maniacs going around wearing fuckin' peace symbols."

While Harrison would later regret the way things ended with the maharishi, his mystical quest only deepened. He would eventually devote himself to the spiritual movement known as Krishna Consciousness through his relationship with Shankar. Apple Records, the Beatles' boutique label, would even release *The Radha Krishna Temple*, an album of devotional chants, and in 1969 the first single, "Hare Krishna Mantra," would reach number twelve in the UK charts. Once the Beatles broke up and Harrison was free to explore his spirituality through his music unfettered, he offered "My Sweet Lord," one of the most explicitly religious songs to ever land as number one on the Billboard singles chart.

To bridge the personal quest with the cultural, it took a band with a public persona inflexibly the same as the bandmates' private lives, a band who wore their spiritual search in the often indecipherable lyrics of their music as well as in interviews with the press. In other words, it took the Beatles to drive home the idea that a new spiritual age truly was dawning, but they were also the band to show that you could only take it so far.

III

In the January 1967 issue of the seminal underground newspaper the *San Francisco Oracle*, a full-page spread announced the Human Be-In, a "Gathering of Tribes" bringing together politics and spirituality, often the estranged bedfellows of the 1960s counterculture. The ad put a stake in the ground. The political revolution must be driven by a spiritual consciousness. Scheduled attendees included Timothy Leary and Allen Ginsberg, with music to be provided by the seminal San Francisco bands of the time, including the Grateful Dead and Quicksilver Messenger Service. The cover of the issue is now iconic, a Hindu holy man with an open third eye resting in a pyramid. LSD was thought to be the tool to open the third eye of a generation. Even academics saw LSD's potential. Some, like Barbara Brown, interviewed for the *Los Angeles Times* in January 1966, likened the coming laws against LSD as being akin to laws against things like witchcraft: "[H]istorically there has always been legislation against magic . . . and LSD can work magic." Musicians were not shy in talking about how it changed their lives. Brian Wilson of the Beach Boys described how it would turn pop music, even his own girl-crazy pop music, into spirituals: "White spirituals. I think that's what we're going to hear. Songs of faith." It was his own LSD trips, he said, that were a "religious experience" that set him on a new path as an artist. But researchers and musicians could not stop the popular tide. In the spring of 1966 the psychedelic drug was made illegal in California in a bill signed by then governor Jerry Brown. The Human Be-In would be the counterculture's tribal response to the new law. It was a howl at the system that consciousness could not be legislated. There was real magic in the air, and it was coming to transform the world whether the People of the State of California liked it or not. The Human Be-In was a warning flare that the psychedelic revolution could not be stopped. The long-term effect would be a popularization of LSD-flecked mysticism that would find its way into every part of pop culture. As a result, Western spirituality shifted dramatically, eagerly pushing past the Christian crowds as people eagerly feasted on every form of Eastern philosophy and religious practice, magic, and every manner of occultism. More important, the Human Be-In would turn rock and roll into the primary means of delivering the message.

The idea for the Human Be-In was born in a conversation between two counterculture occult artists, John Starr Cooke and Michael Bowen, the art editor and one of the founders— along with the poet Allen Cohen—of the *San Francisco Oracle*. Bowen was deeply schooled in theosophy and other esoteric philosophies and his artwork might now be described as belonging to the Visionary tradition. He was an outsider artist who routed his attunement to mystical frequencies onto canvas. Cooke, born to a wealthy family in Hawaii, had started using tarot cards as a child when he inadvertently purchased a deck, thinking it an ordinary pack of cards. As an adult, Cooke became involved in Scientology, Sufism, and eventually Subud, an esoteric spiritual practice using a technique called *latihan*. (During *latihan*, practitioners allow the spirit of the divine to enter them and then to be expressed in whatever manner is particular to the individual. People have been known to shout, laugh, cry, and even dance, but *latihan* is not considered to be a trance state of spiritual ecstasy.) In the early 1960s, Cooke met Bowen, and the two had much to discuss. Cooke and Bowen were both convinced a new age was dawning. Guided by answers received on a Ouija board from an entity known as "One," Cooke "channeled" the images for what he understood to be an important new interpretation of the tarot, one that Cooke believed had been prophesied by Madame Blavatsky. The deck, T: New Tarot (often referred to as New Tarot for the Aquarian Age), was first presented as a series of posters, published by the psychedelic-poster company East Totem West and showcased in the August 1967 issue of the *Oracle*.

The Human Be-In turned into a gathering of over thirty thousand hippies and counterculture elites on January 14, 1967, at Golden Gate Park. It was here that LSD prophet Timothy Leary made his famous pronouncement: "Turn on, tune in, drop out," a message that would become Walt Whitman's "barbaric yawp" of the hippies. Leary later remarked that this was his version of Aleister Crowley's own call to spiritual liberation: "Do what thou wilt shall be the whole of the law." Freedom did not just mean social and political liberation. It meant the freedom of consciousness and of the spiritual quest. But unlike the original Puritan call for religious freedom, which really only meant freedom enough to build your own theocracy, the call of spiritual freedom in 1967 was a call to a transcendent experiential experience, an ecstatic Dionysian gaze into the heart of the sun, no priests or messiahs needed. Even those who attended the Human Be-In for the outstanding musical lineup of the Grateful Dead, Quicksilver Messenger Service, and the Jefferson Airplane were also subjected to not only political speeches, but to the chanting of Allen Ginsberg as he prayed devotionally to the Hindu deity Shiva and a Buddhist bodhisattva, not just bringing the East to the most western part of the United States, but even conflating the various Eastern traditions. The idea of a spiritual revolution underlying the political one would transform the counterculture through the rest of the 1960s, an idea that would come to underlie the remaining years of the counterculture.

Even the most political of the hippies would use the occult in protest pranks. In October that same year, 1967, the radical activist Abbie Hoffman marched on the Pentagon with a group of people, including Allen Ginsberg, where they staged an attempt to levitate the Pentagon using various occult methods such as "consecration of the four directions," "creation of a magic circle," "invocation of Powers and Spirits," and "placing of love articles and clothing onto the pentagon," including but not limited to "rock & roll records." Even as a large-scale put-on, Hoffman's prank had enormous impact. No one believed they would really levitate the Pentagon, but using occult language to political purpose revealed its potential use as a social weapon, as a means of alerting the public that your rebellion goes beyond mere protests—it strikes at the heart of the religious edifice built around the political structure you oppose. Even when politics were removed, the occult continued to function as a sign of defiance, especially for rock culture, which would adopt these symbols in ways not far removed from Hoffman's.

The Human Be-In prefigured the coming Summer of Love that same year, in which hundreds of thousands of disaffected youth poured into Haight-Ashbury. The hopeful, spiritually liberating center could not hold. Hard drugs, poverty, and crime began to skyrocket. In Joan Didion's heartbreaking account of the Haight in 1967, "Slouching Towards Bethlehem," the coming tide of drug addiction and poverty could already be felt seeping through. In October 1967 the original counterculture settlers staged an event called "The Death of the Hippie" in which they carried a casket down the street in a funeral procession. But as things fell apart for the hippies, the mainstream was finally catching the wave and rock's mystical-infused spiritual rebellion would become big business.

Landing first off-Broadway at the New York Public Theater in 1967, and then moving to Broadway in 1968 to sold-out crowds, the rock musical *Hair* offered mysticism to the masses in a finely crafted stage production. It was musical theater after all, not a rock show, and audiences could distance themselves while grooving in the mostly authentic hippie ethos. The full title, *Hair: The American Tribal Love-Rock Musical*, gives a nod to the Gathering of Tribes of the Human Be-In, as well as highlighting the communal and pagan qualities of the 1960s counterculture. It's the musical's book and lyrics, a series of catchy and memorable songs, that lay out exactly what the spiritual revolution was about, in all its authentic power and its naive earnestness. The show's opener, "Aquarius," sums up the astrological prophecy of a new age through slightly nonsensical spiritual platitudes: "Mystic crystal revelation / And the mind's true liberation." Other songs revel in the sex and the drugs of the time, and there is even the necessary Hare Krishna chant to elevate the musical from mere stage show to religious ceremony. The final song, a powerhouse that both derides and celebrates the hippies, offers the simplest message, free of any mystical lingo: "Let the Sunshine In."

Rock bands incorporated the new popular mystical stylings in a variety of ways. The band Gandalf's eponymous album cover is an alien feminine face masked by colorful butterflies and other adornments. H. P. Lovecraft opts for more horror-laden cosmic awareness with their song "At the Mountains of Madness." Ted Nugent's early band the Amboy Dukes offered the chart-topper "Journey to the Center of the Mind" to a land "Beyond the seas of thought, beyond the realm of what." These and other acts continued to perpetuate the commercialization of psychedelic spirituality, and eventually it was so aboveground that it made the dwellers of the underground look like they were behind the times. Most of the major magazines had something to say about the new religious consciousness. Even *Playboy* tried to ensure that the magazine would be seen as hip and had its pulse on the spiritual erogenous zone of the culture: there is the poet and scholar Robert Graves's article discussing the resurgent belief in reincarnation, a feature on what a woman's horoscope can tell you about the best way to seduce her, and a photo gallery offering a look at some of the major trumps of the tarot, with naked girls posing as various characters from the deck, including the Magician, the Lovers, and the Devil.

Popular music was utterly transformed from four-piece bands dressed in three-piece suits to experimental and noisy collaborations, expanding three-minute songs into twenty-minute cosmic jams, turning saccharine, radio-friendly ditties into songs awash with feedback and tape loops, carving up songs about love and teenage heartbreak and serving up enigmatic lyrics about a "white knight talking backwards" and a wind that "cried Mary." Many were trapped in the cycle of doing whatever was popular at the time, such as the Lemon Pipers' "Green Tambourine" and "Incense and Peppermints" by the Strawberry Alarm Clock. It would reach its peak when the manufactured bubble-gum pop of the cartoon act the Archies would entreat fans to "get on the line with love" as they played on a rainbow-paisley decorated stage and electronic pulses and ever-brightening stars flashed behind them. (Even Sabrina the Teenage Witch makes an appearance and apparently slips the adults a magical Mickey, making them feel groovy.) The result was a parade of paisley-clothed bands churning out songs that sounded like they were made in a candy factory. But many knew how to turn all this into art and make it act as a beacon for a spiritual revolution that might not quite change the world, but would change American culture, and rock and roll, forever.

IV

Sitting at a party, strumming his guitar, the Scottish troubadour Donovan came upon a riff that seemed to hypnotize him. He played it over and over again and was told later he worked on it for seven hours. This riff was to become "Season of the Witch," a dark and prophetic song suggesting that the new age dawning brings with it darkness. Something about it stuck. (Since then, the song has been covered by dozens of artists, including Robert Plant and Joan Jett.) "Season of the Witch" was a departure from the other songs on Donovan's 1966 album *Sunshine Superman*, whose titular opener begins "Sunshine came softly a-through

SEASON OF THE WITCH

my a-window today." But "Season of the Witch" was oracular in another way. Something dark was coming for Donovan. The same year, Donovan was arrested for possession of cannabis, and while he wasn't much of a drug user, the British press used him as the poster child to further exploit the middle-class fear that the counterculture was rife with amoral drug fiends.

In interviews with the press, Donovan was nothing like the rock stars who were his peers. He continually pushed back against making any political statements, scandal couldn't stick to him, and he preferred to talk about keeping a neighborly fox away from his chickens. "The fox is a friend, too, but I'll have to have a chat with him," he told the *Los Angeles Times* in 1968. Like they did with many rock musicians, the fans and the media were looking to him to *say something* about the world, about the future of things. By this time, audiences were looking for wisdom, and it seemed rock musicians, by virtue of being incarnations of Bacchic energy, must also have spiritual wisdom. There was obvious power in their music, the way it shaped culture, the way the youth had followed it like a pied piper toward drugs, sex, and other excessive rebellions. But Donovan wasn't having any of it. Donovan grew up among Gaelic mythology and legend, and his music drew from other influences ranging from Bob Dylan to Eastern ragas with which he crafted whimsical and psychedelic pop. *Sunshine Superman* is a walk through a fantastical landscape of wizards, Arthurian legend, jewels and gemstones, and princesses. But "Season of the Witch" became an anthem, and in an interview decades later, Donovan described the song as "ritualistic." Donovan eagerly jumped into the portal the 1960s had opened into Wonderland. There, he had permission to explore musically the idea that divinity was not predisposed to exist only in heaven, but was part of the very fabric of the world. It expressed itself through myth as well as nature. This is pantheism, where God can be found in every tree and flower, every note of every song, every stoned romp in the bed of a lover. It is also pagan, where the world is animated by spirits, where nature is a book that tells the secret story of the world. Of his iconic song, Donovan said, "Maybe it is the first kind of Celtic-rock thing I was doing, a rediscovery of our roots in Britain, which of course became the British sound."

The New Forest of southern England is a protected expanse of woods, once used as a source of lumber as early as the seventeenth century, and long before then, a sacred place to ancient people who left behind burial mounds, called barrows. It is here that a supposed horned deity cult of pre-Christian worshippers passed down their rituals and practices since before Christianity came to dominate Western Europe. In 1939, Gerald Gardner, a retired anthropologist with a personal interest in the occult, met and was initiated into a coven that gathered in the thick of the forest. The story of Gardner is fraught with rumor and controversy, but it is likely that at some point around 1936, he did encounter a group of people claiming to be witches. Indeed Gardner was deeply influenced by Margaret Murray and her thesis that claimed before Christianity (and until the witch trials of the Middle Ages) there was a centralized witch cult that worshipped a horned god by way of various rites and observances. Gardner believed that aspects of this cult survived in modern-day England. He wanted to go "public" with what had been for generations secreted away. Fearful of British intolerance, Gardner's first book was presented as a novel called *High Magic's Aid*. In 1951, the Witchcraft Act, which had been in effect since 1542, was repealed, and Gardner wrote two nonfiction books, *Witchcraft Today* and *The Meaning of Witchcraft*. Gardner also perpetuated Murray's idea that had largely been debunked by other scholars. Pockets of pagan worship might have existed all over Western Europe, but the notion that it was ever a centralized religion that transmitted esoteric wisdom through ciphers was not widely accepted. But Gardner had enough to build his own religion. Using what fragments he could find from those who practiced some form of pagan worship, as well as gloss from his friend Aleister Crowley, Gardner cemented the notion of witchcraft as religion into the popular consciousness, while alerting a burgeoning counterculture that pre-Christian spirituality was alive and well.

Witchcraft, known to its followers as Wicca, was, along with Eastern mysticism, the spiritual system de rigueur among the hippies, and offered a means of rebellion that could steer clear of politics. Still, they couldn't stop the corporate machine from grinding it up and spitting it out as commercialism. The range of 1960s pop culture references to witchcraft was startling in its variety. The fabric maker Collins & Aikman took out a full-page ad in the September 13, 1964, issue of the *New York Times*, with the headline "WE Practice Witchcraft" and an image of a darkly clad woman spinning about in a field, followed by the ad copy: "Here's a gown that looks like black magic." The television sitcom *Bewitched* presented a smart witch who ran a household and presented the worst danger of the witch's craft as a troublesome mother-in-law. Wanda the Witch magically kept her hair liberated in Hidden Magic hairspray commercials. But all this really did was to keep the ideas of occultism alive in the popular consciousness. For every television show and advertisement, there was a new occult book being published.

In 1969, Andrew Greeley, a Roman Catholic priest who moonlighted as a reporter for the *New York Times*, had enough material for a full-length piece on the new religions found on college campuses, offering up examples of the student-run occult-guerrilla group WITCH (Women's International Terrorist Conspiracy from Hell), a coven of warlocks, courses on astrology and Zen, and the best and brightest at MIT meditating, casting the I Ching, and tripping on chem-lab acid. The students claimed a "return to the sacred," a heavy suggestion that not only was science failing to provide meaning, but the mainstream religions had all but abandoned their sacred charge to unite people with the divine. The press was rarely sympathetic. A *Time* magazine article by Greeley bemoans the superstition in the modern age and casts a wide net around the youth who were seeking something beyond the mundane. He writes:

Miniskirted suburban matrons cast the I Ching or shuffle tarot cards before setting dates for dinner parties. Hippies, with their drug-sensitized yen for magic, are perhaps the prime movers behind the phenomenon. Not only do they sport beads and amulets that have supposed magical powers; they also believe firmly and frighteningly in witchcraft. Some of the hippie mysticism is a calculated put-on—as when Abbie Hoffman and his crew attempted to levitate the Pentagon last October—but much of the new concern with the arcane is a genuine attempt to find enrichment for arid lives.

Greeley's cynicism misses the point and fails to ask the most essential question: Why was the occult in vogue, and why were so many young men and women the disciples of a new age? On the surface, the answer is not at all complex. What had Christianity offered them? Churches appeared to hate rock (in 1966, WAYE, a Christian radio station in Alabama, had organized the burning of Beatles records), hate sex, and love war. Many denominations, including the Catholic Church, supported the American troops in Vietnam. While reactions to organized religion were not always sophisticated, the youth were not wrong to see the mainstream Christian Church as something generally opposed to change and to a kind of self-determination. Freedom had to mean more than democracy, which was also not doing a bang-up job as far as race, class, and war were concerned. Atheism would not do, either. There had to be meaning beyond the mundane, the artificial, and the dogmatic. But it had to be new, even if by way of the very old.

The 1960s' potent mix of LSD guru sycophancy and occultism opened a door into the popular consciousness that could never be closed. Even more so than the Occult Revival of the fin de siècle, the 1960s performed a powerful conjuration of a spirit that was all but banished when Christianity quieted its song and put it in a cage to stop its rutting. But the spirit of Pan or Eshu or whichever manifestation best represents the archetype at any given moment, could not be locked up. The god Dionysus was often called "the god who comes," or "the god who arrives," because he will find a way home no matter how he might be cast out, barred, buried, or even burned. He is on the margins, sometimes just out of sight, but with rock he came to the fore, his power in the rhythms of rebellion and defiance.

While the occult in its broadest sense is a set of spiritual practices that provide direct communion with the divine, often called gnosis, it is also an ancient human drive through which the spirit of the dancing gods, the noisy gods, the trickster gods, and the gods of intoxication, madness, and ecstasy manifest themselves through history. Before the advent of Christianity, the mystery cults of the ancient world promised initiates and acolytes that the gods were ever present, and through certain ritual activities, would share their secret knowledge. The destruction of their temples and their icons might have buried their altars, but what they offered could never be entombed forever. Just as the *orisha* of Africa made themselves known through the popular and religious music of African Americans, this Dionysian spirit found a perfect vehicle through rock and roll of the 1960s, and from there was enfolded into the whole of popular culture.

Unfortunately, violence, war, heroin, and an overall cultural burnout eventually left little room for the revolutionary and transformative promise of spiritual liberation by way of LSD, yoga, and tarot cards. The spiritual sixties would give way to the excess of the 1970s, characterized by disco and cocaine. But the die had been cast. Mysticism had changed rock and roll, and no matter how far it sometimes got buried, it would continue to manifest, first in the cosmic mythology of progressive rock, and later in the experimental electronic sounds of trance, house, and underground ambient. But before mysticism's resurgence, rock would undergo another kind of change. Like all great myths, the occult story of rock involved a descent into the underworld, a transformation, and an ascent. But Orpheus's journey into Hades was not without dangers, and the long walk back to the light required sacrifice. At least he got to play music all along the way. Rock and roll would do no less, even in its darkest moments.

CHAPTER 3

THE DEVIL RIDES OUT

I

The event was billed as the Rolling Stones Rock and Roll Circus, with a heavyweight lineup, including John Lennon, Eric Clapton, the Who, Jethro Tull, the Rolling Stones, and replete with trapeze artists, fire-eaters, and midgets. The Circus was recorded for BBC Television and would be the first of its kind, a true rock spectacle aimed directly at living rooms. By 1968, Mick Jagger had styled himself as something of a dandy-in-devil's-clothing, a master seducer out to ruin civilization, or, short of that, at least your daughters. The Stones had just released *Beggars Banquet*, a return to their roots after the much-maligned *Their Satanic Majesties Request*. The *Beggars* opening track, "Sympathy for the Devil," a strongly political song that at once celebrates and mourns the evil that had befallen the 1960s, is Jagger in full-on swagger. Although there was still hope, Jagger's performance was a prophetic moment. Woodstock was still a year away and popular culture was decorated in paisley prints and primary colors. The Rolling Stones were not hippies, though. Their music was a conscious attempt to recover rock's blues-based origins, and in doing so reconjured Legba-turned-Satan, reminding everyone who the real patron saint of rock really was. Jagger's bold public recognition that the devil was alive and well, not only in the roots of rock and roll but in the stormy clouds darkening the whimsical mysticism of the counterculture, would shift rock and roll once again. The occult imagination would begin its slow turn away from gurus and astrological love charts toward a more sinister horizon, charting rock's course anew and saving it from what was becoming a neutered psychedelic commercialism.

During his rendition at the Circus, filmed before a live audience, Jagger becomes a man possessed. His Lucifer is all physicality, smoldering sex appeal with a hint of madness. At the peak point in the song, when Jagger screams over and over again "What's my name?" he begins to writhe on the floor. Back up on his knees, he bends over and slowly pulls his tight red shirt up his back, over his head, and then completely off. The camera zooms in on his arm, revealing a devil tattoo, and then pulls out to show a full devil head on Jagger's hairless chest. He then prostrates himself, appearing as if to pray to the underworld. The crowd cheers wildly as the tattoos make known exactly who Jagger is personifying in the song: Lucifer-cum-Satan, the prideful—and beautiful—fallen angel who turns hell into a kingdom, casts off his feathered wings, and bends his halo into horns.

The show never aired. The Stones were displeased with the way the footage turned out and kept it in a vault until its release on VHS in 1996. No one but the audience at the time saw Jagger's temporary tattoos. But it didn't matter. This was merely the unnecessary spectacle of what had already been decided by the media and his fans. In a 1969 concert review in the *Washington Post*, the writer named Jagger "the closest thing to an incarnation of evil that rock music has."

A band could easily become seduced by its own mythology, and trying to parse what had been a passing interest to something that becomes the defining part of a band's mystique could become difficult. Beyond the music a band makes, part of rock fame includes the rumors that surround their personal lives. In the 1960s, things like LSD use, drunken escapades, and sexual exploits could elevate interest in a musician far beyond what their talent might warrant. But even more controversial was an interest in any kind of alternative religious practice. Fans would feel the exciting flutter of reading lyrics that might hide taboo, esoteric secrets, while parents fretted and Christian groups took to burning albums. Playing up rumors was good for sales, but for a band like the Rolling Stones—who found themselves bumping up against every intellectual, artistic, and spiritual fad—it would become difficult to know where having sympathy for the devil was merely a trendy idea or where having tampered with unseen forces might have actually darkened their lives. In any case, the timing for Jagger's persona could not have been better. The devil was becoming ascendant in popular culture.

In the 1968 Hammer film *The Devil Rides Out*, Christopher Lee investigates the disappearance of his nephew and his snooping leads him to stumble upon a cult of devil worshippers who conjure Satan during a sacrificial rite of a naked woman in the woods. One of the better horror films of the time, and one of Christopher Lee's favorite roles, the plot perpetuated one of the most far-reaching misconceptions about the occult.

When the devil appears, he of course looks exactly like the god Pan in his classical representations. The movie is based on the book of the same name by Dennis Wheatley, the popular British author who the writer Phil Baker describes as the man responsible for creating the image of the devil worshipper: "[Wheatley] virtually invented the popular image of Satanism in 20th-century Britain, and he made it seem strangely seductive."

Sex, occultism, and Satan would become synonymous in various pockets of pop culture, and more films would follow, the most sensational being *The Wicker Man* (1973), directed by Robin Hardy and also starring Christopher Lee in a role diametrically opposed to the Christian occult expert in *The Devil Rides Out*. Here he plays Lord Summerisle, the leader of a pagan cult that benefits economically from their fruit crops. But a successful harvest requires a sacrifice to the gods. The devout and celibate Sergeant Neil Howie, played by Edward Woodward, is lured to the island under the pretense of a missing girl. Unlike many films in the genre, Howie's Christian entreaties do not save him from immolation inside the giant construct of a wicker man. Rather than upper-class Satanists, the people of the island are free-love hippies. Even the father figure Christopher Lee sports long hair and a bright yellow turtleneck, looking not unlike an older Brian Jones from the Rolling Stones, a dandy come to worship the old gods and serve you your doom.

While the "heathens" of Summerisle do not venerate Satan or the devil, their religion is decidedly hedonistic and, when necessary, murderous. Pagan religion is cast as a dreadful and malevolent force. While it makes for a fine horror movie, it deepens the line in the sand between the supposed mature rationality of the Judeo-Christian tradition and the irrational, youthful, and oversexed traditions of any alternative religious practice. And while this might have not been good for a nuanced understanding of the occult, it was great for rock and roll. These kinds of representations would inspire both the performance and presentation of rock music and elevate it to a mythical status.

Colloquial associations of the word *occult* with Satan and devil worship in film would fuel the rebellious whims of teenagers as well as the obsessions of certain Christian groups. But movies were not that easy of a target. Being fictional, films were less likely to be taken—or taken seriously—as personal attacks on the general public. Rock and roll, on the other hand, involved real-life, flesh-and-blood musicians making music that was being sold by the millions to impressionable kids.

Rock stars' lives were seen as pure debauchery, their music a mix of anger, sex, and defiance. These often coded, sometimes explicit occult messages would be the ruin of a civilized (e.g., Christian) world. Certainly, some bands gave over to the devil's embrace with lyrics and a presentation that were decidedly satanic. But even for those musicians, how much was a put-on—a musical role-playing of Hammer horror films—or an earnest spiritual path was not always clear.

Firmly entrenched in the rock and art scene of the late 1960s—a time of heavy barbiturate use and high fashion—the Rolling Stones met the avant-garde filmmaker Kenneth Anger, who had an idea to push the boundaries of cinema. He would make a movie that would be a magic ritual, filled with pagan gods, incantations, and his first serious attempt to channel his hero, Aleister Crowley. In 1963, Anger had completed his film *Scorpio Rising.* The thirty-minute movie—a hostile series of biker culture, homoerotic, Nazi, and occult images—was to be Anger's first real counterculture success. Over the next few years he firmly planted himself in the underground arts culture and became a darling of the hippies.

Anger's fame gave him the confidence he needed to put down on celluloid the film he had wanted to make since he was a teenager. And he had the money he needed from the lucrative publication of *Hollywood Babylon,* a scandalous account of Hollywood debauchery he first published in France in 1959, and then in the States in 1965. (The book was quickly banned and not rereleased in the United States until 1975.) To make the film, Anger first cast a musician by the name of Bobby Beausoleil, a handsome goateed fellow with a boyish face and devilish eyes.

Beausoleil would also write and perform the soundtrack. Anger was feeling on top of the world and decided to stage a public ritual in Haight-Ashbury he billed "The Equinox of the Gods." The event took place at the Straight Theater on September 21, 1967 (the date of the autumnal equinox). Beausoleil and his band, the Magick Powerhouse of Oz, headlined. Much of the ritual was filmed, and Anger wanted to include the footage in the film he would call *Lucifer Rising.* After the show, Anger and some friends went to get ice cream. Returning to the theater, they found the box office receipts and the footage stolen, taken by Beausoleil. Anger was distraught and the next day took out an ad in the *Village Voice* announcing the "death of Kenneth Anger." Beausoleil

THE DEVIL RIDES OUT

disappeared, only to show up later on charges that he murdered his music teacher, Gary Hinman, on orders from Charles Manson.

With the loss of Beausoleil, Anger immediately saw Mick Jagger as the perfect acolyte for his lead in *Lucifer Rising*. Jagger and company were intrigued by Anger and the allure of the dark arts, and Anger believed the Stones capable of producing powerful magic through their music. Anger became particularly close with Anita Pallenberg, Keith Richards's girlfriend. Theirs was a scandalous arrangement since she had been with Brian Jones before. Anger wanted to perform a pagan marriage ceremony for Richards and Pallenberg, but it seemed that Anger wore out his welcome in their lives when he set up their room for the ritual while Richards and Pallenberg were sleeping.

According to Tony Sanchez, the band's assistant (and rumored dealer) who was in the apartment at the time, they awoke to find their door painted completely gold on both sides, suggesting that Anger had been able to come and go in the dead of night without anyone the wiser. Sanchez recounts that this just made everyone uneasy, and from then on Richards was starting to feel less enamored with the occult in general, and Anger specifically. Eventually Jagger also felt pressured by Anger regarding *Lucifer Rising* and decided not to play the titular role after all.

Anger was taking it too seriously, and while Jagger was interested in the charm of the devil as a metaphor, he was really interested in what he felt that metaphor referred to. As Tony Sanchez tells it: "It was power that fascinated [Jagger], the ability to control individuals, audiences, even societies—and he knew Satan wasn't to thank for his strength in that direction."

Even their 1967 album *Their Satanic Majesties Request* came about not as an attempt to musically unlock any infernal doors as much as it was a (and some say a cynical and ill-advised) response to the Beatles' *Sgt. Pepper.* The bands had been continually and good-naturedly competing for the top spot in the public eye, but *Sgt. Pepper* changed the game completely. Art and rock finally converged in a way not thought possible and the pressure was on for the Stones to produce something as good. So they abandoned their tried-and-true blues-based rock and produced a psyche-delic grab bag replete with string arrangements, sitars, and horns.

The album title suggested something dark and malevolent inside, but the cover was almost a parody of the whole endeavor. The Stones are outfitted in Renaissance clothing, with Jagger in the middle, the grand magus with a pointy wizard cap. They are surrounded by a collage reminiscent of the *Sgt. Pepper* cover, but without the symbolic palimpsest that gave the Beatles al-bum an aura of hidden meaning and occult associations. The songs are mostly generic psychedelic manifestos, a Candy Land board where "the trees and flowers were blue." There are a few standouts like "She's a Rainbow," but the only decidedly occult song is "The Lantern," in which Jagger beseeches an unnamed traveler to leave a clear and well-lit path through an impene-trable magical forest, a likely metaphor for the vast and some-times inexplicable spiritual landscape of the sixties.

When the Aquarian Age ended not with a whimper but a stabbing at the Rolling Stones' 1969 concert at the Altamont Speedway, Jagger no longer had any use for an image of himself as the Prince of Darkness. The Stones wanted to move away from mystery and magic and return to their deep rock roots as enter-tainers and chart toppers. In the end, it's not clear how much influence Anger had on the Stones. Anger has said that the idea for "Sympathy for the Devil" came from him, but Jagger has only ever said that he was influenced by Baudelaire, who once wrote, "The finest trick of the devil is to persuade you that he does not exist," as well as Mikhail Bulgakov's novel *The Master and Margarita*, in which Beelzebub visits Moscow. Christian conspiracy theorists might tell you the Stones' relationship with Anger is all you need to know about the infernal power behind rock and roll. There is a truth here, but not quite the one they think.

While Anger's occult theology does not actually encompass a belief in the Christian conception of Satan, the overarching dark and ominous edge to his films was seductive to people like Mick Jagger. Jagger had long been cultivating an image of the decadent bad boy, a Baudelaire-like figure who projected a debauched and vaguely Mephistophelian vibe.

But to what end? What did the occult offer that fame, money, and creative freedom didn't? Much has been made of the Rolling Stones' association with Anger, but their relationship with him was also a symptom of the endless quest for meaning that characterized the era. Jagger in particular would continually find himself rubbing shoulders with the more bizarre and experimental aspects of spiritual discovery. He even ended up on the cover of the magazine put out by the Process Church of the Final Judgment, a group formed when two high-ranking Scientologists decided that they wanted a bit more personal will on their spiritual path. Robert and Mary Ann DeGrimston developed an apocalyptic vision that promised a time when Satan and Christ would join hands and usher the world into a new era. They drew heavily from the hippie aesthetic, and their magazine, while filled with foreboding and fascist imagery, still looked like a typical underground rag. Jagger was never a member, but his face on the cover of the issue titled "Mindbending," with the Process logo looking strangely reminiscent of a swastika right below his iconic face, deepened his persona as someone wicked.

Satan would continue to be a spiritual muse for those seeking a symbol of spiritual rebellion, not for his reputation as anti-Christian, but as a representation of sex, power, and ecstasy. This is not the devil whose true face is that of Pan and the other trickster gods that have possessed human beings since the earliest religions. This is the Antichrist, the destroyer, come to seduce your children. Musicians would find the persona and image of the devil to be a mighty force, not only inspiring their fans to feel empowered by the simple act of rebellion that can come with an upside-down pentagram hung on a bedroom wall, but by the fierce sexual and ecstatic energy their music inspired.

This is a prime example of where occultism, by its nature, is indefinable, a tabula rasa that becomes a projection of whatever fears, desires—spiritual or otherwise—that culture needs, and do not fit within a mainstream (read Christian) context. It didn't matter, for example, that Anger's Lucifer was not the fallen Satan of Milton's *Paradise Lost* and Christian mythology. For the Stones, the association was enough to engender an idea that they walked in darkness.

The irony of the Stones in the context of this narrative is that, except for Jagger's almost faddish interest in the occult and the hobnobbing with people like Anger and the Process Church, the band had no abiding spiritual motivation beyond that of making music, which is no small impulse, to be sure. But their reputation as somehow sowers of the flowers of evil was as much a dandyish and Baudelairian persona that Jagger eagerly cultivated as an agreement between fans and the media to crown them satanic majesties. The culture of psychedelic rock and flower power hippie culture needed its serpent in the garden. Everyone—the band, the public, the media—acknowledged that the devil seemed to have more of a role to play in the history of the world than any colorful LSD-fueled mysticism.

The innocent belief in the cosmic power of love was undermined every day by a continuing war and the gruesome faces of people like Manson staring out from a commune, once the ideal example of a utopian possibility. The Rolling Stones were the soundtrack to the feeling of unease, as well as a reminder that no matter how bad things got, there was still great music to be had. Rock and roll was now becoming a thermometer for every temperature of the culture, bands and performers perfectly representing the associated hope or fear.

II

Terry Manning was hunched awkwardly over the master vinyl disc of the album that would be called *Led Zeppelin III*, his hand preternaturally steady as he engraved the words on the runoff— the smooth inner ring where no grooves had been cut. A special platter was placed on top of the disc that exposed only the area he was working in, so he was prevented from accidently scratching the vinyl and ruining the master. Guitarist Jimmy Page, excited and stoned, looked on. It was Page who'd implored Manning to carve the message that would end up on every copy in every record store and in the hands of every fan. Unless you looked for it, the words would essentially be invisible, but their very existence on the record would impress a great truth that Page was convinced the world needed: "Do what thou wilt." This single moment serves as a microcosm of the entirety of the influence the occult would have on rock and roll. It would spread out into rock's atmosphere in ways neither Manning nor the band could have predicted. The timing was perfect. Music fans were anxiously waiting for the next incarnation of Dionysus to remind them that the god was not dead. He was merely biding his time while the astral trails of psychedelic rock dissolved. Led Zeppelin perfectly encapsulates the power of the occult imagination, how it continues to see expression, and how it was able to completely propel rock and roll into electrifying new directions.

Manning, an old friend of Page and a veteran of the still fairly young rock industry, had been called in to engineer the record. On a July day in 1970, at the Mastercraft studio in Memphis, he and Page did the final mix and then the master. It was going to be a slightly different album, Zeppelin's hard rock edge softened with British folk influences. But the opener, "Immigrant Song," was pure Zeppelin, a Viking-inspired revelry about cold Nordic winds and the halls of Valhalla. At the time, Page was obsessed with Aleister Crowley, whose notorious turn-of-the-century magical and sexual escapades were idealized by much of the sixties counterculture as brilliant feats of radicalism. Page believed Crowley was a "misunderstood genius" and thought he had a duty to spread Crowley's prime directive: "Do what thou wilt shall be the whole of the law." While Page's own passion could be infectious, it was not always easy to know when he was just looking to stir things up. Manning later said he never knew of Zeppelin's guitarist ever actually trying to cast a spell or perform a ritual. But Page had invested a huge sum on rare Crowley manuscripts, and even went so far as to buy Crowley's home on the shore of Loch Ness—a mansion rumored to be haunted by the spirits the dark magician had conjured. By agreeing to inscribe the Crowley line on the master pressing of the album, Manning decided to humor his friend even though the risk of damaging the master was great.

Twenty years later—almost to the day, as he remembers it—Manning was flipping channels when he came across a televangelist preaching on the devil's influence on rock and roll. He held up a vinyl copy of *Led Zeppelin III*, an album by then considered one of the greatest rock records of all time by critics and fans. As the camera zoomed in on the album, the televangelist's fingers began to trace the words engraved on the runoff. The TV preacher explained that these were the words of one of the most devilish men who ever lived, the black magician and Satanist Aleister Crowley. Manning sat back, smiled. He said to himself, "I did that."

By the time Manning saw his handiwork raised up as a symbol of the demonic influence in rock and roll, Led Zeppelin's reputation as a band that had trucked with Satan was cemented. That idea was provoked by both the band and by the circumstances of their tumultuous rock star lives and would spread across the entire spectrum of popular music. Page's interest in the occult and Crowley is where this all begins, and it has been widely documented. And Crowley has been written about even more than Led Zeppelin. While the artistic and spiritual merit of his ideas are up for debate, his impact is undeniable and deserving of the word count devoted to trying to get a handle on the man and his legacy. What makes Crowley in equal measures fascinating and frustrating is that he's impossible to pin down. Was he a serious magician, hoping to transform the world through his work, or was he merely a charlatan, using his gift for crafting baroque rituals to seduce men and women alike?

Crowley was born in 1875 in England, just as the Occult Revival was starting in earnest and Spiritualism and the Theosophical Society (founded the same year as Crowley's birth) were gaining popular notice. Crowley was a rascal as a child and his mother called him "The Great Beast." He would later put this phrase on his business card. Crowley wore many hats. He was a formidable mountain climber and chess player, but his greatest talent was that of the libertine. The core of his system of magic, which he related in dozens of books and articles, relied on the notion that norms related to sexuality and other behaviors were keeping mankind from achieving true spiritual liberation. To the dismay of many of his peers in the Golden Dawn and other occult fraternities, Crowley developed a system of "sex magick" (Crowley added the *k*, he said, to differentiate the "great work" from stage magic) that did not shy from any form of sexual expression.

The rumors of both magical and sexual excess, as well as his taste for drugs, helped Crowley develop a reputation as a devil worshipper. But the truth is that Satan appears very rarely in any of his writings. What does appear, however, is the idea that God is man, that there is no deity beyond what the individual desires to make manifest. For Crowley, the figure of Lucifer was merely a stand-in for the Miltonian idea of self-determination. Lucifer's pride is not simply a middle finger to the heavens, but a willful intention to be responsible for one's own destiny. Magick is the means by which one dives into one's own self. It's no wonder, then, that Crowley would become not only an icon to the sixties counterculture, but that he'd also be embraced by those who enjoyed his reputation as Satan's best human advocate. Over time, Crowley stopped being an actual person, instead becoming a cipher that could be interpreted in whatever way was needed. Timothy Leary once remarked that he believed his own attempt to make the exploration of consciousness via drugs an inalienable right was an extension of Crowley's "Do what thou wilt." The Beatles included him in the roster of characters on the cover of *Sgt. Pepper,* while occultists, Wiccans, and magicians of every stripe would borrow liberally from his ideas for their own thoughts and practices.

Today, Page tends to dismiss his interest in Crowley as just one of many novel curiosities he's explored in his life. In a 2012 interview with *Rolling Stone,* he even seemed a bit annoyed to have to keep answering questions about it all these years later: "What attracted me to [the Pre-Raphaelite poet and painter] Dante Gabriel Rossetti? You won't be asking me questions on that. But you would ask me about Crowley. And everyone is going to prick up their ears and wait for great revelations. . . . It's taken out of all proportion. There was a balance to it. I wouldn't be here now if there hadn't been." But no matter the force of his protestations, in the accepted history of Led Zeppelin, the story of Page's magical dabblings is indispensable.

In *Hammer of the Gods,* one of the earliest and most popular biographies of the band, author Stephen Davis quotes a much younger Page saying something a bit less "balanced": "Magic is very important if people can go through it. . . . I think Aleister Crowley's completely relevant today. We are still seeking for truth—the search goes on." No source is provided for the quote, but it certainly echoes the thoughts of a typical young man in the early 1970s for whom taboo and dark things held a special appeal. Let's chalk it up to his age and the context of his life as a rock star. In a 1976 *Rolling Stone* interview, he talked candidly about his interest in Crowley, but was wary of coming across as proselytizing. He notes Pete Townshend's name-checking of the Indian spiritual leader Meher Baba in the title of the song "Baba O'Riley" as something he never wanted to do with Crowley. But he was not shy in proclaiming that he incorporated Crowley's ideas into his "day-to-day life." Here, Page is more mature, less gushing, likely feeling he no longer has to convince anyone of anything. His 2012 interview, where he almost seems exasperated with the question, is just as indicative of a long life where one's ideas have mellowed.

Page's willingness to discuss his fascination with Crowley and magick ebbed and flowed. But over many years of interviewing Page, *Guitar World* editor Brad Tolinski was able to gain confidence with the reticent guitarist, and in their conversations a clearer picture emerged. With Tolinski, Page admits that his esoteric inquisitiveness was not limited to Crowley, but took in the whole spectrum of "Eastern and Western traditions of magick and tantra." But the media found Crowley an easy mark for referencing a sinister figure par excellence, and he made for more interesting interview questions than, say, an obscure grimoire. Nevertheless, Crowley did represent for Page the very best example of "personal liberation." As a young man with unlimited money and access to drugs, Page took it literally: "By the time we hit New York in 1973 for the filming of *The Song Remains the Same,* I didn't sleep for five days!"

But the cultural truth is much more important than even how Page talks about the occult at different stages in his life. Culture is where the story of the occult and rock is created, not in coy interviews with musicians. Along the trajectory of a band's life, the facts are akin to mythology, a grand narrative that is as much about how the myth gets transmitted as it is about how the myth gets made. But for Led Zeppelin, their mystique was grounded in something intentional, something that was as much a part of what they conceived and gave birth to as it was the frenzied media and fan speculation. Page tells Tolinski, "I was living it. That's all there is to it. It was my life— that fusion of music and magick."

Page first encountered the writings of Aleister Crowley when he was eleven years old and, while intrigued, he couldn't really penetrate Crowley's often impenetrable and assertive prose. When he returned to the magician's writings as an adult he was taken by Crowley's philosophy of self-liberation. In the late 1960s, Page began collecting rare Crowley works and in 1970 purchased the home once owned by the magician, known as the Boleskine House, on the southeastern shore of Loch Ness in Scotland, a place that would continue to attract legends of mystery and monsters. Crowley purchased the house in 1899, as it was, according to the magician, situated in a place that was particularly conducive to magical experiments. Crowley was, at the time, attempting a ritual by which a magician meets his or her Holy Guardian Angel, a yearlong operation that requires chastity, intense prayer, and the conjuration of spirits both good and evil.

The ritual is found in a medieval grimoire known as *The Book of the Sacred Magic of Abramelin the Mage*, a text filled with complex and decidedly religious invocations ("In the name of the blessed and holy Trinity . . ."), list after list of infernal and heavenly names ("Akanef. Omages. Agrax. Sagares . . ."), and byzantine rules ("Take of myrrh in tears, one part; of fine cinnamon, two parts; of galangal . . ."). Nevertheless, the practical purpose of the grimoire is disappointingly prosaic: becoming invisible, discovering treasure, and even locating a misplaced book. Crowley believed, however, that the Holy Guardian Angel was not, in fact, an external divine presence, but a stand-in for the "higher self." He never completed the ritual at the Boleskine House. But the attempt was enough to charge the grounds with a current of ominous radiance.

Prior to Crowley, the house was already considered a place of ill repute. A church once situated there is said to have burned down, killing all the people inside. Crowley's reputation for black magic made the place twice haunted. It's uncertain what Page actually did there except hold lavish parties. The guitarist eventually sold the house and opened a bookstore in London called *Equinox*, named after Crowley's book series (an attempt at a literary journal for the occult set). Page worked hard, and spent a lot of money, to keep the store from looking like a typical musty bookstore or a head shop, an establishment just then beginning to line store shelves with quartz crystals. Page, ever the romantic dandy, had an architect design the shop in the style of a nineteenth-century occult lodge, replete with Egyptian motifs and Art Deco trappings.

Page's burgeoning curiosity with Crowley coincided nicely with Robert Plant's own love of Celtic folklore and fantasy, particularly by way of J. R. R. Tolkien. References to Tolkien's hobbit-populated Middle-earth in Led Zeppelin's lyrics were fairly explicit, with Plant name-dropping Tolkien's delightfully grim locations, such as Mordor and the Misty Mountains, as well as the nefarious Gollum and the black riders called Ringwraiths. Plant also wanted his lyrics to hold mythological meaning, and he once described Celtic mysticism as the vital source for the spirit of Led Zeppelin. "[Those are] the lyrics I'm proud of," he told a reporter for *New Musical Express* in 1973. "Somebody pushed my pen for me, I think."

Plant grew up in West Bromwich, an area of England rich with folklore and legends. Pre-Christian mythology was at his doorstep. And Page's magick guitar work was the perfect vehicle to hitch to folk fantasy lyrics. "Immigrant Song" offers a powerful example. The song is a dragon's fiery breath unsealing the new decade of the 1970s, a period that would fuse mythology, fantasy, and the occult in exactly the same way the band would with their music. Lester Bangs, the frenetic genius of rock criticism, prophesized this union of imagined worlds carved out of ancient myths and the spiritual rebellion at the heart of rock and roll in his review of *Led Zeppelin III* for *Rolling Stone* in 1970.

Bangs makes special note of Page's opening cry with its "infernal light of a savage fertility rite." Even more so in "Immigrant Song," Bangs identifies the future of rock: "You could play it, as I did, while watching a pagan priestess performing the ritual dance of Ka before the flaming sacrificial altar in *Fire Maidens of Outer Space* with the TV sound turned off. And believe me, the Zep made my blood throb to those jungle rhythms even more frenziedly." Led Zeppelin rapidly became the touchstone for all the weird and occult permutations of the 1970s. From Tolkien to Crowley, from pulp fantasy to pop magick, the darker edge of the 1970s occult leanings was found everywhere.

Book publishers such as Ace and Ballantine were putting out cheap paperbacks of old sword-and-sorcery stories, many of these in anthologies, including the popular *Swords Against Darkness*, published by Zebra Books in 1977. While much of the literature and comics of the genre were consumed by a dedicated group of fans, by the mid-1970s, images of magic and fantasy, often with a dark tinge, would come to dominate the pop culture landscape. Chain bookstores began carrying inexpensive art books showcasing the talents of artists such as Boris Vallejo and Frank Frazetta, whose paintings featured Viking-like warriors battling giant serpents, with scantily clad maidens at the heroes' feet. In the same mall as the bookstore, gift shops sold small pewter statues of wizards and dragons.

The filmmaker Ralph Bakshi released two major animated motion pictures—*Wizards* and *The Lord of the Rings*—and the company Rankin/Bass produced a widely popular made-for-TV feature-length cartoon of *The Hobbit*. Led Zeppelin gave these shadowy fantasies an aura of the real. Sure, role-playing a wizard in D&D is just a game, but Page talks about the magick of Crowley in interviews the way the Beatles talked about the benefits of Transcendental Meditation as taught by the maharishi. Tolkien wrote fiction, but the same song that mentions the Misty Mountains also describes real-life hippies getting stoned in a park. Was there some hidden magic peak that Plant knew about, a retreat where he communed with the spirits, away from pretense and fame?

All of this was solidified by the vaguely sinister vibe the band gave to their music and lyrics. The ghost of the supposed crossroads bargain made by Robert Johnson became attached to the band by way of their appropriation and celebration of the blues. Their essential sound is the driving twelve-bar blues found in some of the most important blues and early rock songs, including Muddy Waters's "Train Fare Blues," Gene Vincent's "Be-Bop-A-Lula," and Elvis Presley's "Hound Dog."

Led Zeppelin's oeuvre includes luminous interpretive covers of songs by Howlin' Wolf, Willie Dixon, and Memphis Minnie. In a 2012 interview by Tolinski with Jimmy Page and guitarist Jack White, White describes Led Zeppelin's ability to express the power of the blues: "When you have a vision like Jimmy's, I think that's the aim. To make everything as powerful as you can make it." Page agreed, but took it one step further: "But it wasn't just power—atmosphere was very important for us as well. We wanted to create an atmosphere that was so thick you could cut it with a knife. Our goal was to make music that was spine-tingling." It was precisely this atmosphere that gave the band its dark mystique, and it's why Led Zeppelin so perfectly embodies the uncanny synergy between rock and the occult. Led Zeppelin contains all the elements unearthed so far.

We see the medieval bard as if through a scrying mirror, a crystal used by the Elizabethan astrologer and magus John Dee to try and communicate with the spirit world. The figure stops to eat a mushroom he finds at the base of a tree, where he sits and then begins to dream. He is now on a horse, a sword at his side, riding along a landscape of beaches, hills, and valleys. The dashing hero rides through a forest until he comes upon a castle. A falcon flies from his wrist and into a window where it scares a group of guards. Our hero then battles a dark knight and vanquishes the villain into a moat.

This is, of course, a scene from *The Song Remains the Same*, the Led Zeppelin concert movie interspersed with fantasy sequences, one for each member of the band. The brave adventurer is Robert Plant, and he eventually finds what he was looking for, a princess held in the castle against her will. Plant fights the guards and saves her from whatever terrible fate was about to befall her.

The Song Remains the Same, released in 1976, mixes sword and sorcery, Tolkien, Arthurian lore, and Celtic mythology in a snapshot of the 1970s: a fantasy-imbued mysticism that is darker than the hippies' pastoralism, a place where great battles and romance, not vegetarianism and yoga, characterize the spiritual quest. Plant's sequence also further refines the Led Zeppelin mythos as a grand epic, where each member functions as an archetype. Plant as romantic hero might seem in opposition to the almost androgynous and steamy Dionysian sexuality he exhibited in his stage performances, but this kind of image is the glamour of rock, and precisely how rock managed to so effectively combine spiritual ecstasy and danger with a rich phantasmagorical aesthetic.

In another sequence, the haunting strains of an electric guitar being played with a cello bow leads into the scene of a foggy night. A desperate seeker, Jimmy Page, climbs a dark and lonely mountain, his way treacherous. What he is looking for awaits him at the top. At the summit stands an elderly hermit—almost ancient—who guides the man's final steps with the light of his lantern. The young man reaches toward the elder and looks into his eyes. Page watches as the hermit's face transforms into his own, and then to that of a child, and finally to an embryo, a moment reminiscent of the star child in *2001: A Space Odyssey*. The vision then begins the movement back again until we gaze upon the face of the wizard, who raises his staff and waves it, producing a trail of prismatic color.

This image of the hermit first appears in the inner artwork of the gatefold cover of Led Zeppelin's untitled fourth album, often referred to as *Led Zeppelin IV* or *Zoso*, a creative means to pronounce the unsayable sigils that decorate the album. Taken almost whole from the famous Rider-Waite tarot deck, the hermit stares down into the village, the only light coming from his lantern, his frail body supported by a long walking stick.

If the band was trying to deepen the occult aura around themselves and their music, they couldn't have come up with a better, more potent means than the sigils. Indeed, the whole package of *Led Zeppelin IV* as an album and as an artifact serves as one of the most perfectly magical moments in rock history. While the Beatles' "Paul is dead" rumors set the stage for the album cover to become an occult emblem and Manson's homicidal exegesis of the *White Album* gave song lyrics a sinister weight, *Led Zeppelin IV* functioned as a kind of grimoire, a magical text, each song a spell, the vinyl disc a kind of magic circle in which to perform the invocations, and the album cover the altar on which to make sacrifice (or de-seed your weed, as the case may be).

Adding to rock's reputation as a vehicle for subliminal Mephistophelian control were the persistent rumors that musicians were recording secret messages with a technique called backmasking. When played backwards, songs would reveal their true meaning, such as the clues to McCartney's death supposedly "masked" in Beatles songs. *Led Zeppelin IV*'s prime mover, the leviathan of rock and roll, "Stairway to Heaven," is thought to be the backmasked song extraordinaire, a literal love song to the devil with its infamous line: ". . . to my sweet Satan . . ."

Subsequent album covers would continue to inspire occult speculations. *Houses of the Holy* (1973) shows naked children crawling across stones toward some unknown terrible glory. The inner gatefold is more disturbing. Up on a hill of ancient ruins, a naked figure holds a child aloft as if to throw it off. The cover was designed by Aubrey Powell of the design company Hipgnosis, responsible for some of the most iconic record album covers of all time, such as Pink Floyd's *The Dark Side of the Moon*. Powell claims the idea for the artwork came from the book *Childhood's End* by Arthur C. Clarke in which extraterrestrials, who hide their appearance since they resemble human conceptions of the devil, interfere with humanity in a way that helps push earth toward extinction; only a group of children who have evolved and share a single hive mind survive. But truth rarely gets in the way of speculation, especially when it comes to rock. And it's difficult to image that, whatever Powell's inspiration for the cover, the band enjoyed the way it continued to ignite rumors of perverse magic. The late music critic Keith Shadwick proposes nothing less in his discussion of *Houses of the Holy* in his book on the band: "The images gave the strongest suggestion yet that Page and Plant's interest in legend, mythology, and esoterica was beginning to help form their overall notion of what the band and their music was about."

Later in 1970, the same year of the Royal Albert Hall concert, Led Zeppelin pushed the Beatles out of the number-one spot in a British music poll. The Beatles had held that title for eight years, but Led Zeppelin brought with them the spirit of change, an insistent driving rhythm that dethroned the previous monarchs of rock. The reflective and melancholic mysticism of the Beatles—delivered by way of a message of love (it's all you need), peace (give it a chance), and the giggling spirituality of the maharishi—could no longer speak to the cynicism and disappointment that characterized the end of the 1960s. Rock's soul would need to be newly forged on Surtur's anvil. Led Zeppelin was the hammer.

For detractors of rock, it didn't take long to diagnose the post–Aquarian Age as a time of excess exemplified by popular music. Religious leaders saw rock and roll as the worst form of hedonism; it contained all the wickedest offenses: intoxication; sex and gender fluidity; loud, aggressive music often drawn from the blues (a troublesome "primitive" form of music); and social rebellion. In 1971, Ezra Taft Benson, a leader of the Mormon community in Salt Lake City, told the *Washington Post* that even the debauchery of ancient Greece and Rome paled in comparison to a rock show. Rock festivals, Benson said, are "Satan's greatest successes."

Adding to the devilish aura around Zeppelin specifically

was Page's meeting with Kenneth Anger. In 1973, at a Sotheby's auction of Crowley memorabilia, Anger was outbid by Jimmy Page, then twenty-nine years old and exceedingly wealthy. Anger and Page met, and their shared interest in magick led Anger to ask Page to write the neglected soundtrack to *Lucifer Rising*. Page agreed, excited to be working with this famous underground filmmaker. But the next few years would be difficult ones for Page and the rest of the band. By 1976, Page was addicted to heroin, and Anger believed this was the reason for the guitarist failing to deliver on his promise. Page was finally able to produce twenty-three minutes of music, but Anger was not pleased. The two had a falling-out, and Page would eventually call upon an imprisoned Bobby Beausoleil to complete the soundtrack from his cell.

For many people, the name "Lucifer" necessarily refers to the biblical Satan, but for some occultists the image of Lucifer is used to represent that aspect of being human that seeks "light" or knowledge. As Anger once explained to Mick Farren in *NME*: "Lucifer is the hero. He shouldn't be confused with the Christian devil. Lucifer is another name for the Morning Star, the bringer of light. He is the one who helps man in his search for truth and enlightenment." It would be this devilish association— strengthened by Page's Crowley interest—that would eventually be impossible to unglue from the band, however. Even their sympathetic fans began to wonder what was true when tragedy and calamity were on Zeppelin's heels like a hound from hell. Bad things started happening. In 1975, Robert Plant was almost killed in a car accident, and two years later his young son died from a virus. Three years later, their beloved but out-of-control drummer, John Bonham, died of a drug overdose. Rumor, public persona, and private life became a kaleidoscopic blend, hypnotizing both fans and detractors: To be as good as they were for as long as they were, Led Zeppelin must have made a deal with the devil, and that would eventually require the contract to come due.

In 1982, during a meeting of the California State Assembly's Consumer Protection and Toxic Materials Committee, members listened intently as "Stairway to Heaven" was played backwards. Stoned teenagers everywhere had already grooved to this sonic mirage for years, but an armchair neuroscientist named William Yarroll was convinced of a satanic conspiracy, and claimed that Led Zeppelin purposefully recorded the song so that the subliminal message "Here's to my sweet Satan" would be absorbed by the unsuspecting public. This would be the beginning of a movement to put warning labels on rock albums to ensure that people were not unwittingly turned into "disciples of the anti-Christ."

The patron deity of Zeppelin is not Satan, but "the god that comes." He has been called Dionysus, and the lead singer Robert Plant seemed to channel whatever power remained of him centuries after the last of the maenads ran into the hills at the drunken god's side. Dionysus's entourage featured satyrs, those perpetually rutting half-goat/half-human flautists whose leader was Pan, child of Hermes and Dionysus's older brother. While Dionysus is the frontman, the one who demands nothing less than total religious intoxication from his worshippers, Pan is the piper, the true musician who tethers that ecstatic state to the earth, who reminds us that no matter how subsumed by the gods we allow ourselves to become, there are still the essential things we need: sex, libation, a romp with a nymph through the woods. This is where the real magic is, and why Pan's image will be superimposed on images of devils, adopted as the god of the witches, believed to be the Horned One, the Green Man, and then Baphomet, the symbolic god of magicians.

This is where Led Zeppelin exists, midway between Dionysian, intoxicating madness and the sexual earthiness of Pan. And like the mystery cults that worshipped these gods, Zeppelin's concerts are communal, driven by similarly tribal rhythms banged out on drums and timpani. Their fans grooved to their individual rhythms as much as to the collective consciousness of the audience, prompted by the theatrical gestures of the gods incarnate in the band. Just as the earliest forms of theater were to pay tribute to Dionysus, the spectacle of a Led Zeppelin show reignited that ancient urge. But let's not forget Pan, whose attributes were celebrated in the ancient Satyr plays, a joyous romp in the field of the darker and tragic aspects of life, exemplified in the open tuning of Page's guitar and Plant's unearthly high-ranging voice. And just as the satyrs proudly displayed their tumescent phalluses, the band exhibited their own cocky gesture by way of pelvis and upright guitar.

III

During the early 1980s, at the peak of his solo career, Ozzy Osbourne's brilliant stage show involved the singer sitting on a throne at the top of a large staircase, torches igniting in balls of flame, as he makes his way down the stage. The set was bookended by two large "stone" arches, and overhead a light show drew a batlike demon flapping its angry wings. Ozzy would appear holding a large cross, and this would become a staple for not only Ozzy, but for gothic rock bands as well. The use of the cross in the context of a musical horror-movie performance was an inspired bit of malevolent whimsy.

Is the cross in defiance of its Christian context or is it a talisman to keep any real evil at bay, from being summoned by accident? That Ozzy would opt for the cross to become his representative symbol, rather than, say, a pentagram (which would become the ubiquitous metal icon), exposes an essential contradiction that Ozzy was able to use to his advantage. His young fans would listen to the song about "Mr. Crowley" (which itself is on the fence about whether or not the infamous magician is someone to revere or lament) and light black candles in their wood-paneled basements. But Ozzy would often say he was a Christian, and insist the demonic bombast was all showmanship. In interviews, Ozzy lamented—perhaps disingenuously—that even if he sang about birds, people would hear it as "Satan." Even to his audience he felt the need to remind them before his shows began: "It's just music." But no matter how he protested, Ozzy Osbourne would be seen as Satan's little singer.

Once he left Black Sabbath, which was his original band, Ozzy Osbourne would deliberately cultivate a dark and fiendish persona with his onstage antics, such as biting the head off a bat he later claimed to believe was rubber (the subsequent rabies shots taught him to be careful about what he put in his mouth). His lyrics would invite speculation of every sort, and they would even result in a lawsuit claiming Osbourne urged teenagers to commit suicide in his song "Suicide Solution." The covers to his first two solo records, *Blizzard of Ozz* and *Diary of a Madman,* are both suggestive of Osbourne practicing some kind of wicked magic. Fans loved it. They were a generation of kids witness to a gruesome parade of pop culture artifacts during the 1970s. Horror was not limited to film. In toy stores, parents bought their kids some of the most macabre products: In 1971, Aurora Plastics Corporation introduced its line of Monster Scenes models, including the Hanging Cage (complete with hot-coal pincers) and the Pain Parlor, with a nefarious-looking machine and an examination table. Later, in 1975, Milton Bradley produced the Shrunken Head Apple Sculpture kit, the box showing Vincent Price—the then most recognizable face in horror movies—in a lab coat, holding up two tiny withered heads. Monsters were used to market everything to kids, from chewable vitamins to cereal.

The monster craze really started in 1958 when James Warren launched *Famous Monsters of Filmland,* an unabashed celebration of horror movies, including interviews, still photos, and reviews. From the first magazine under Warren Publishing, and from there on in, Warren revived the lost art of gory sequential art in the tradition of EC Comics, such as *Tales from the Crypt,* which had been discontinued due to the heavy-handed moral weight of the Comics Code Authority, a self-governing agency of comic publishers that approved—or censored—comic book material depending on the level of violent, sexual, or even supernatural content it contained. Gaining approval meant getting a stamp on the upper corner of the comic. This meant better distribution in drugstores, magazine stands, and bookstores. By making his comics the size of regular magazines and unable to fit in the spinning comic book racks, Warren avoided the Code.

Warren published three essential horror comic magazines, *Creepy, Eerie,* and *Vampirella.* The stories were written and drawn by a remarkable stable of writers and artists who took gleeful advantage of their newfound freedom. In the 1970s, the Warren magazines offered dozens of occult-themed stories and offered the comic book–reading audiences a gloomier panel-by-panel look at the world, one in extreme opposition to the colorful superheroes that had come to dominate the 1960s with the ascension of Marvel Comics' lively aesthetics of Spider-Man, the Fantastic Four, and the Hulk. The tide was turning away from the psychedelic pastels of the Aquarian Age toward something more foreboding. Marvel Comics wasn't immune, either. In the 1970s, the company introduced their own version of Dracula in *The Tomb of Dracula,* the supernatural antihero Daimon Hellstrom in *The Son of Satan,* and the undead motorcyclist *Ghost Rider.* Other titles included *Werewolf by Night, The Legion of Monsters,* and *Morbius, the Living Vampire.* The magazines and comics accumulated a nice cult following, prompted by the distribution to local television stations of *Shock Theater,* an inexpensive package of horror movies by Universal Studios.

Monsters and occult movies received another boost when they moved from late-night programming featuring costumed hosts, such as the Boston-based *Simon's Sanctorum,* to the late morning and early afternoon in the 1960s and 1970s, with UHF stations running *Creature Features* and *Creature Double Feature* on Saturday and Sunday mornings. American adolescents were getting their first taste not only of the main quorum of monsters—

Frankenstein, Dracula, Wolfman, and the Mummy—but the darker, more esoteric chills of movies like *The House That Dripped Blood* and *Dr. Phibes Rises Again.*

Ozzy Osbourne's Black Sabbath would embrace this exaggerated horror-movie sensibility. Even their name was inspired by the film *Black Sabbath* starring Boris Karloff, which the bass player, Geezer Butler, noticed on the marquee of a cinema and who then decided to write a song with the same title. At the time, the band went by the name Earth, but opted to change it to better reflect the sound they had in mind. This doom-laden and riff-heavy sound, along with their dark lyrics, would give the band a reputation for having made an infernal pact. Black Sabbath, the very name evoking a perverted notion of holiness, was the de facto Luciferian messenger. Black Sabbath became the new mantle of hard rock, fueled by marijuana and afterimages of Vietnam and Charles Manson with songs like "War Pigs" and "Iron Man."

The irony of Black Sabbath is that a close listen to their lyrics will reveal a warning cry during a time when it looked like the world was going to hell, more than an embrace of the devil they seem to portray. "War Pigs" (a song that includes the worst couplet in the history of rock, rhyming "their masses" with "black masses") explicitly names Satan, but he laughs and "spreads his wings" because of warmongering and genocide. The song is a mirror, not a conjuration.

Nevertheless, Black Sabbath would create a legacy of rock and roll demonism, altering the presentation and aesthetic of rock. The band presents an interesting problem in rock history, since they played with both extremes of the occult manifestation in rock. On the one hand, their music and performances can be seen as nothing more than a deliberate attempt to court media attention by turning up the evil persona to eleven. This playacting didn't always go over well with critics. In 1975, for *NME*, Mick Farren called their horror-movie bombast nothing but a carnivalesque put-on: "This isn't psychodrama. It's an amusement park ghost train. It has the same cheap, lowest common denominator, dubious thrill quotient while totally lacking the kind of gaudy innocence that might make it redeemingly charming." Osbourne didn't try to pretend otherwise. In 1978, the singer told *Rolling Stone* magazine: "People think we're into black magic and voodoo, which we never have been. . . . A lot of that had to do with the initial drive to sell the band. We created a brand, if you like, a package."

On the other hand, Black Sabbath employed musical elements tapping directly into the deeper well forming rock's essential spiritual motivation. Often held up by detractors as proof of their brimstone-blackened souls is the use of what is called the tritone, or the "devil's interval." The chord was first noted for its extreme dissonance, and for early composers was deemed ugly and best avoided. Rumors persist that the Catholic Church banned the chord due to its sinister associations, but there is no evidence that there was in any way a concerted effort to prevent or punish its use. It wasn't until later composers such as Richard Wagner and Franz Liszt—who used the tritone in his pieces "Dante Sonata" and "Mephisto Waltzes"—that the chord was connected to the figure of the devil.

Black Sabbath's virtuoso guitarist Tony Iommi told the *BBC News Magazine* in 2006 that he was trying for an ominous sound,

SEASON OF THE WITCH

but he had no intention of creating an aura of evil around the band: "When I started writing Sabbath stuff it was just something that sounded right. I didn't think I was going to make it Devil music." Nevertheless, Satan and his legion make numerous appearances in the songs of Black Sabbath. Whether by design or accident, the band's sound and themes gelled perfectly, offering up the perfect and original Luciferian heavy metal affect.

"Black Sabbath," the band's first and most explicitly satanic song, mentions the devil by name, but the narrator is anything but thrilled to see him, calling out, "Oh no, no, please God help me." "The Wizard," the second song on their eponymous first album, introduces a magic user who banishes demons and "turns tears into joy." "War Pigs," one of their most legendary songs, bears witness to an ecstatically happy Satan looking over the bodies of fallen soldiers. Almost every reference to the devil or evil doings is met by a warning. In this respect, Black Sabbath is more like a biblical prophet than the tempter who mocks Jesus in the desert.

As Michael Moynihan writes in his book on black metal, *Lords of Chaos*, Sabbath's lyrics "reveal an almost Christian fear of demons and sorcery." It didn't matter. Sabbath sang about evil and Lucifer often enough that they performed an actual feat of magic. It's all in the name. Just as the ceremonial magician constructs a magic circle and conjures demons by calling out their names, Black Sabbath invoked a dark spirit that possessed the popular consciousness. In another example of how music in general, and rock in particular, functions as a particularly potent vehicle for transmitting the occult imagination, Black Sabbath became a code that could be read with whatever key you wanted. If you were Christian you could see them as the devil's emissary. Teenagers saw them as agents of rebellion. The reality was that they were a group of young musicians who wanted to make great rock and roll that had relevance and power. Black Sabbath was able to discover where in the culture there was a vacuum easily filled by an occult principality. Led Zeppelin led the charge by leveling psychedelic rock and rebuilding a darker, heavier, and esoterically rich musical foundation. But Black Sabbath called it by name, a moniker attaching itself to the whole of the 1970s, a decade characterized by excess. This was not the romantic Lucifer that shadowed Mick Jagger, nor was it the lawful evil of the devils found in the Dungeons & Dragons *Monster Manual*. This was a Satan come to storm the castle of rock, the anti-Christian beast whose foul breath would smother the planet in doom.

From the beginning, Sabbath would swing wildly from admission to denial when it came to their interest in the occult. In an early interview with *Rolling Stone*, Geezer Butler appears annoyed when asked about the name of the band, citing, as he often would, the name of the Boris Karloff movie he saw was playing at a local cinema. Almost forty years later, in a documentary about the making of their album *Paranoid*, Butler is asked the very same question. This time he explains that he was deeply interested in the occult when they were first forming the band. And then in 2013, Tony Iommi told the *Guardian* that the band "dabbled in the occult," but this could have meant merely playing with a deck of tarot cards while drunkenly bored on a tour plane.

Retroactive memory is an important aspect of rock's relationship to occultism. For a band like Black Sabbath, running triage against every manner of rumor and accusation, the members often had to claim ignorance about any occult influence. But once the mythos of the band was set in stone, it was safer to come clean. Or maybe the truth is the other way around. It is just as likely the band really wasn't interested in the occult at all and only later, when the association had helped make them rich, did it make sense to embrace it. It's more probable, however, that the truth is somewhere in between.

In *Louder Than Hell*, the remarkable narrative history of heavy metal by Jon Wiederhorn and Katherine Turman, Butler describes a book on witchcraft Osbourne had given him as a gift, which he claimed was "at least three hundred years old." That night, Butler decided to keep the book in the bathroom, worried about having it too close to him. But its magic was powerful. "I woke up and there was this black shape looming over the bottom of the bed," he said, and he knew then the occult was not something to take lightly. The incident must have inspired the rest of the band, however, because Ozzy describes reading occult books and realizing it was very different from the horror-movie affect they had decided on for themselves. And despite the lyrics in the band's songs suggesting the listener be wary of playing with dark magic, they attracted all manner of people who were looking for both kindred spirits and occult gurus. Black Sabbath represents the most perfect example of how occult manifests in rock and roll culture. Sabbath members were young men when they started out. Music was a way to reach beyond their English working-class neighborhoods. Rock was a kind of rebellion against fate, a way for them to say there was more to the world than jobs as carpenters and plumbers. And as youths looking for something more, the occult by way of Aleister Crowley and books on witchcraft offered another means to explore defying convention. The darker spectrum of occultism was a perfect fit. Social and spiritual rebellion are the touchstones of rock, and infusing their music with a sensibility challenging and critiquing what is normal was exactly what made Black Sabbath so powerful, and would influence so many bands to come.

On the other side of the curtain were the media, the public, and the fans, all of whom needed the band to represent for them whatever they most wanted or were most afraid of. Black Sabbath took up the gauntlet willingly. They could honestly deny any real satanic fealty, while churning up enough abysmal vapors to satisfy their fans and scare fundamentalist Christians, both of whom were equally obsessed with the band's supposed evil intentions. This was rock's supposed original bargain after all, a pact made with the devil in order to seduce teenagers away from clean family values by giving them music that stoked a sexual fire in their loins and a blaze of rebellion in their hearts. From the very beginning, rock urged teens to turn their backs on their parents and priests, their teachers and ministers, clothing Satan's message in songs about dancing and young love. Black Sabbath was simply more forthright about who was really in charge of rock's governing principles. Fundamentalist Christians, defenders of morality, and conspiracy theorists had proof. Devil worship was just fodder for scary movies and gory comic books. Satanists could be living right next door, driving their children to school, mowing their lawns, doing all the things normal people did. They even had a church.

In 1966, the same year that the world looked up in awe as

Russia landed the first man-made object on the moon with the spacecraft *Luna 9*, an ex–circus performer named Anton LaVey was staring into the underworld where he heard "a call" to start the Church of Satan. In the beginning, the church saw itself as a place for the over-thirty set to feel naughty, and the media enjoyed the spectacle—for instance, in 1967 when LaVey performed the first satanic wedding. LaVey wore a devil costume and a woman lay naked on the altar while LaVey chanted a black mass that beseeched the devil to bless the (un)holy matrimony. Later that year, he had his then three-year-old daughter baptized in what he said was a ritual in opposition to the Christian belief in original sin.

The Manson murders changed everything. Newspapers ran stories linking Manson to devil worship, first by trying to associate him with the Process Church and later by pointing out every instance where Manson may have told someone he was the devil. In the public consciousness, the Church of Satan was one-stop shopping for anything related to the devil, and so LaVey was quickly peppered with questions about the murders.

The stylishly bald and charismatic leader of the church then became much more explicit about what his brand of Satanism actually stood for. The church was not, as some thought, the worship of the actual Antichrist. Satanism, LaVey explained, is an extreme version of spiritual libertarianism with Satan as a perfect symbol for strength of will. All religion favors the weak, LaVey believed, and he looked to the Church of Satan as an island of free thought. LaVey even saw the hippies as nothing more than conformists, their minds addled by drugs and terrible music. As he told the *Los Angeles Times*: "[I]t's just Ayn

Rand's philosophy, with ceremony and ritual added." LaVey goes on to explain that his church believed in law and order, a strangely Apollonian view in the midst of what he sold as a Dionysian hedonism.

Despite LaVey's insistence, one he would continue to make, that the Satan of his church was not a literal personification of evil, but rather a stand-in for "the spirit of discovery, freethinking and rebelliousness," he still offered the perfect icon for rock's enduring need to spiritually rebel, an energy that would continue to push the music into new territories. It's important to stress how spiritually bereft young people felt at the end of the 1960s. The New Age movement had not yet offered an abridged but comprehensive spiritual encyclopedia for the mainstream that pulled together the various practices that had been embraced in the 1960s. Many historians and critics cite the violence at the Rolling Stones' Altamont concert because there really is no better metaphor for how the artistic and spiritual revolution that prefigured in festivals like the Human Be-In was completely undermined by the gross machismo and drug-addled aggression that was on display that day in 1969.

People on every step along the cultural spectrum agreed something had utterly changed. In an editorial for the *Boston Globe*, the conservative pundit William F. Buckley called the event the "corpse of Woodstock Nation," and *Rolling Stone* magazine said that Altamont was "perhaps rock and roll's all-time worst day." Worse yet, Altamont was also a warning sign of a greater disease.

The bands Coven and Black Widow, who released the first deliberately devilish rock albums in 1969 and 1970 respectively, are important examples of this malevolent edge that began creeping its way into popular music. They are also instances where even those who professed a belief in black magic were also keying into the exploitive and historical errors regarding magic, paganism, and their relationship to Satan.

Coven's first album, *Witchcraft Destroys Minds & Reaps Souls*, is a pretty terrific rock record, with singer Jinx Dawson's Grace Slick–like delivery on the back of a psychedelic/jazz vehicle swathed in a sinister atmosphere. The album mixes folktales and legends and closes with the song "Satanic Mass," a thirteen-minute spoken-word ritual that claimed authenticity, but was a mix of popular novels on Satanism, some medieval sources, and even some Crowley for authority (the mass ends with "Do What Thou Wilt, Shall Be the Whole of the Law!" just before the final refrain of "Hail Satan!"). Coven is also credited with being the first band to "throw horns," the hand sign with up-raised index finger and pinkie that would become the staple gesture of heavy metal fans.

Black Widow's debut album, *Sacrifice*, offered some trappings similar to Coven's *Witchcraft Destroys*, but in a 1970 interview with *Beat Instrumental*, Black Widow claimed they were more interested in the theatricality of staging something like a satanic mass than actually being practitioners themselves. *Sacrifice* offers a lineup of songs that read more like Hammer horror films than actual devil worship, with titles like "In Ancient Days," "Come to the Sabbat," and "Attack of the Demon."

Through their manager, the band became associated with the English witch Alex Sanders, having been named by his followers King of the Witches. Sanders had been part of Gerald Gardner's coven, but eventually formed his own tradition (Alexandrian Wicca as opposed to Gardnerian) and quickly became the public face of witchcraft, even going so far as to release his own album, *A Witch Is Born*. On it, Sanders performs an initiation into his coven. Not only does Satan not make an appearance, but the ritual is exceptionally positive, filled with earthly images. The initiation even includes a prayer known as the Charge of the Goddess, written by the Wiccan Doreen Valiente for Gerald Gardner. Unlike the figure behind supposed satanic masses, this deity is not in need of blood: "Nor does She demand sacrifice, for behold, She is the mother of all living, and Her love is poured out upon the earth." So while it's surprising that Sanders would associate with Black Widow's darker occult vision, he does so in a way that was largely in keeping with the time, when every flavor of occultism was mixing into an almost tasteless stew, save for its ability to shock and create media scandals.

Instead of tapping into an ancient stream of occult knowledge, Coven and Black Widow used ideas and imagery that arose first in the Middle Ages and were also apparent during the American witch trials conducted by religious authorities. For example, the idea of the witches' sabbath as a rite in which witches meet with Satan to be initiated and to dance ecstatically was a fiction, one that painted fertility rites not only as a non-Christian ritual but as one that was diabolical as well.

This belief persisted, given its most iconic form in a famous 1798 painting by Francisco Goya, *Witches' Sabbath*, in which a magnificently horned goat appears to bless a group of women and infants. Earlier and less well-known, but equally influential, was the illustration from the 1608 witch hunters' manual *Com-*

pendium Maleficarum showing a woman being initiated into a coven of witches by bending down and literally kissing the devil's ass. Coven's song "Pact with Lucifer" offers the same devilish pastoralism: a poor farmer sells his soul to Lucifer only to have the devil return in seven years to take his only son.

While Coven and Black Widow were not presenting what some might say is an accurate depiction of Wiccan practice at the time, their music and performances are still authentically occult along the vast spectrum. Just as occultism is not a single stream from a single ancient source, the varieties of ways the occult is expressed have always pulled together sometimes eerily similar, sometimes completely disparate, elements. For the Renaissance mages, it was the *Corpus Hermeticum*—itself a conglomeration of Egyptian, Gnostic Christian, and Neoplatonic ideas—mixed with Jewish Kabbalah, astrology, and what was called natural magic to create a complex but hugely influential form of esoteric lore. By the 1970s, there was already a rich historical vein to tap, then applied to contemporary cultural media. Ancient and premodern sources were blended with comic books, horror movies, and other more contemporary magical elements such as Wicca to help generate a new occult identity, one that was carved into vinyl records, erected onstage, and chanted by fist-raising fans, all of it feeding the fears of parents, urged on by mass media.

By the late 1970s and into the 1980s, nobody in popular music was immune to accusations of devil worship. One example is Heart, with band members and sisters Ann and Nancy Wilson often seen as oversexed pagan priestesses. A profile of the band in the *Washington Post* noted the absurdity: "More recently, the gypsy motif on the cover of 'Little Queen' gave rise to rumors of the band's involvement in Satanism and the occult, which prompts from [Ann] Wilson a somewhat exasperated laugh." One of the most overplayed songs of all time, "Hotel California" by the Eagles was believed to be a metaphor for hell. Some claim Anton LaVey can be seen on the balcony in the gatefold photograph showing the band and their entourage in a hotel courtyard, but a close inspection merely shows a blurry figure that could be Saint Paul if he is who you're hoping to find.

The idea of the devil would continue to supply the power to rock's electric current, both in terms of marketing aesthetic and as spiritual fodder. Just as occultism had the power to awaken new spiritual ideas, it also had the power to shock, and the early 1980s phenomenon of heavy metal made sure the devil was walking the earth, guitar in hand. Instead of curbing the type of lyrics that prompted warning labels to be put on their albums, many bands were happy for the kind of attention that only making something taboo can create. Many heavy metal bands, already under fire for their own brand of sexual and violent lyrics, ramped it up by giving their music an aura of devilish intensity and a darkly apocalyptic sensibility.

For a while Satan and his legion would appear almost comical as heavy metal bands adorned their album covers with horned demons and upside-down pentagrams and sang in falsettos about infernal deeds and other wickedness, while their fans "threw horns." They also made some pretty great music, and it raises the question as to whatever was giving them inspiration and such fierce energy was due in large part to the dark occult mystique they clothed themselves in. While the number of heavy metal bands using some form of sinister occult imagery was substantial, bands such as Venom, Pentagram, Slayer, and even the punk band the Misfits didn't bother with subtlety or claims of misunderstanding. They each had a slightly different take, however.

Slayer's brand of Satanism, for example, was inspired by Anton LaVey. The late Jeff Hanneman told *NME* in 1987: "A lot of its principles are just about being yourself, if you want to do something you do it, if you wanna have affairs you can. But we never hold daily rituals or anything." Despite their intense and powerful dark metal music, with album covers and song titles that could be the names of lost 1970s devil movies ("Evil Seed," "The Ghoul," "Bride of Evil," "Vampyre Love"), the repentant and currently sober lead singer Bobby Liebling claims Pentagram took a more moralistic stance by setting up a world in which the forces of good and evil are both vying for your soul: "The band's showing you . . . you've got to make a choice."

Sometimes, though, the air needed to be let out of the bombast. The punk band the Misfits tried to remind everyone how much of rock's devilish sneer came from those black-and-white horror movie double features and slasher films. The Misfits painted their faces in the likeness of B-movie monsters and performed songs with titles like "Devil's Whorehouse" and "Astro Zombies."

For the most part, however, all of them would ultimately claim it's just rock and roll, an art form whose audience often demands to be charmed by the illusion of malevolent intent. It is the spiritual rebellion at the heart of rock, whose blood is oxygenated by the occult. There is no better way to announce you are dangerous and a force to be reckoned with. As boringly ubiquitous as it would become, an upside-down pentagram on an album cover became a not-so-coded message that inside the record sleeve (or CD jewel case) was music not governed by mundane sensibilities. Even when these bands were simply play-acting, their message was still the same. People will not stop long-ing for ecstatic experiences, and even if it only takes place a few times a year at a heavy metal show, padded by weekend hang-outs in the basement with friends and a record player, or on a cassette player at bonfire parties in the woods, the urge to wor-ship the old gods who danced and drank and fornicated with abandon will still need expression.

The fear of the devil lurking between the grooves of rock albums—the musicians his secret emissaries—exacerbated by the playful and oftentimes ridiculous satanic decorations of heavy metal bands, would begin to have some very real conse-quences beyond whatever fights teenagers were having with their parents or other authority figures.

IV

At a U.S. Senate hearing in 1985, the Parents Music Resource Center (PMRC)—a lobbying group made up of high-profile women in Washington whose members included Tipper Gore, wife of Al Gore—met for the first time. Well-funded and even well-connected, the group was able to stir up outrage by focus-ing on a handful of songs they found particularly objectionable, including Prince's *Purple Rain* song "Darling Nikki"—featuring a woman who is seen "masturbating with a magazine." The group wanted a range of changes, including the lyrics of every song printed on album covers. While the emphasis was on sex and violence, of the fifteen songs the PMRC deemed the worst offenders, two were called out for explicit references to the occult. The song "Into the Coven" by the Danish heavy metal band Mercyful Fate describes an initiation into Lucifer's coven (another example of musicians conflating witches with Satan worshippers), and "Possessed" by the proto–death metal band Venom is a graphic exhortation of the devil with all the right references—whores, priests, blood—to make a parent cringe.

The PMRC imagined a label system for albums with a letter alerting parents about the lyrical content: X (sex), V (violence), D/A (drugs and alcohol), and O (occult). The PMRC was not affiliated with any religious groups, and so the addition of "occult" as a category might appear to be an anomaly. But by 1985, the country was awash in stories, many of them recounted in court testimony, of what was called satanic ritual abuse. Stories unfolded, each one more horrific than the last, of children being sexually and physically abused and repressing the memories. Dramatic moments of hypnotic recall were evidence of satanic cults flourishing and using children for their debauched and evil purposes. The scare began with the 1980 publication of the book *Michelle Remembers*, a supposed transcript between a woman named Michelle Smith and her psychotherapist, Lawrence Pazder.

Smith recounts in sensational detail her abuses by a satanic cult her mother was a part of. Not only is the Church of Satan named as an organization older than Christianity, Smith details the appearance of the devil during a ritual, and even gets divine intervention from the Virgin Mary. The panic reached its peak during the trial of owners of a preschool who were accused by prosecutors of performing every manner of terrible abuse on their young charges. Hundreds of children acted as witnesses, and despite the outrageousness of the allegations, the public eagerly ate up the sordid details. While much of the "satanic panic" has since been debunked, the fact that so many Americans accepted the idea of a satanic conspiracy with agents everywhere was not unlike the Red Scare of the 1950s insofar as it was believed anyone could be a secret devil worshipper. If even our most trusted members of society, such as preschool teachers, bowed at the feet of the devil, then who could we trust?

Even law enforcement officials got into the game. In a 1989 report, "Satanic Beliefs, Criminal Actions," written for the International Association of Chiefs of Police in Arlington, Virginia, the author named an interest in heavy metal (along with role-playing games) as one of the signs of a possible criminal personality. That same year, the infamous Jack Chick—known for his illustrated religious tracts left in train stations and on bus seats—published *"Angels?"* in which a struggling rock band learns that the entire popular music industry is secretly managed by the devil and that even "Christian Rock is a powerful demonic force controlled by Satan." The contradiction here is if Satanists worked best in secret, hidden in the banality of daily life, why would they give themselves away by erecting huge upside-down pentagrams during rock concerts?

But the devil really was thought to be everywhere. The first edition of Dungeons & Dragons' *Deities & Demigods* didn't help. The book presented a variety of divine pantheons with which to interact and what one Sacramento televangelist in 1981 said was "exactly like witchcraft." The *Monster Manual* was

SEASON OF THE WITCH

even worse. It listed twelve demons and eleven types of devils, including Asmodeus and Baalzebul, the latter of which could cast these spells: "symbol of pain, symbol of insanity, and (un)holy word." D&D would be seen, along with rock, as one of the primary means through which the devil got a hold of children. The company that published it, TSR, was so concerned about public perceptions that in the second edition the words *demon* and *devil* were removed from the rules and replaced with *tanar'ri* and *baatezu*. Stories describing troubled youth playing D&D often made sure to mention their obsession with heavy metal. The belief in Satan walking among us would help sell albums, but it would also damage the lives of those who just wanted to listen to those same records and let their imaginations soar beyond the Christian mainstream.

The devil is not the only source for an alternative path toward unconventional spirituality, though. Just as mysticism would alter rock music in ways unimaginable, fusing rock's synapses with a drug-induced spirituality continuing to find expression for decades to come, and the devil gave rock its malevolent sneer, magic would dress rock in a fantastic wardrobe, giving musicians the tools to turn the rock performance into ritual and shamanic ceremony.

CHAPTER 4

THE TREE OF LIFE

I

It was 1968 and the Crazy World of Arthur Brown's single "Fire" had reached number one in the UK. Robb Baker, writing for the *Chicago Tribune*, said Brown was likely to become "a priest of new black cult in pop music." Brown himself felt like he was on fire, having emerged from the British underground with a hit song and then embarking on a raucous tour of the United States. His stage performance was radical, even for the hippies. Brown would open the set garbed in billowing red robes, face painted white, teeth painted black, head adorned with a brass helmet dowsed in oil and set aflame. The song begins with Brown calling out, "I am the god of hellfire!" Brown believed he was heralding in a new age for rock and roll, one where the musician was a kind of shaman, hypnotizing the audience and shaking their souls anew. Arthur Brown got his start under the colored lights on the stage of the UFO Club in

London, but he had a vision for something more than acid-rock transcendence. Brown wasn't channeling swamis or Satan, but rather became a vessel for the occult's original expression in ancient magic, performed ceremonially in religious rites and taking other forms throughout history in the medieval magician's secret room, the Renaissance magus's workshop, and the nineteenth-century magical order's temple. Brown would bring magic to rock and roll, elevating it with new sounds, new imagery, and an even headier mystique much different from what came before. Brown would show that, like the early magicians, rock could be cast like a spell, transmuting the consciousness of fans, spellbinding them all with a powerful glamour.

Later that year, with a bit of swagger from the effects of fame, Brown was walking home with groceries. A few neighborhood kids recognized him. Even out of makeup he cut quite a figure; skinny and sinewy, with a large nose and chiseled face. The boys gathered round him, teasing him at first with taunts.

"Hey, we hear you are the god of hellfire?" they asked. "That must make things difficult." Brown felt himself slip immediately into character, the spirit of whatever entity he channeled onstage possessing him right there on the London street corner. "On the contrary. It makes everything easy!" They continued to follow him and Brown kept working the spell. Eventually they got to his front door. Brown didn't have his key and had to ring to be let in. There was the voice of his wife through the intercom, and Brown responded, "Oh, I'm sorry, I forgot the milk." The street kids erupted, "This is no fucking god of hellfire!" Brown later said of the moment: "The god of hellfire apologizing for forgetting the milk must have been quite disturbing."

While the tremendous cultural and spiritual shift from the 1960s to the 1970s was often characterized in rock mythos by a gloomier visage, Brown might seem at first to be just another musician taking advantage of the devil's insistent meddling in rock's aesthetic. But Brown was after something deeper. As a child he had seen a film of African priests and identified with how theater and spectacle are a means to transmit wisdom. He was also inspired by Walter Pater's idea that "all art constantly aspires towards the condition of music." Brown explains it like this: "[M]usic goes straight into a particular lobe of your brain, which bypasses thought or what we normally call thought." Brown likens his music to a Zen master using a stick to whack a student needing the sudden jolt back to awareness. Brown's god of hellfire was not intended to be in opposition to Christianity, but rather a messenger demanding your attention and one that will use any means to get it: "If you think that you can impress something on people's minds by shocking them, then you should *shock* them."

When Brown was a teenager, his father introduced him to Transcendental Meditation, which would place a young Arthur on a spiritual quest that found its way into his songs. But he quickly discovered that audiences weren't paying attention to the lyrics in the way he intended.

"Devil's Grip" was the song that made him realize he wasn't singing about things people were used to hearing. This was not a song about love or a hippie cry for freedom; it was about a precipitous spiritual journey: "Born from wonder / I soon slipped under." Brown sought a vehicle to turn rock and roll into an occult passion play. Culling from his interest in African shamans,

Brown added theatrical elements to his performances to conjure a sense of otherworldliness, thereby giving the music and lyrics a mythic quality. He painted his face and wore robes embroidered with symbols, in an effort to reshape a standard rock performance into something more like the creation of a new world. Multicolored strobe lights, his infamous flaming helmet, and sometimes his stripping naked brought accusations of "degrading public performance."

Brown's first tour of the United States was panned by the critics. After his 1968 show at the Anaheim Convention Center, the *Los Angeles Times* called him a "poseur whose rites were a tinseled hoax." Nevertheless, in his hotel room Brown would find half a dozen or so fans waiting for him. They would ask him questions about life, death, and the universe. For weeks during the tour he grooved on the attention and the thrill of keeping the performance going—even offstage. And then one night, Brown said, he couldn't keep it up. He realized he didn't actually *know* anything. Brown started his own spiritual quest in earnest. His experiences would only deepen his commitment to the stage, perfecting what Brown's biographer, Polly Marshall, called "a truly theatrical paganism."

At the UFO Club he had found an audience willing to be initiated into his magical order. Those who flocked to the club every week in 1967 were already apprentices of the spectacle of rock. This was, of course, the home base of Pink Floyd and Soft Machine, two experts in using projection, lighting, and sound to zap the already LSD-soaked crowd further into the astral plane. Brown's first album, *The Crazy World of Arthur Brown*, is a musical "book of shadows," each song a spell intending to invoke a different entity inhabiting his mind and soul. Brown describes creating and listening to the album as an "inner journey" in which he would call forth "gods and presences" through each song. Brown was interested in dualities, in the tension inherent in the gods of mythology. He saw his own role as trickster, mediating between humans and gods, showing the hazards of breaching the divide. Here again is the story of Dionysus's birth, where the god's coming into the world was a result of his mother getting too close to the divine fire. There is also a Christian connotation in the quagmire: Does hellfire burn or cleanse? Is hell a place of eternal suffering, or does redemption await on the other side of punishment?

Incorporating all this into a Saturday night rock show was profoundly original but also part of a lineage; Brown was integrating elements of spiritual questing that the avant-garde had tinkered with almost a century earlier. As noted with regard to composers Claude Debussy and Erik Satie, many artists and musicians in the 1800s were pushing up against the mainstream, innovating in ways that sourced both spiritual and creative sustenance in magical fraternities such as the Hermetic Order of the Golden Dawn and various Rosicrucian orders.

Rosicrucians mysteriously appeared in Germany in the early 1600s via a series of pamphlets circulating around the country. The believers eventually made their way through Europe, ultimately inspiring many seventeenth-century thinkers, including astronomer and mathematician Giordano Bruno and physician-turned-mystic Robert Fludd—two men who would go on to have a profound impact on magic and occultism in the West. The first of the Rosicrucian writings, the *Fama Fraternitatis*, announced a mystical fellowship born out of the exotic travels of someone named Christian Rosenkreutz, who would help usher in a new age for the spiritual health of humanity. Possibly nothing more than an elaborate hoax, the idea of a secret brotherhood fired the imagination, particularly among those for whom Christian teachings had become stale. While the Protestant revolution promised an unmediated salvation free from the interference of priests, it still functioned as a hierarchy with a minister behind a pulpit facing the congregation. The mystical Christianity of the Rosicrucians promised something more like the mystery cults of the ancient world, where initiates were put through a series of trials, each one revealing more and more until at last the great secrets of the universe are revealed.

By the 1800s, a number of groups claiming to be direct descendants of the original Rosicrucians sprouted up in France and England. Members were often already schooled in the traditions of secret fraternities by way of Freemasonry, known for its complex and elegant series of rituals. Each degree presented the member with new teachings, secret handshakes, and passwords. These secretive elements inspired nefarious and ultimately debunked (but everlasting) conspiracy theories, but others saw Freemasonry as a basis from which to develop esoteric fraternities emphasizing ancient mysteries, occult powers, and magic. The means to teach these divine truths was nothing less than the theatrical.

It was the Hermetic Order of the Golden Dawn, however, that incorporated the occult sensibility of the Rosicrucians into the ritual grandeur of Freemasonry to create an occult belief system that would become the most influential magical organization in the Western world, still seeing an active membership today. The order began in England in 1888, when, it was told, three Freemasons looked out at the horizon of human culture and saw only two possible paths forward for history: a purely materialistic science, with a strong positivist bent giving no quarter to mystery; or a strict religious banality, void of wonder. William Robert Woodman, William Wynn Westcott, and Samuel Liddell MacGregor Mathers had met while members of the same Rosicrucian order, the Societas Rosicruciana in Anglia (SRIA), but they were not satisfied it could provide what they sought to establish—a path beyond the opposing pillars of science and Christianity.

Occultism was not altogether unfashionable in England at the time; spiritualism made for spooky and titillating salon and sewing circle activities, and Blavatsky's Theosophical Society had started to gain followers, as well as skeptical notice by the press. But the three Freemasons were after a more rigorous spiritual system, one that deepened the mystical associations they found in the SRIA. Westcott claimed to have come into possession of a series of papers he referred to as the Cipher Manuscripts, a collection of writings laying out rituals intended to teach a method of occult psychology linking tarot cards, astrology, astral projection, and the Kabbalah. Westcott and company founded the first Golden Dawn lodge and over time attracted a diverse membership, many of whom were women, as the Freemasons and other societies typically excluded them. As the writer Francis King explains, the Golden Dawn's system of initiatory ritual magic didn't manifest anything original other than how to "synthesize a coherent logical system," inspiring occultism to this day, all of it dressed in ritual finery that depends on performance to spellbind the initiates.

Borrowing heavily from Freemasonry, the Golden Dawn rituals begin with a candidate dressed in simple robes and blindfolded. The blindfold itself is called a "hoodwink," an idiom denoting being tricked or duped. The initiate is meant to feel disoriented, thereby heightening their other senses. Members of the lodge wear their own ritual garments, often incorporating Egyptian motifs, specific to their level and office, with each one given a prescribed role in the initiation. Over time, as members achieve higher grades (the degrees in Freemasonry), the rituals become more and more complex, and the added use of lights and sounds enhances the experience.

Similarly, Arthur Brown's stage shows utilized these elements, including robes, masks, "huge costumes with these geometric patterns," and a specific dance routine for each song. Brown's light show was controlled by the mood of the music, an idea originally developed in the nineteenth century by Russian composer Alexander Scriabin. Other composers had played with the idea of controlling light with sound; there was even a U.S. patent filed in 1877 by Bainbridge Bishop in which he described: "The combination, with a musical instrument, of a device arranged to exhibit a series of colors corresponding with the notes played, substantially as specified."

For Scriabin, combining music with color was more than a technical problem to be solved. The art scholar James Leggio explains how Scriabin was intrigued by the phenomenon known as synesthesia, in which some people see sounds and hear colors. The notion that colors have a specific corresponding note was in line with Scriabin's other interest: theosophy. As Leggio points out, theosophy as presented by Madame Blavatsky taught that human beings have both physical and astral bodies, the latter of which can be seen as aura. The person's mood or level of spiritual wisdom can be understood in the color of the aura.

For his symphonic piece *Prometheus: The Poem of Fire*, Scriabin included in the score instructions for the projection of colors controlled by a color organ. The occult themes of the piece are highlighted by Scriabin's use of what he called the "chord of the pleroma," a dissonant drone dramatically rising during the opening movement and intended to correspond to the divine totality existing beyond normal human perception. The chord *is* the bridge to the divine, and the colors are the divine echo.

Brown describes his own performances in much the same way but from the point of view of a pre-enlightened Gnostic. The darker, spookier aspects of the Crazy World and his next band, Kingdom Come, were an attempt to show how humanity is disconnected from the divine source: "The experience we give is alienation in its modern concept of the human mind being removed from its true central joining point with the emanations of the divine spirit by entrapment in its own creations of systematic self-deception."

The idea of isolation from a divine source is at the heart of the modern Occult Revival of the nineteenth century. The Golden Dawn understood magic to be the way to reintegrate the human with its godlike destiny. Aleister Crowley, an early member of the Golden Dawn, defined magic as "the Science and Art of causing change to occur in conformity with the will." This definition was amended by a later Golden Dawn member and magician, Dion Fortune, who wrote that "magic is the Science and Art of causing change *in consciousness* [italics mine] to occur in conformity with the will." These two additional words are essential, as they put the emphasis on what actually happens, if anything, as a function of the mind. This, of course, is where the real magic takes place. It is the grand illusion that can only happen when the aspirant wants to be hypnotized.

When Brown's band broke up in 1970, he continued on with Kingdom Come, a progressive rock outfit producing a trilogy of albums, each one a key to his deepening quest to use music as a means of spiritual initiation. Brown had almost given up on music altogether, now drawn toward spending his time in a Tibetan monastery. But during a mescaline trip, he had a vision of a warrior angel right out of a William Blake drawing, replete with armor and sword, filled with what he described as a "mortal terror." For Brown, this meant one thing: start a new band. Kingdom Come turned up the theatrics to "11," performing with a giant pyramid set, flaming crosses, druids dancing in the audience, and each of the band members decked out in robes and makeup, including the guitarist dressed as a clown for good measure. Brown sought spiritual nourishment in multiple ways, from acid binges to all-apple diets. But the music, an innovative but too often flaccid progressive rock, failed to get him to the next commercial level. Kingdom Come did well on the festival circuit, but band members changed often. The last album was recorded without a drummer, and Kingdom Come was forced to become the first band to use a drum machine. It could be that audiences wanting to be entertained via an occult transmission during a concert weren't ultimately willing to commit wholesale to Brown's somewhat scattershot shamanistic vision.

But Brown might have understood this, as well. After Kingdom Come broke up, Brown traveled to Turkey to study Sufism and eventually landed in Austin, Texas. It was here he was inspired to pursue music as a means of psychic transformation through less bombastic methods. Brown received his master's in counseling psychology and started a music therapy practice. The patient would talk about their phobias or fears, and Brown would then compose a song on the fly with a guitar in hand, the lyrics drawn from the patient's own words. The patient would take a tape of the song home and listen to it whenever the anxiety or depression set in. Here is the location where hypnotism and magic meet.

One of the first proponents of hypnotism was the eighteenth-century German doctor Franz Mesmer. He believed in a kind of supernatural invisible fluid with magnetic properties coursing through human beings, and, with the proper training, a practitioner could manipulate this fluid to a healing effect. Mesmer called this "animal magnetism" and, while the idea was quickly discredited, the technique, first called "mesmerism" but later changed to "hypnotism," has become a genuine and powerful means to induce trance states by way of suggestion.

Brown's music therapy practice was not unlike hypnotherapy, with the song becoming a means of suggestion that the patient can then use to return themselves to the hypnotic state first induced in the therapist's office. Hypnosis is indeed a form of altered consciousness, and while more subtle than an LSD trip, it may have more profound and long-term effects. Suggestion might be the most powerful tool in the stage magician's bag of tricks, as much as it is for the tribal shaman and even the Free-masons' rituals. Brown might have taken off his robes and makeup, but his therapy technique is the same, and it is also the key function of rock and roll's occult power. The question of whether or not the supernatural is real is irrelevant. The occult doesn't need arcane forces to give it reality. It only needs a means of transmission and a willing audience. Mesmer's ghostly fluid might not really exist, but the current running between the practitioner and the patient, the high priest and the neo-phyte, and the musician and the audience is valid and evident.

While Brown was never quite able to maintain the spell over the mainstream, the ideas and traditions he drew from would find popularity in other acts. Visionaries rarely make it across the desert, and Brown was no different. It would be others—Alice Cooper and Kiss—who would deliver more easily digest-ible versions of Brown's shamanic magic. There is an apocryphal tale of how Alice Cooper got his name. Born Vincent Furnier, he was a young man who dreamed of his high school rock band becoming famous. He and his bandmates were playing with a Ouija board, and the mysterious force controlling the board communicated that he was in fact the reincarnated soul of Alice Cooper, a seventeenth-century witch who had been burned at the stake during the Salem witch trials. (Another version has him learning the secret truth of his destiny from a fortune-teller at a carnival.)

The band became known as Alice Cooper, but soon there would be no separation between the lead singer and the name of the band. Furnier became known as Alice Cooper, and he eagerly embraced the nom de guerre. Cooper liked how simple and sweet the name sounded and how antithetical it was to his stage act. Alice Cooper turned rock into a theater of the macabre, incorporating bloody baby dolls, guillotines, electric chairs, mock hangings, and a boa constrictor named Yvonne. All these props were used to extravagant effect by a Cooper garbed in dresses, leotards, or leather, with his signature Harlequin-painted eyes. Cooper did not see himself as a shaman inviting the gods into the world, but as a rock and roll scapegoat, a gathering of the entire miasma humans have hidden inside them. Cooper made it all visible. He projected it back to the audience and turned it into spectacle.

The band Kiss (which some Christian groups believed was an acronym for Knights in Satan's Service and hence rejected the music) took the theatrics of Alice Cooper and crafted them into a perfectly oiled machine, a living mystery cult. Sylvie Simmons, writing for *Sound*, told how a Kiss performance was what Alice Cooper's band "always wanted to be but weren't." For every tour, Alice Cooper created a new set piece, trying to outdo himself each time. Kiss learned that what their teenage fans really wanted was something to emulate, a mostly unchanging ritual, except for a new song now and again.

So the band adopted perfectly crafted personas: the Demon (Gene Simmons), the Cat (Peter Criss), the Spaceman (Ace Frehley), and the Starchild (Paul Stanley). Their makeup was never altered, allowing their fan-cum-followers to don the same look. This "army" of devotees, as it was called, wanted the direct confrontation with their gods, and Kiss gave it to them by way of drum sets on hydraulic risers, mortar-rigged explosions, fire and more fire, and Gene Simmons's ungodly long tongue. Their music, panned by music critics, was not complex. Under all the histrionics, it was just pop after all, but the music was not the thing. Kiss was a phenomenon, fueled by preteen hormones stirred into the frenzy by that ancient craft Arthur Brown had worked so hard to bring to the rock stage.

Even today, Brown appreciates what these other acts were trying to do, but believes their work is undermined by the banality of their subject matter. It wasn't merely theatrics. Brown likened his dramaturgy to the performance of tribal priests and shamans. Their playacting was a form of magical practice intended to draw down the divine to reveal itself to the community. Elements such as masks are particularly powerful. Masks are, as Walter Otto explains, "nothing but surface. . . . Here there is nothing but encounter, from which there is no withdrawal—an immovable, spell-binding antipode." The representation of the spirit in the mask cannot be mistaken for something else. Add to this chanting and the ecstatic sound of drums and other instruments, and something like mass hypnosis could easily occur. And when an audience is willingly giving themselves over to be in the presence of the god, the trick is even easier to pull off. This could serve as a definition for all of rock's performances, but with someone like Brown, and the later acts who would incorporate his ideas, it is even more fitting. However, Brown felt that songs like Alice Cooper's "School's Out," for example, didn't merit shamanic theatrics. Musicians like Cooper and Kiss turned it into pure entertainment, with shock as a means to an end: fame and fortune. Brown admits he could be shocking also, but it was merely a method to alter consciousness, just as shamans had done, to open up a space to let the gods in.

II

When a nineteen-year-old Cameron Crowe visited David Bowie for a *Rolling Stone* magazine interview in 1975, he found a coked-out Bowie lighting black candles to protect himself from unseen supernatural forces outside his window. Bowie had just finished filming *The Man Who Fell to Earth* with director Nicolas Roeg. It was a heady time for UFOs and alien encounters, and it was easy for Bowie to mold himself to the role. He had long before been singing about the existential dread of outer space and the descent of alien rock stars, but he was way ahead of the cultural consciousness. When *The Man Who Fell to Earth* was released, current pop culture was being heavily invaded by cosmic entities. The number of books and TV specials on UFOs might very well have outnumbered actual sightings at that time. But by then, Bowie was channeling something more enchanting than ancient astronauts. He was mixing his science fiction with magic and cocaine. While the results would supply rock with an occult-jolt, continuing the trend of transforming popular music, Bowie's sanity would be the casualty. Luckily, the artist made it through mostly intact, but the legacy of that battle between the forces of magic and sanity would be the next phase in rock's continuing occult transformation. Bowie's exploration of his consciousness by way of costume, drama, and an unstoppable creative drive showed musicians and audiences once again that the music should never settle for any trend. The occult imagination made sure rock would never die, and Bowie injected it with the pure speedball to keep it awake, no matter the consequences.

While many of his lyrics drop references to various shades and types of occultism—often filtered through Nietzschean imagery, strange fascist ideology, and alien messiahs—the form in which this shaped rock culture is not as clear as Harrison's use of the sitar driven by his devotion to Eastern mysticism, for example, or Page's interest in magic adorning album covers and compounding the sinister vibe of Led Zeppelin's music. It's not enough to focus on Bowie's mercurial interest in mysticism and other esoteric practices. Bowie's role in this larger narrative is much more subtle, but in some ways the most far-reaching. In the history of rock, there is likely no truer magician than Bowie, as he has come to personify how magic works. As noted, in stage magic those in the audience allow themselves to be tricked, to be seduced by the illusion, just as in ritual and cere-monial magic, where a similar phenomenon is at play and is an important effect in conducting the events and rituals within the context of a group, community, or fraternity. There is a shared, often tacit, language agreed upon by the group; its power evi-dent in the way a neophyte will accept the language or other coded acts implicitly, such as when an apprentice Freemason is given the first handshake, or "grip," and without hesitation ac-cepts it as so.

Despite his dark occult interests and the almost tragic ending to a still-remarkable career, Bowie's cosmic and magical perso-nas lifted rock music onto a new stage. Bowie used glamour—both in the fashion and magical senses—to convert rock audiences into accepting a bisexual and binary sense of self. This was not simply the androgynous sexuality of someone like Jagger. Bowie's sexual self is a method of transgression illuminating something universally and perhaps subconsciously human. Bowie was a cultural seer, not unlike Tiresias, the prophet in ancient Greek myth and theater who by punishment of the gods lived as a woman for seven years. Tiresias walks both worlds, both female and male, and through this wisdom is able to intuit the shape of things to come. Tiresias appears in many Greek plays, often foretelling tragic endings, or as a follower of Dionysus in *The Bacchae*, prefiguring Pentheus's own transgendered moment in acquiescence to the god.

Bowie outfitted his transgendered themes with what was cutting-edge fashion at the time—aliens, magic, and mysticism—but his tones were somewhat bleak. In the time between 1970 and 1975, there was an aura of troubled messianic and apocalyptic fervor. It was difficult to know if Bowie offered warnings or celebrations in his presentation and performance. As his drug use became more severe over time, he might not have known himself.

Bowie's first album, the 1967 *David Bowie*, was a strange bit of British whimsy, a fluff piece of pure sugary pop with an obvious intent to reach Top 40 recognition. Once he recast himself as a cosmonaut with his second outing, *Space Oddity*, in 1969, Bowie began his ever-shifting transmutations, a living alchemical elixir becoming more potent and dangerous with every experiment. Music critics agreed that *Space Oddity* was unique. The opener is a song by the same name, an existential space journey in which Major Tom finds himself untethered from both his rocket and reality, free-floating through the astral planes.

A writer for *Disc and Music Echo* swooned: "I listened spellbound throughout, panting to know the outcome of poor Major Tom and his trip into the outer hemisphere." Here was a rock song in 1969 that looked from within the starry void down onto the closing of the decade with a melancholy detachment. The song "Memory of a Free Festival" gives a generous nod to the music festivals of the 1960s, but the ultimate hope was not for the energized gathering of hippies. Salvation is otherworldly, and comes by way of "sun machines," interplanetary starships piloted by Venusians. But hope was not everlasting.

The imagery of forbidden fruit would underpin his next album, *The Man Who Sold the World*, in 1970. Something was stirring in Bowie, a kind of eerie decadence, plainly seen in the UK cover version: Bowie lounges in a dress and leather boots on a silk-draped couch, the floor in front of him littered with a deck of playing cards. The songs are heavyweight, some sounding like early heavy metal, and the themes are equally menacing and explicitly sexual. Bowie imagines himself being initiated into a forbidden sect offering salvation by way of musical Gnosticism: to know yourself, you must cast aside the illusion of convention, freely eat what the serpent offers, but never be ashamed of the knowledge you find. Themes of superhuman masters haunt the entire album, but it's unclear if Bowie imagines himself their equal or their pawn.

It's on his 1971 album, *Hunky Dory*, that Bowie's fascination with magic becomes less opaque as he makes reference to things fairly well-known by other seekers in the early seventies. Crowley gets his necessary nod on "Quicksand"—a downbeat song about a spiritual crisis. Bowie's biographer Nicholas Pegg makes particular note of the song "Oh! You Pretty Things," with its warning that "Homo sapiens have outgrown their use." Pegg believes this is a nod to the writing of Edward Bulwer-Lytton. In his 1871 novel, *The Coming Race*, a man finds an entrance to the hollow earth where he discovers an ancient superpeople described as a "race akin to man's, but infinitely stronger of form and grandeur of aspect" who use an energy called "vril" to perform wondrous feats, such as controlling everything from the weather to emotions.

This delightfully strange story might have gone the way of other quaint nineteenth-century fantasies if not for *The Morning of the Magicians* by Louis Pauwels and Jacques Bergier, first published in France in 1960 and translated into English in 1963, which created a wave of esoteric speculation and occult conspiracy theories still being felt today. The authors were inspired by the writer Charles Hoy Fort, who, in the first decades of the twentieth century, used an inheritance to spend his time in the New York Public Library, collecting stories and data from a wide range of sources, all of which suggests an underlying and connected web of paranormal and supernatural phenomena. Using Fort's method, Pauwels and Bergier outlined a secret history in which important historical figures intuited their own role in shaping a cosmic destiny for mankind, aliens had visited mankind during the first days of Western civilization, and alchemy and modern physics were not in opposition. The seventies also needed a messenger who could personify astronomical dreams and occult permutations, a figure of decadence and wisdom who could deliver a rock and roll testament to what it's like to fall between the worlds. Only Bowie could imagine such a creature.

Bowie's next release would create one of the most iconic and powerful rock personas of all time: Ziggy Stardust. Forgive the hyperbole, but in what is one of the greatest rock and roll albums of all time, *The Rise and Fall of Ziggy Stardust and the Spiders from Mars*, Bowie subverted the grandeur of spaceflight along with the wonder and excitement over the moonwalk and turned the cosmos into a place of ominous mystery, where fallen alien messiahs would learn to play guitar. Bowie synthesized the spiritual hopes and fears of the seventies without ever resorting to New Age platitudes. Ziggy is not here to experiment on humans, he is here to experiment on himself, seeking forbidden knowledge in the urban wastes of earth.

In 1973, *Rolling Stone* arranged a meeting between the two poles of cultural transgression: William Burroughs and David Bowie. Burroughs occupied a central place in the underground pantheon. Both gay and a drug addict, he explored these aspects of himself through some of the most challenging and disturbing novels written in English. Bowie was his Gemini twin, a wrecker of mores who was reaping fame and fortune as the deranged but beautiful creature of pop music. Burroughs might have been looking for a way into the mainstream, and might have believed rubbing elbows with Bowie would get him closer.

During their talk, Bowie describes the full mythos behind Ziggy, describing a race of alien superbeings called the "infinites," living black holes that use Ziggy as a vessel to give themselves a form people could comprehend. Burroughs countered with his own vision to create an institute to help people achieve greater awareness so humanity will be ready when we make eventual contact with alien life-forms.

Bowie's fascination with alien Gnosticism gave way to a return to the decadent magic of *The Man Who Sold the World*, particularly with the album *Diamond Dogs*, one of the most frightening albums of the 1970s. The warning of an imminent apocalypse in the song "Five Years" on *Ziggy Stardust* is realized in the dystopian urban wasteland where "fleas the size of rats sucked on rats the size of cats." The only hope is in the drugs and the memory of love. The track "Sweet Thing" is a beautiful killer of a song, Bowie's voice hitting the high notes as if desperate: "Will you see that I'm scared and I'm lonely?" *Diamond Dogs* might be a fictional vision, but the truth underlying it was Bowie's increasing and prodigious cocaine use, and an even deeper curiosity with the occult. Supercharged by coke, a drug known for its side effect of throat-gripping paranoia, Bowie's interest in magic could only turn ugly.

By the time Crowe met with him, Bowie was convinced he was cursed, possibly by Jimmy Page, and took to drawing Kabbalistic symbols on the floor of his studio. Crowe listened as Bowie talked lucidly about his music and then suddenly began describing an apocalyptic future where rock's pretense of evil and darkness would become reality and give Bowie a kind of dictatorial power: "I believe that rock & roll is dangerous. It could well bring about a very evil feeling in the West. I do want to rule the world." While he didn't mention it to Crowe at the time, Bowie believed his plans were being thwarted by witches set out to steal his semen (the substance needed to magically create a homunculus).

A few months later, Bowie and his then wife, Angela, bought a sprawling Art Deco house in L.A. And in a perfect bit of non-fiction plotline, Bowie discovered that the previous owner, the dancer Gypsy Rose Lee, whose life inspired the musical *Gypsy*, had painted a hexagram on the floor of one of the rooms. Bowie fell apart, and began claiming the devil lived in the home's pool. The only way to stay in the house would be to perform an exorcism, so Bowie gathered together all the necessary accoutrements, and he and Angela stood in front of the pool and performed their own private ritual. In a later interview, Angela claims that despite her disbelief in such things, she was witness to the water beginning to bubble and a stain appearing at the bottom of the pool. The exorcism wasn't enough for Bowie; they moved out a few weeks later.

In a 2009 interview with his biographer Marc Spitz, Bowie revealed what cocaine was doing to his already occult-addled mind: "My psyche went through the roof, it just fractured into pieces. I was hallucinating twenty-four hours a day." Bowie's coke-stimulated interest in the occult was mostly concealed in his private life, but an astute listener can find a myriad of clues in his music. Occultism in the 1970s was concerned primarily with ideas of the devil. Culturally, one couldn't escape his grip, even if it came by way of the family pet (*Devil Dog: The Hound of Hell*); the strange quiet child next door (*The Omen*); or the local motorcycle gang (*Psychomania*). But Bowie was able to bypass the devil for a more authentic and maybe even more dangerous kind of occultism. While Arthur Brown saw his musical performance as a form of shamanism, Bowie saw magic as a form of self-actualization, but guided by a commonly misunderstood notion of magical perfection.

The occult in the 1970s was also dominated by the resurgence of magic instruction manuals used by magicians to conjure demons and other unlikely allies in their search for knowledge of the divine. The genre became so popular, publishers began printing fictional tomes as if they were recently excavated ancient texts. Other books were intended to actually teach the public something about the art of magic.

The two most popular books on magic, Israel Regardie's *The Golden Dawn* and *Psychic Self-Defense* by Dion Fortune, provided hands-on application in the context of the magical society, particularly the Hermetic Order of the Golden Dawn, of which both authors were members. Regardie's book was the first time the Golden Dawn rituals were made public in such a systematic way (he was accused by other members of "breaking his oath"), but the book itself is almost impossible to follow without knowing something firsthand about the order. *The Golden Dawn* offers both individual and group exercises, but it's not unlike a book on trying to learn card tricks without knowing the maneuvers first: "Go to the West, make the Pentagram, and vibrate EHEIEH."

What it does provide is a glimpse into the practice of magic not bound in the popular notion of Satanism or even witchcraft. *The Golden Dawn* is a book of nonfiction fantastic realism, igniting the occult imagination of the 1970s and providing the basis for the founding of a number of Golden Dawn–related groups still active. Fortune's book, on the other hand, is much more pragmatic, offering cookbook wisdom, including how to ward off curses and magical attacks.

While Crowley certainly had his influence on Bowie, the mercurial singer smartly did not exploit him, or use his name to conjure an image of a black magician, as Ozzy Osbourne would later do in his 1980 song "Mr. Crowley." Bowie was attracted to Crowley as a figure of Luciferian grace, in the sense described earlier, wherein Lucifer represents a kind of self-realized dandy, a Baudelaire-like poet who is not afraid to explore the more taboo aspects of sex, will, and intoxication. But this notion of a perfected spiritual man, an image Bowie had been playing with since "Oh! You Pretty Things," was easily conflated with the idea of Aryan perfection. This formulation has long posed a problem in understanding the history of the occult.

Madame Blavatsky is often cited as the location where this tension first manifested. Her book *The Secret Doctrine* lays out a taxonomy of "root races," an evolution of humanity's spiritual destiny. The first of these is ethereal, without form, and the root races evolved over time. Blavatsky would provide pulp fantasy writers with a deep well to draw from with the next races, the Hyperboreans, Lemurians, and Atlanteans. The fifth root race is the Aryan, which Blavatsky claimed was the peak of humanity at that time. A sixth would rise above the Aryan, and then the seventh would see the final and perfect human being.

Gary Lachman, in his biography of Blavatsky, explains how race was a deeply important topic during Blavatsky's time and, while we might find some of her ideas to be troubling, they were part of a larger cultural milieu. More disturbing, Lachman writes, is how racists used her ideas to further their own bigoted occult ideas. The Thule Society, for example, was a group of Germans—including Rudolf Hess—with decidedly anti-Semitic views who believed a racially pure people arose in the mythical land of Hyperborea.

The Thule Society would become the inspiration for an entire industry of books purporting that the Nazis sought occult power, believing they could create a perfect and deadly Aryan being. Pauwels and Bergier's *The Morning of the Magicians* was the first book to bring this to popular awareness, and their occult–Nazi link was replete with strange science and the quest for legendary objects imbued with great power. If not for *Morning of the Magicians*, it's unlikely the Nazis in *Raiders of the Lost Ark* would have sought the biblical ark as a means to wield the power of God as a weapon. And while those villains meet their fate in no small part thanks to Indiana Jones, others would write the Nazis back into history with a romantic idealism.

Through a reading of *Morning of the Magicians* it would be easy to connect the dots from Lytton's occult fantasy of hollow-earth superhumans found on *Hunky Dory* to the Nazi-inflected ideas of homo superior. Bowie would find himself getting mired in this kind of thinking. The image of Nazi occultism offered a perfect storm of shock and awe for a rock spectacle and a persona both beautiful and deadly. All of these ideas would merge into the apocalyptic fervor, but because Bowie was such a brilliant artist, he could channel it into music.

In an interview with *Arena* in 1993, Bowie looked back on this time with regret. He understood that, while made delusional by drugs, a yearning for God was the driving motivation behind all of his occult dabbling. Bowie had become fascinated with the book *The Spear of Destiny* by Trevor Ravenscroft (you couldn't make up a name this good), which claimed Hitler was obsessed with finding the spear a Roman soldier used to pierce Jesus during the crucifixion, a supposed artifact of deadly mystical power. This, along with the legend that Hitler was also looking for the Holy Grail (also later popularized by the third Indiana Jones movie, *The Last Crusade*), so captivated Bowie that he put aside the reality of the Nazis' deeds to instead imagine them on some great, holy quest. "And naively, politically," Bowie said, "I didn't even think about what they had done."

Bowie's self-destruction was in service to the fascist mythology of the palingenesis. In Bowie's case it was his person, not a nation stripped of its preconceptions, desires, loves, and fears, becoming nothing more than a shell, and resurrected in perfection through a means of rigorous reprogramming. Bowie was not looking for a perfected inner self so much as a perfected outer self, his art an expression of his perfected will. There is no better means of carving up a persona than cocaine, and mixed with the Kabbalah and racial occultism, Bowie couldn't have picked a more effective formula. Fascism, for Bowie, was less about a political accent than it was about fashion.

All this evocation of various personas was heightened by Bowie's uncanny sense of fashion that, even beyond his music, would stand out and inspire other musicians. In the press, Bowie would continue the construction and deconstruction of his character, as when he told a reporter for *NME* that he was not a musician but an artist using music as his means of expression. With statements like this, Bowie intended to keep himself apart from the pure rock persona to better establish himself as the next character he might inhabit. In the same interview, Bowie also wanted to stand clear of being lumped in with someone like Alice Cooper. Bowie admitted to a kind of theatricality, but he eschewed the use of props or sets, claiming he was the "vehicle" for his songs. This also meant that when he was ready to move on to the next thing, he wasn't saddled by the production itself, as when during the final show of his Ziggy tour with his band the Spiders from Mars, Bowie returned to the stage for his encore and introduced the song "Rock 'n' Roll Suicide" by telling the audience it was the last time the Spiders would play together. His bandmates were just as shocked as the fans.

Bowie once commented that Marc Bolan was "Glam 1.0," and without Bolan's all-too-brief tenure leading the band called T. Rex (Bolan died in 1977, weeks before his thirtieth birthday), Bowie would not have known which stage door to walk through. Bolan had transformed himself from hippie troubadour—a minstrel with a vibrato voice who sang about fairy tales and magic spells—into a glamorous and decadent rock star, trading in his paisley for high-heeled boots and sequined jackets. But he retained a mystic aura, particularly in the steamy androgyny he brought to his performances.

Fans of his earlier band Tyrannosaurus Rex called him a sellout, and music critics saw his glam pretensions as just that, a cynical showmanship devoid of any real artistic merit. But Bolan found a generation ready to embrace glam's mix of old and new, simple pop stripped of psychedelic extravagance but dressed up in cosmic finery. Glam would provide a template for a new kind of occult imagining, one where the rock star was merely a cover-up for a secret identity—alien or monster.

Brian De Palma found glam, as well as the entire culture of rock, to be ripe for a horror parody in his film *Phantom of the Paradise*, a movie that could only have been made in 1974. Swan, a record executive played by Paul Williams (who also wrote the film's music), sells his soul for eternal life and acts as the devil's agent, soliciting others to sign away their own souls in return for record contracts. Swan discovers the musician Winslow Leach and believes his music will be the perfect backdrop for his new rock club. Swan frames him, and Leach is put through all terrible manner of tortures, including having his teeth pulled and replaced with metal, and having his face burned by a record-pressing machine. He takes to wearing a mask and black cape, haunting the nightclub, enacting his revenge on those who destroyed him.

Rock culture would continue to utilize the concept of secret identities hidden behind masks and makeup. Mercyful Fate would make its mark on the 1980s with occult and satanic imagery buoyed by a fairly generic metal sound. Their lead singer, King Diamond, gave the band its power. King Diamond was said to be a devotee of Anton LaVey's brand of Satanism, and he took to painting his face white like the bastard love child of Alice Cooper and Kiss. He often wore a top hat and a funereal morning suit, and would perform holding some bones; sometimes these were tied together to form a cross attached to his microphone. These elements signaled to rock audiences that the musician was a messenger for arcane secrets, delivered in the language of rock.

Marilyn Manson followed Bowie's template, as each one of his albums presented a new persona, but he maintained the overall Alice Cooper School of Makeup program. In 1998,

Manson told *Kerrang!* that Bowie was a crucial influence, particularly on his album *Mechanical Animals*, whose cover, the article's author notes, looks uncannily like *Aladdin Sane*. Bowie had a clearly traceable effect on popular music, but his overarching influence was more subtle. So many of his constructed personalities paralleled his real life in the 1970s, each of them depicting desperate spiritual seekers, looking toward both inner space and outer space for spiritual sustenance. But as much as Bowie was a conduit for the decade's excess, he was also a mirror.

The last song on *Diamond Dogs* is "Chant of the Ever Circling Skeletal Family," and it mimics a locked groove on an album, when the needle gets stuck and repeats the same groove over and over. It's a frightening bit of macabre whimsy but musically is the perfect metaphor for the risky nature of occult pursuits. More so than exaggerated and often false rumors of devil worship, the true dark side of the occult is the ever-circling loop of meaning.

Because the occult is not a system, but rather a messy accumulation of bits of tradition, synthetic beliefs, and even pure fictions in the service of commercialism, there is no final word, no final wisdom. And even for some, it becomes the ruthlessness of seeking signs, where everyday things begin to take on occult connotations, each one a reference to some deeper meaning, which again only points to another possible inference. What makes Bowie the great magician is that, even as his psyche fractured under the strain of this self-imposed mission, he was able to cause "change to occur in conformity with the will." Bowie's personas were rarely that of a magus. Instead, they were otherworldly characters from beyond space and time: Major

SEASON OF THE WITCH

Tom, the space oddity whose voyage into outer space reveals an inner loneliness within an opiated dream; Ziggy Stardust, a messianic figure not unlike Valentine Michael Smith from Robert Heinlein's counterculture science fiction classic *Stranger in a Strange Land*; the futuristic glam visage of *Aladdin Sane*; and the grotesque hybrid dog creature prowling an apocalyptic landscape of *Diamond Dogs*.

With *Station to Station* in 1976, Bowie emerged as the Thin White Duke, a character most critics agree was a husk, the burnt-out shell of a man who had tried to touch the sun. Everything but the glamour had been burned away. The song "Station to Station" is a harrowing admission of an occult obsession fueled by drugs. The quest for divine truth turns into a Sisyphean task: "Got to keep searching . . . Oh what will I be believing." Bowie makes direct references to the Kabbalah, turning over and over the hope that keeps slipping away: "One magical movement from Kether to Malkuth" that he insists is not just "the side-effects of the cocaine."

This is an occult image to be sure, the destitute and craven lich-king, a necromancer whose soul was the last thing to be sacrificed in the search for secret knowledge. But there is also something romantic about this image of the decadent magician. He's a Faust-like character inhabiting a gothic landscape, like those imagined in the German Expressionist motifs depicted in F. W. Murnau's 1926 film of the fabled scholar who sells his soul to the devil in search of hidden wisdom. Out of this image would come two other rock movements, one that embraced the darkness as a means of psychological and spiritual subversion, another that saw walking in the shadows a kind of authenticity, dressing it up in leather, lace, and beautiful silver crosses.

III

Milk and urine enemas, live intercourse, masturbating with chicken heads—all to the soundtrack of Charles Manson's singing, and interspersed with the roar of trains. This was a typical performance of COUM, the artist and musician Genesis Breyer P-Orridge's London-based performance art collective. Founded with Cosey Fanni Tutti (the name a play on Mozart's comic opera) in 1969, initially COUM was an avant-garde hippie band making noise with violins and drums. Theatrics during performances gave them the means to directly challenge the mainstream. It was the underground's turn to show off its magical acuity, using occult techniques as a means of transgression and inspiring other subcultures to do the same. The occult was not just for show, not merely a marketing ploy or a fad made possible by access to unlimited amounts of money and drugs. It was a weapon of the imagination and would illuminate the outer fringes of rock in ways that would cascade toward the middle.

Public funds were available if, as Simon Reynolds explains in his book on postpunk, *Rip It Up and Start Again*, "they described what they did as 'performance art' rather than rock music." The band's peak—and the public interest peaked—happened during a 1976 gallery show at the ICA in London. The installation featured porn magazines, strippers, tampons, and music provided by P-Orridge and Tutti, along with Chris Carter and Peter

Christopherson. Carter was a sound and lighting engineer who worked with a number of high-profile bands, including Yes, but was becoming interested in experimental performances using homemade synthesizers. Christopherson was working with the design firm Hipgnosis (his idiosyncratic vision is on display on Peter Gabriel's first three albums, particularly the iconic image of Gabriel's face melting). The exhibit was met with outrage. The British parliament called COUM "the wreckers of civilization," and as a result they were no longer allowed to apply for arts funding in England.

COUM was an early attempt at cultural transfiguration by way of transgression. As Richard Metzger, the founder of the *Dangerous Minds* website, explains, the COUM performances were "about freeing themselves (and the spectators) of their own taboos by performing benign exorcisms of a sick society's malignancies." This meant having to skirt the edges of whether or not they were celebrating or merely putting a mirror up to what they perceived as these "malignancies." P-Orridge and company would heighten this tension with the formal creation of Throbbing Gristle, soon the standard-bearer of industrial music—a genre heralding in an underground movement in music without peer, and whose influence would extend into the mainstream by way of acts such as Nine Inch Nails and Godflesh.

Throbbing Gristle was to music what COUM was to art. Pure provocation by way of fascist imagery and songs about serial killers and sexual deviance poured out like avant-garde slurry. Their music was a pastiche of blistering electronics, mechanized dance music, ambient landscapes, and impenetrable experiments in Gysinian cut-ups. The cut-up—an artistic technique of cutting pieces of text and allowing elements of chance and stream of consciousness to re-form them—that William Burroughs and the artist Brion Gysin had developed together—was a powerful means of manipulating both consciousness and culture. It was magic: a willful intent to change reality.

The members of Throbbing Gristle were each interested in occult subjects in their own way and in Crowleyan ideas of willful intention—as well as Burroughs's magical ideas—but they eschewed using occult imagery as their primary means of eliciting a reaction from the public. Bands often employed pentagrams and satanic imagery to signal to their audiences or the media their danger or dark spiritual intentions. Throbbing Gristle never felt compelled to use arcane symbols in that way. As Cosey Fanni Tutti explains: "When your work is created from a deep connection with the spiritual, its power is manifest so using symbols is an unnecessary overstatement. I think public gratuitous display tends to reflect a weakness and insecurity, in both the work and the person behind the work."

In 1971, P-Orridge had found a kindred spirit in William Burroughs, whose novels such as *Naked Lunch* set decency on fire. During one of their first conversations, Burroughs related a story kindling P-Orridge's entire future vision (and changing the course of Western occultism). Burroughs frequented a certain diner, where one evening he was treated very poorly. He had the perfect means at hand for revenge. Burroughs would utilize the idea of the "cut-up" for a form of sympathetic magic: a system of occult practice relying on the idea of "like as to like." For example, a doll shaped into the likeness of a particular person could be cursed, stuck with pins, thrown under a bus.

All you needed was a good enough resemblance and the willingness to see the spell through. With this method in mind, Burroughs took a picture of the block where the restaurant stood. He developed the film and used a razor to cut the restaurant out, taping the two pieces back together. He recorded the ambient sounds of the diner's neighborhood, and then he cut in recorded sounds of guns firing, sirens, and explosions. A few weeks later, without warning, the diner closed.

Burroughs told this story to P-Orridge during their first meeting. P-Orridge had sought out Burroughs as a kindred soul intent on subverting what Burroughs called "control," the powers seeking to contain human consciousness, to limit its freedom. The tools available to undermine control were available all around them: hallucinogenic drugs, art, and magic. Burroughs's magic shunned grimoires and ceremony, ritual and conjuration, in favor of photographs, recordings, music production, and film. He believed magic had to adapt to the technology at hand, not rely on the same old texts and traditions. Preserving the rituals of the Golden Dawn or other occult orders might be keeping those methods alive, but it wasn't doing the practice of magic (or art) any good, in his mind.

Jennie Skerl, one of Burroughs's many biographers, explains it like this: "The cutup is a way of exposing word and image controls and thus freeing oneself from them, an alteration of consciousness that occurs in both the writer and the reader of the text."

Burroughs was introduced to the cut-up as a magical means of subversion by his friend and artistic collaborator Brion Gysin. The two had met when Gysin was the proprietor of the 1001

Nights, a restaurant in Tangier that Gysin co-owned between 1954 and 1958. Burroughs and Gysin reconnected again in Paris and worked on reenergizing a technique used by the Dadaists in the 1920s. The Dadaists are often framed as being against any kind of system, believing in nothing but the pure play of their idea. But as the writer Nadia Choucha explains, their quest for a pure "experience of consciousness" meant that they were indeed sensitive to the occult imagination. Collage and other cut-up techniques used by the Dadaists allowed them to tap into the unconscious and listen in to the "unknown." Burroughs recognized that what made the cut-up so potent was how easily it could be adapted to any technology, even those not yet realized. Burroughs could not have imagined the MP3, but the cut-up can be applied to 0s and 1s just as easily as to Polaroid pictures. Cut-ups, Gysin believed, were a working of the higher self, making connections that normal waking consciousness is not able to apprehend. Together, along with the filmmaker Antony Balch, they sought to show how the cut-up was the perfect weapon in the war against control.

P-Orridge met Gysin through Burroughs in 1980 and became even more convinced Gysin's art and ideas were a form of magic that could be used to break free of the stranglehold "control" had on consciousness and liberty. P-Orridge was not the first musician who wanted to utilize Gysin's somewhat isolated artistic vision. In 1967, while waiting to return to court to face drug possession charges, the Rolling Stones took off to Morocco in search of a spiritual cleansing. What they found were better drugs and more debauchery. But Brian Jones had a vision quest of his own. At Gysin's restaurant, Brian witnessed the astonishing trance-inducing music known as the Master Musicians of Joujouka, a group of highly trained Sufi musicians performing as the house band for 1001 Nights. They were a select group of musicians trained from childhood. Their instruments—flute, horn, and drum—caused people to believe their music was channeled from the god Pan and their discipline passed down like an ancient mystery through initiation. Gysin grew to be a true devotee of the musicians, believing their craft to be a type of "psychic hygiene." Jones returned to Morocco in 1968 and together with Gysin convinced the musicians to allow them to record their music in a ceremonial context. Their collaboration would result in a daring album of the Masters' music, produced and mixed with rock's sensibilities, titled *Brian Jones Presents the Pipes of Pan at Joujouka*. This essential album would inspire generations of musicians to incorporate indigenous music and trance elements into their compositions.

What P-Orridge understood was how practical Gysin's magic was; there were actual tools, not just abstract techniques for conjuring demons or meeting with your Holy Guardian Angel. The cut-up had already been applied to literature, to words on a page, particularly in Gysin and Burroughs's collection and user guide, *The Third Mind*. Maybe even more potent, however, was Gysin's invention known as the "dreamachine," a revolving cylinder cut with holes and fitted with a bulb producing a stroboscopic effect. Gysin conceived of the idea on a bus ride. His eyes were closed, but the sun, flickering along a tree-lined street, put him into a trance state, which for Gysin was a "transcendental storm of colour visions." His friend, the technical wizard Ian Sommerville, assembled a simple device that could generate the same effect, and Gysin quickly built his own to recapture the experience in order to use it and share it as a tool of transcendence. The dreamachine has since been used by artists and musicians from Iggy Pop to Michael Stipe in their own work. Gysin believed the dreamachine tapped into the alpha waves of the human brain, a locus that "contains the whole human program of vision," including the entire history of myth and symbol. The cut-ups could destabilize culture, but the dreamachine opened up consciousness, an even more subversive act in a world P-Orridge believes wants us to "fit in with and comply with the overriding culture."

When Throbbing Gristle disbanded, P-Orridge and Christopherson went on to form the band Psychic TV. It was first conceived when P-Orridge saw a television documentary about David Bowie, in particular an unremarkable scene showing David's arrival at a train station and him then stepping into a vintage livery car from the 1930s, a type the Nazis had driven in Berlin during World War II. The ambiguity of Bowie's persona, along with the image of him in this car, made it seem to P-Orridge that Bowie was one step away from appearing like a National Socialist intent on making a power grab. In the scene, the train station was mobbed with teenage fans hoping to catch a glimpse of the musician. The voice-over was commenting on the power Bowie had at that very moment, a power to potentially unify all those kids for a political reason. "So that was the final trigger," P-Orridge remembers: to start a band that might actually use the music and recording as a "platform for radical ideas."

Utilizing more pop elements in their music than P-Orridge

had previously, Psychic TV decided to infect the system from within: "We used the idea of the rock band to prevent as much as we could from the establishment realizing what we were really doing was very urgently saying to people you can change your behavior, you can be as creative as you choose no matter what your original skills if you wished it." To this end, Psychic TV called upon fans to create a magical collective, a virtual secret society with its own language, passcodes, and rituals. Instead of a traditional fan club, Psychic TV would create what P-Orridge calls "a very laissez-faire libertarian occult network." They called themselves Thee Temple ov Psychick Youth (TOPY), a magical youth culture, one part sex, one part drugs, and a huge dose of magical energy borrowed from the nineteenth-century British artist Austin Osman Spare, who had developed a technique known as sigil magic.

Sigils had been used for centuries, and they were made popular when Samuel Liddell MacGregor Mathers, one of the cofounders of the Hermetic Order of the Golden Dawn, translated and published *The Key of Solomon the King*, a medieval grimoire outlining a complicated system of ceremonial magic to conjure angels and bind demons. The grimoire lists the sigils (called seals) of many of the entities, which appear as abstract symbols, not unlike alchemical and astrological signs but more complex, surrounded by a circle. These are essentially the spirits' signatures, which can be used to control them. Like the story of Rumpelstiltskin taught to every child, once you know someone's name you have power over them.

Sigil magic was Spare's greatest contribution to the occult imagination. He first gained recognition in 1904, at the age of fourteen, when he was invited to participate in the prestigious British art showcase, the Royal Academy Summer Exhibition. Spare's work was not unlike the other fin-de-siècle illustrators, such as his predecessor Aubrey Beardsley, with lush pen-and-ink works commissioned by book publishers.

But Spare's work is more personal, and otherwise more grotesque; his use of occult symbols is much more explicit. His drawings are filled with horned creatures and contorted nudes surrounded by fiery swirls. Spare found much of the art establishment distasteful and by midlife went mostly underground, his artwork becoming a sole practice dedicated to pursuing magical wisdom.

For a time, Spare become involved with Aleister Crowley's magical orders, but Spare believed that magic needed to break free of the fraternal grip (and all its attendant handshakes). Spare's genius was to remove the quasi-religious quality from his own sigils by emphasizing their personal nature. His formula for sigil making involved writing down a word representing a specific desire, often placing the letters on top of one another, and erasing extraneous marks until what was left would be "a simple form which can easily be visualized at will, and has not too much pictorial relation to the desire." The form can then be conjured up until the desire is manifest.

In their own investigations of magic, Psychic TV came across this curious British practitioner of magic and urged their fans to create their own sigils. But the band took it one step further, encouraging fans to smear their sigils with blood, semen, and other bodily fluids. Fans then mailed these to the band, who kept a file of them in the hopes that collectively they would energize one another and bring their desires into form and being.

Magic needed to be demystified, P-Orridge argued, so that new, unfettered spiritual cultures could be created. Anything can become a magical battery, says P-Orridge, "stuffed animals, or Hershey chocolate bars or whatever. You can develop your own language of symbolism, language of magic that for you maximizes the efficiency and effect of the ritual." When the band opened a piece of mail for the first time to find a sigil smeared with an unknown fluid, P-Orridge knew this could be the start of new occult thinking, the ultimate expression being ten thousand people worldwide creating sigils on the same day at the same time. "Not everybody could coordinate their clocks but a hell of a lot did," P-Orridge recalls. "Nobody had done that before."

Peter Christopherson eventually left Psychic TV to form Coil with John Balance, who also played frequently with Psychic TV. The two men in this new iteration combined heavy electronic sound with cut-ups, percussion, and Balance's powerful vocals to produce a number of critically notable albums of the 1980s and 1990s, including *Scatology*, *Horse Rotorvator*, and *Love's Secret Domain*, along with numerous live releases, side projects, seven-inch singles, and cassettes. Coil made no distinction between their art and their spiritual (and sexual) affinities. They used magical techniques such as the I Ching and herculean amounts of psychedelics in order to create states of altered consciousness, for themselves and their music. Balance had come to see the magic associated with Psychic TV and TOPY as cultlike, too dependent on the group energy, and he wanted to follow even more directly in Spare's footsteps as someone whose occult practice was solitary, as in the path of the shaman. In an interview with Mark Pilkington for *Fortean Times*, Balance decries the cultlike approach to magic of the Church of Satan. Any accusations that Coil used satanic imagery were just ignorance, he'd say, Coil's true patron deity being Pan. And for celebrities and musicians like Anton LaVey and Marilyn Manson, Balance had no patience: "That's showbiz Satanism, I don't buy into any of that at all. Pan is certainly one of my deities, one that I find solace and power in."

Coil's first single, the 1984 "How to Destroy Angels" (a title Trent Reznor of Nine Inch Nails would borrow as the name of his side band), was packaged with a wordy description of the music that begins: "Ritual music for the accumulation of male sexual energy." The song was an attempt to remind their listeners that music had once been used "as a tool for affecting man's body and spirit." "How to Destroy Angels" could be described as ambient pulses, punctuated by gongs and the scratching of metal on metal—sounding both deliberate and "cut-up."

It's an intensely powerful piece of music, but the presentation of "How to Destroy Angels"—with its emphasis on male sexuality—would front-load Coil's identity and with what Balance called their "solar" aspect, characterized by their use of what is called the Black Sun, a symbol linked to the Nazis. (During World War II, the SS held meetings within the Wewelsburg castle in which the Black Sun symbol had been tiled into the floor. The symbol was later adopted by other neo-Nazi groups, particularly those emphasizing occult motivations.) The symbol's history is actually quite complex. It can even be found in the writings of Blavatsky. Nevertheless, its association with Nazi occultism is impossible to sever. And later, Coil would allow for a lunar (read feminine) occult influence. While Balance claimed this was a natural progression of their music's evolution, it might also have been a response to the problems of being associated with any kind of actual fascist ideology.

Coil collaborated with Boyd Rice, an underground noise musician and acquaintance. Rice later became embroiled in a controversy over a photograph of him with Bob Heick, the leader of the neo-Nazi group American Front, both wearing American Front uniforms. Coil decided it was best to separate themselves from any association with Rice. While fascism had been part of the arsenal of symbols that Throbbing Gristle (and sometimes Psychic TV) used for shock effect, Coil wasn't interested in moving beyond the use of music to undermine "control," and instead pushed themselves into untrodden areas of magic and consciousness exploration.

One night before a Killing Joke show in Ireland in 1982, the singer and keyboardist Jaz Coleman failed to show up. His bandmates learned later that he had fled to Iceland, believing an apocalypse was imminent. They found out that he had sought out a magical order, corresponding by mail. Coleman was able to convince his friends of a coming doom, and more joined him, only to find they had been duped by a cult looking to increase their membership with rock star personalities. Coleman would later claim that he just needed an extended vacation, to "study classical music, study sacred geometry, and antiquities—just break out of the corny, clichéd rock 'n' roll lifestyle." But his leaving seemed intimately tied into his deep interest in the occult and to Killing Joke's music, which the band had once described as "nature throwing up."

Killing Joke had come to believe their group was a magical fellowship. Their interest in magic began as teenagers, after joining the Hermetic Order of the Golden Dawn. Later, as Killing Joke, the group staged magical rituals that were helped along by Dwina Murphy Gibb—second wife of Robin Gibb of the Bee Gees—who would draw and bless magical circles on the stage. Killing Joke wanted to be more than a rock band. Like the serpent in the garden, they wanted to be an oppositional force to both mainstream music and Christianity. When a young fanzine editor interviewing the band described them as "punk," Coleman spat back, "Well, that's just ignorance, isn't it? Because we don't play 'punk-rock,' we just reflect what's happening and endeavor to be honest with ourselves." Killing Joke believed they couldn't fit into the definition of rock, or rock culture. During a hostile interview in 1980 with the critic Paul Morley for *NME*, Coleman accused Morley of being too enamored of "pop" to get what Killing Joke was about. During their heated exchange, Coleman described what he thought the band was about: having the will to survive the future, one that he believed would likely include natural disasters or World War III.

Killing Joke's 1980 eponymous debut album is a powerful bit of postpunk spittle, a driving rhythmic set of songs, one part tribal, one part futurist vision. They broke the punk model by incorporating electronics. After their return to England from

Iceland, their music became more commercial, less confronta-
tional, and by 1986 Killing Joke sounded more like a synth-pop
new wave band, their once-fiery guitars dowsed by synthesizers. Despite the somewhat neutered sound, Coleman's occultism
was more mature, less reactionary. Perhaps he had found a way
to separate his spiritual practice from making music and performing, putting that energy elsewhere. Nevertheless, the band's
reputation as heralds of a rock apocalypse would continue to
precede them, and rightly so.

The macho image of rock was often softened by the androgynous and pansexual face attached to even the most masculine of performers, but Killing Joke, as Simon Reynolds puts
it, was "reveling in male energy." Magical practice, especially as
derived from Crowley, is often driven by a phallic-oriented
view of sex. The other aspect of this male-focused energy is,
Reynolds rightly points out, sometimes akin to fascism. Fascism,
clothed in the camouflage of occult mystery, characterized certain aspects of industrial's effete cousin, gothic rock. As Reynolds explains, this was troubling for the gothic scene, which for
the most part saw itself to be thoroughly egalitarian, especially
when it came to gender.

Reynolds points to three other bands that form goth's cor-
ners: Bauhaus, led by Peter Murphy, would deliver goth rock's
first manifesto, the droning masterpiece "Bela Lugosi's Dead";
Birthday Party—whose deep-voiced Nick Cave would go on to
form the influential Nick Cave and the Bad Seeds—played
tribal, abrasive postpunk; Siouxsie and the Banshees started
as sneering British punks, but softened into a goth band that

skirted the edges of the occult by using the aura as a way to construct an attitude and a fashion.

Goth cannot be compared to heavy metal's upside-down pentagrams and brandishing of Aleister Crowley. Instead, goth rock inhabits a mood, just as the original literary genre did. Goth's aesthetic is more like the tragic beauty of the Victorian Era's memento mori. Even goth's embrace of death is not about gore, but about the melancholy loneliness of the graveyard, crumbling ancient tombstones, and, sometimes, vampires. Goth rock's literary antecedent, gothic literature, grew out of the Romantic tradition, but rather than an idealistic longing for the myth and values of the past—often by way of the natural world—the gothic story is one in which the loss of the past solicits melancholia and an inward retreat. The past is a ghost that haunts the present. While there might be supernatural or otherworldly goings-on, the emphasis is on the setting, often some decaying castle or ancient family home.

In *Dracula* by Bram Stoker, the character of Lucy Westenra—beautiful and pure of heart—is visited nightly by the vampire. He slowly drains her of blood, but to her friends she appears to be sickly anemic, dying a slow, inexplicable death. She eventually becomes a bride of Dracula. The entire subplot of Lucy's transformation is one of the most terrifying in the novel, but it is also the most strangely erotic. The taking of her blood—her innocence—at night while she is in her bed is an extreme sexual metaphor. It is an image like this, the tension between desire and purity, that forms the heart of the gothic novel. In this novel, evil is not a moral dilemma but an existential one. A novel like *Dracula* served as a template for goth subculture, and vampires represented the perfect antihero, particularly when Anne Rice's best-selling Vampire Chronicles series gave them such elegance. But despite the eroticism, vampires are asexual.

The contemporary gothic subculture dressed itself in dark finery, disdained normative gender roles, and no longer believed music needed to change the world. It could merely mirror the inner life. Similarly, the occult is largely a fashion statement, an affect that alludes to something taboo but is only really visible as a shadow, a half-remembered dream. But while goth did not use magic as a weapon like its industrial rock cousin, it still recognized that the occult imagination is powerful all on its own. One need not cast a spell, divine the future, or hold a séance. The mere intimation of a hidden, mysterious reality can set the heart afire, ignite the creative spirit, and transform culture, and popular music, forever.

CHAPTER 5

SPACE RITUAL

I

A large inflatable tent was erected just beyond the main fairground, christened Canvas City. From there you could still see the crowd of at least half a million people at the Isle of Wight Festival. Two bands from the UK underground—the Pink Fairies and Hawkwind—simply decided not to play the game at all and staged their own free concerts in Canvas City. Hawkwind would provide not only free music, it would also offer an experience in altered consciousness that received little attention at the time. Nonetheless, it was an essential moment in the transformation of rock and roll. Under this tent, Hawkwind began their decades-long interstellar mission to explore the occult mysteries of the cosmos. They would never achieve commercial success, but their influence on other musicians—particularly in regards to crafting a science-fantasy mythology—would give the occult imagination a new vessel for shaping rock and roll.

The year was 1970, and the pioneers of 1960s rock, along with some of the new breed, had done two previous successful festivals in 1968 and 1969. The muddy utopia of Woodstock in America had inspired the Isle of Wight promoters to make sure this would be comparably glorious. Over the course of five days, the kings and queens of rock and roll performed to their worshipful subjects. The acts included the Who, Joni Mitchell, Jimi Hendrix (who would die from an overdose a few weeks later), Joan Baez, Miles Davis, and the Doors, among many others. But the revolutionary spirit of the 1960s had not completely faded. Many believed the festivals should be free, and thousands ended up squatting in an area they called Desolation Row, which, to the dismay of the organizers, offered a fine view of the festival. During Joni Mitchell's set, a man by the name of Yogi Joe snuck onstage and interrupted her performance in an attempt to remind the crowd that the festival "belonged" to them and to congratulate the peaceful anarchy of Desolation Row. He was forcibly dragged off and Joni Mitchell gracefully, albeit shakily, finished her set.

On display and being played out was little more than rock's crass commercialization, an end to the free-festival spirit of the 1960s, a metaphor for the sad conclusion to the decade. Something within rock's consciousness had changed. The devastating spectacle of violence at Altamont might have prefigured the end of Aquarian Age idealism, but Yogi Joe's mad dash to get his word out was not merely the action of a raving acidhead. Joe was something of a prophet who saw the terrible truth on the horizon. Rock was selling out, and soon the festivals would become the domain of promoters and sponsors.

By the end of the five days, as Dave Smith writes, "It had become painfully clear to those still clinging on to the various philosophies of hippy culture that the shift to the commercially dominated events we recognize now was both well in motion and unavoidable." Amid this tension, Hawkwind's music and performances functioned as a time-travel device through space and time, looking toward the future, where a new rebellion might take place and keep rock's soul spiritually intact. Just as Arthur Brown saw rock shows as shamanic rites that could transmit ideas, Hawkwind understood that the very electric currents they discharged through their music could also function as a kind of mesmeric device. After the Isle of Wight Festival, where the band had generated what Jerry Gilbert for *Sounds* magazine in 1970 would describe as "arcs of sound" using electronic noise generators, the lead singer and guitarist David Brock knew something potent had taken place. He told Gilbert that, after seeing the audience's reaction, he had a new responsibility: "You can force people to go into trances, and tell them what to do; it's mass hypnotism, and you're really setting yourself up as God."

Hawkwind, considered the first space rock band, came to prominence in the British underground with their first, eponymous album, an intoxicating brew of psychedelic and hard rock with a nod toward what would become the overarching theme of their career: science fiction mysticism both sincere and tongue-in-cheek. They were through with the hyperidealism of the hippies' psychedelic values but still believed rock had the power to be a spiritual beacon, and even made it clear in the liner notes of the album: "We started out trying to freak people (trippers), now we are trying to levitate their minds, in a nice way, without acid . . ." Their second album, *In Search of Space*, included a minifanzine as the liner notes, complete with astrological tables, psychedelic collages, and pulp-comic artwork, along with logs of the "spacecraft Hawkwind." The logs document the travels of stoned alien astronauts who listen to Jimi Hendrix on their way to planet earth. The final entry is a religious evocation of space: "And now I believe in the supreme and mystic darkness of nothing, in the deepest reaches of the immaculate void . . . in the incomprehensible infinity of untold nothing, in absolute nothing." *In Search of Space* could be considered the first truly great work of rock sci-fi, and yet the songs tell tales of journeys into the psyche. This would characterize much of space rock and later progressive rock, where the metaphors of inner and outer space are interchangeable. But Hawkwind's live elements were largely fantastical, a "sonic attack" by way of strobe lights, lasers, projectors, and Stacia, the band's nude dancer who improvised moves to the rhythm of the music.

Just as 1960s alternative spirituality emphasized the religious possibilities of the LSD trip, the 1970s would see a turn toward the heavens for meaning. Certainly, as we saw, the devil played a starring role during this decade, but images of Satan were more symptomatic than representative of any real spiritual path. But what to do about the failed 1960s Aquarian promise? If salvation wasn't found in the gathering of the tribes here on earth, then maybe outer space held the key. Moreover, a belief in a future-cosmic deliverance was not without precedent. A glimpse into the past was all the proof you needed to know outer space held the key to humanity's ultimate transfiguration.

Admit it (it has been said). It would be impossible for the ancient Egyptians to have built the pyramids. They had neither the technology nor the resources for such an astonishing feat of engineering. And even if they had, would they have really done all that dangerous long work merely to bury a king and his toys? It seems preposterous. A better, maybe even more reasonable, theory is that the Egyptians were helped. And this help came from the stars. Ancient people recognized these beings from other worlds as deities, and drew their likeness on the walls of the pyramids. In other places around the world, the alien visitors left their mark in other ways: in the giant malformed heads of Easter Island, in the great pagan stones known as Stonehenge. The Dogon people, an African Mali tribe, had mapped out astronomical charts they could never have discerned from looking at the sky with the naked eye. What we now call civilization, often driven by the massive force known as Christianity, buried these ancient people and their scientific wonders. But they were far more advanced than us, helped along by "sky-people" who still secretly visit earth, waiting for when we are again ready to accept their spiritual and technological gifts.

These ideas were first made popular in the 1968 book *Chariots of the Gods* by Erich von Däniken. Deeply criticized and largely debunked, von Däniken's work nevertheless helped usher in a new wave of belief in aliens and UFOs and sell a lot of books. Von Däniken turned the hostile Martian and the otherworldly body snatcher into quasi-divine beings who not only helped humanity achieve greatness during certain moments in history, but might one day allow us to participate in a great galactic future.

Other books would follow, such as the 1976 book *The Sirius Mystery* by Robert Temple, that concluded the Dogon people had contact with extraterrestrials. These books and still more would set off a UFO craze that would come to dominate the rest of the 1970s. In the bookstores, interest in UFOs was in high demand and publishers kept up a steady stream, with titles like *We Are Not the First, UFO Exist!*, and *Beyond Earth*. Space and aliens also became the stuff of some of the most inventive speculations and narratives during the late 1960s through to the latter part of the 1970s. From *Star Trek*'s space-fearing utopian Federation to the star child of *2001: A Space Odyssey*, the pop culture imagination looked upward for a way to save humanity from itself.

Decades before Hawkwind dressed up space exploration in psychedelic whimsy, the jazz musician Sun Ra had already taken the journey beyond the heliosphere. Sun Ra, born Herman Blount in Birmingham, Alabama, in 1914, moved to Chicago, where, in the 1950s, his exceptional piano playing brought him into the circle of the thriving jazz scene. He became, as the *Independent* lovingly put it after his death in 1993, "one of the more convincing jazz nutters who also managed to make a serious contribution to the music." This reputation as someone possibly slightly cracked was the result of his pronouncements regarding his own outer space origins and a cosmic spiritual theology that would herald in a new age for mankind. Blount changed his name to Sun Ra and in 1956 formed a band called the Arkestra, a literal vessel of musicians taking audiences toward a new vision of music. His music was avant-garde, a future-facing music trying to break free of jazz conventions. But Sun

Ra rarely talked about his music in the context of the jazz tradition. Sun Ra believed his work was the enfolding principle, the necessary method to find true happiness: "Now, my music is about a better place for people, not to have a place where they have to die to get there." In other words, it was heaven on earth.

Sun Ra believed people had to understand the spirit behind the music, and so developed what he called "myth science." The basis of this is a kind of Gnosticism that sees our planet as a trap. Sun Ra once told a reporter, "I hate the idea of being on this planet. It's a terrible place, and I always knew when I first arrived here. But what can I do about it?"

Along with the Kabbalah, numerology, and science fiction, Sun Ra constructed a complex theology easily simplified by just listening to his music: "So I'm gonna take this music and give people a touch of something else, to enlighten them, so they can see how insignificant they are, and how very important they are at the same time." At first these ideas were tied into race. Sun Ra's quasi–science fiction film, *Space Is the Place*, tells the story of a starship and its crew, the Arkestra. Powered by music, the spacecraft is traveling to a new planetary home for African Americans. A pimp, a symbol for the internal forces keeping young black Americans down, is Sun Ra's nemesis, and after a duel it is revealed that the pimp is actually a pawn in the white power structure seeking to keep African Americans spiritually and economically impoverished. Eventually Sun Ra would believe his message was for all people. Onstage, Sun Ra would wear robes and Egyptian headdresses, surrounded by musicians on bongos, drums, and guitars, half a dozen horn players, and ecstatic dancers, all of them writhing and moving as if possessed by alien entities. But these are not individual egos, each vying for attention. It is a true collective, drawing from their bandleader's energy, offering what John Sinclair, writing for *Creem* in 1972, called "the supreme example of dedication and commitment to a common purpose that can be found in the whole music world." Sun Ra's hope was for the whole earth community to aim for heaven, by way of a starship filled with two of every kind, as the means to escape this perpetual flood of affliction.

It wasn't in a vacuum, then, that Hawkwind saw their own spaceship as a way to craft a music and mythology that was one part occultism, one part science fiction. Their famous album *Space Ritual*, recorded in Liverpool in 1972, is the most perfect realization of a heavy rock cosmic odyssey; the liner notes refer to the band as "musicnauts." The band had intended the live show to induce sensory overload. They added more dancers to accompany Stacia, as well as a slide show that included pulsing lights along with images of Stonehenge and sharply angular shapes. The music itself is fierce, riff-driven soundscapes accelerating as they go along. It's infectious stuff, even today, and while the science fiction lyrics are somewhat dated, they are a pulp lover's dream.

Much of this sensibility came by way of their patron saint, the author Michael Moorcock—inventor of two of the most remarkable characters to inhabit the genre: Jerry Cornelius (a time-traveling, perpetually stoned assassin whose meta-adventures are a cynical look at the shuttering of the 1960s), and Elric of Melniboné (a morally troubled sorcerer-king of a race of debauched elves who wields Stormbringer, a demon-inhabited sword). Moorcock became fast friends with the band after seeing them live. Moorcock later told Hawkwind's biographer Ian Abrahams that the band seemed to be "like the mad crew of a long-distance spaceship who had forgotten the purpose of their mission, which had turned to art during the passage of time." In the 1960s, Moorcock reinvented science fiction when he took over as editor of *New Worlds* magazine. Moorcock wanted to save science fiction from what he saw as the staid old guard whose imagination was limited to outer space adventures. Moorcock believed science fiction could serve as a template to explore what he called "a new literature which expressed our own experience." Moorcock was born at the outset of World War II and being haunted by what the critic Theodor Adorno called the failure of the enlightenment. Reason gave way to suicidal irrationality. Science fiction could become a tool of the counterculture, a way to capture in literature the fantastical hopes and fears of a generation for whom rock music and LSD were methods of liberation. Under Moorcock, *New Worlds* published J. G. Ballard, M. John Harrison, and Roger Zelazny. *Lord of Light*, Zelazny's 1967 novel, tells the story of colonists living on another planet who augment themselves and take on the likenesses and personalities of Hindu deities, a story that would inspire a Hawkwind song of the same name.

Moorcock began performing with Hawkwind in the late 1970s and in the 1980s, providing not only themes and lyrics for songs, but backing and spoken-word vocals. Hawkwind went to the Moorcock well often, and the essential song "Black Corridor" on the album *Space Ritual*, a poem about the "remorseless, senseless, and impersonal fact" of space, is taken directly from Moorcock's novel of the same name.

Moorcock believes, like Arthur Brown, that when art takes on the function of myth, it can actually transform consciousness: "I believe that the artist is a shaman, in that you provide your public (tribe) with images, resonances, stories which symbolise their relationship with the physical world and its questions." The idea that science fiction could serve to help understand aspects of humanity would have a profound effect not only on the music of Hawkwind, whose sci-fi pretentions were continually rooted in very human, albeit mystical, concerns, but also on the popular consciousness as it related to outer space. *Star Trek*, of course, would use science fiction as a way to say some quite radical things about race, politics, technology, and even religion. Moreover, the notion of aliens functioning as religious emissaries is a far cry from the destructive tripods that raze London in *The War of the Worlds*. But the future was also about technology, and rock and roll would soon find the means to express the future.

II

It was in the early 1960s, at an Acoustical Society conference, that Robert Moog demonstrated his strange new instrument, a collection of electronic filters and oscillators that could be controlled to make sounds not previously heard by the human ear. During a question-and-answer session, a journalist asked him, "Don't you feel guilty about what you've done?" Others balked, too. The critics, often classically trained composers, saw the synthesizer as an affront. Robert Moog talking about making music with electronics is not unlike listening to a mystic describing an encounter with the ineffable quality of the divine. In documentary interviews about his life and work, Moog did not believe his own abilities as an engineer would help how he solved problems with circuitry: "I opened my mind up and the idea came through me." His understanding of the synthesizer aligns to a spiritual idea of music as something that exists already in time and space but needs to be channeled into a prepared receptacle. The world was quickly changing, and people's minds were changing along with it. LSD helped, as did explorations of alternative religions; the synthesizer was the perfect instrument to express the paradigm shift. Moog and his radical device opened up a completely new path for musical consciousness, and the sounds it made were otherworldly enough to align with the occult interests that were becoming part of mainstream culture. Rock and almost every one of its extended genres would become invigorated by electronic possibilities, and they would all be underscored by Moog's spiritual vision, one that had been a consistent part of experimental music long before him.

At the time, Moog was angered when a journalist accused him of ruining popular music, but the inventor was not deterred. Not only was his synthesizer a real instrument to be played by real people, it was an instrument capable of revealing the very essence of music, how it rises out of consciousness and becomes real. Moog also believed the synthesizer could show students something beyond theory and the staff and the clef. The Moog synthesizer requires manipulation, and, as such, there is something deeply personal that takes place. Moog's co-inventor, Herbert Deutsch, believes that Moog's invention was able to capture a shift in consciousness that had begun with LSD and mysticism but needed a push to the next level, a physical tool perhaps, and a look toward the future that did not reject the advancements in technology all around them.

There had always been a tension about technology for hippies, and rightly so. The release from all our energy-sourcing worries—the splitting of the atom and the horizon of the nuclear age—was a great deception, providing nothing more than the ultimate weapon for the military-industrial complex. Stewart Brand, founder of the *Whole Earth Catalog*, remarked how the conflict over the role of technology could be seen in the difference between Berkeley hippies and Stanford hippies. "We were all taking the same drugs," he said, but the protestors at Berkeley didn't have a solution. More LSD wasn't the answer, unless it was going to help you write computer code. And it seemed to be doing just that for the counterculture nerds at Stanford. In the section titled "Purpose" on the second page of the *Whole Earth Catalog*, first published in 1968, it reads, "We are as gods and might as well get good at it." Brand and his colleagues saw technology as the most powerful tool in the counterculture arsenal. Many musicians were also beginning to look beyond what had once been the perfect quartet of rebellion (guitar, bass, drums, and vocals) as becoming unable to carry the weight of what they wanted to express.

During the summer of 1965, Deutsch and Moog meandered their way in Moog's VW Bug to the University of Toronto in order to demonstrate their new instrument. It was packed into two large boxes in the backseat. One contained oscillators and amplifiers, the other filters. When they arrived at the border, their car was searched and the English-speaking guards were mystified by the equipment and would not let them cross the border. Moog tried to explain to the guards that these electronic components were the parts of an instrument. They were not convinced. A French-speaking guard came over after he heard Moog explaining his new invention, smiled, and said, "Ah! Musique concrète." He then went on to explain to the other guards that this was indeed a way of making music and the two were allowed to pass. Once at the university, they were brought down to the basement where the school's computer was housed, a massive mainframe in a giant room. In the center of the room was a larger piece of equipment that Moog and Deutsch were to plug their synthesizer into. They were asked not to bring a keyboard, since the computer would "play" the music. And indeed they heard Bach in F minor from the electronics of their synthesizer, controlled by a computer. Deutsch recalls being mystified: "This was all magic." Nevertheless, Moog and Deutsch were not yet interested in the computer as musician. They didn't view the synthesizer as different from a piano or even a violin.

The Canadian border guard had called Moog's synthesizer "musique concrète," and while the synthesizer is a different beast, their driving ethos and origins are closely linked. The father of musique concrète, Pierre Schaeffer, founded La Jeune France (Young France) in 1940 during the Nazi occupation of France. During an earlier incarnation of the group, one of the cofounders, the composer André Jolivet, believed young artists should reframe music in opposition to neoclassicism. Neoclassicism wanted a systematic music, relying more on formal technique than emotion. Led by the interests of Jolivet, La Jeune France believed authentic composition was that which drew on music's original intention: ritual and magic. Schaeffer's vision for the group had a political bent, formed as it was during the occupation, when France's very cultural identity was being challenged. By 1942, the Nazis would no longer tolerate ideas about culture that they could not control, and they disbanded the group. But Schaeffer's rebellious instincts were powered by the occupation and after the war he continued with his musique concrète experiments.

Musique concrète creates music out of voices and sounds from nature and instruments. Using tape, these sounds could then be manipulated by cutting and splicing, and music was "composed" using the recording studio as the instrument. Schaeffer would play the works for an audience via speakers, a radical endeavor, since it was assumed that if you went to hear live music, you would see the source of the sounds and the conductor of the musicians. Schaeffer called this "acousmatic" and, according to cultural theorist John Mowitt, he was influenced by Pythagoras, the Greek philosopher known for his method of teaching students while hidden behind a curtain. Music becomes subjective, and the composer of musique concrète cannot assume the music will be received in any predetermined way.

Moog began his career as a teenager when he started selling theremin kits, the instrument best known for its use by soundtrack composer Bernard Herrmann in films such as *The Day the Earth Stood Still*. Moog's interest in electronic music began to shape a vision for his own future, but it wasn't until he met Deutsch in 1963 at a music conference that a practical idea emerged. Subsequent meetings resulted in an ongoing conversation and collaboration. They initially talked about the possibility of a "small and affordable music synthesizer." But their first units were extremely large, complex, and expensive. Each sound required a different module patched together by cables. Keeping them in tune made the devices difficult to use as a live instrument. Eventually, Moog combined them into one portable—and relatively affordable—synthesizer instrument known as the Minimoog. Released in 1970, the Minimoog made its public debut on tour with Emerson, Lake and Palmer during their *Pictures at an Exhibition* tour.

Moog was the meeting place between two poles of electronic music: the serious and the popular. The music journalist Mark Brend argued, "Indeed, many advances in early electronic music came from the energy created by an overlap between the two." Though Moog began as a hobbyist—and even his first business selling theremins was for the amateur and the tinkerer—when he began working with Deutsch, already known as an experimental composer, Moog could begin to imagine a new possibility for electronic music. He would have to first unmoor it from the inert critique that electronic music is unnatural and inauthentic. As Moog would explain, his synthesizer is analog, not digital, and therefore "analogous" to instruments made of wood, brass, and string. Vibration is the phenomenon that allows music to take place, be it via the movement of a bow or the flow of current through a resistor; both require human actions, but it took time for the listening public to hear that playing a synthesizer was indeed "a human activity," and not another symptom of the dehumanization of culture, a scary move into an unknown future.

And indeed, before it could be heard as a human activity, as music, the sounds produced by the Moog synthesizer would become the soundtrack of the otherworldly, outer space, or the supernatural. Some of the first Moog composers packaged their albums in occultism, such as a popular series released after the success of *The Zodiac: Cosmic Sounds*, performed by Paul Beaver and composed by Mort Garson, in 1967. Garson was commercially successful, arranging songs for easy-listening records. But after hearing the Moog for the first time, he decided to use it on other albums. He produced a number of albums using the Moog, but his occult interests peaked with his *Black Mass* (under the name Lucifer) in 1971, and later with *Ataraxia: The Unexplained (Electronic Musical Impressions of the Occult)* in 1975. On *Black Mass*, Garson did his research. The first piece, "Solomon's Ring," refers to the fabled ring that King Solomon used to control the demons that built his temple to God. The ring, or seal, was found mentioned in various magical grimoires and was an important idea in Kabbalistic magic. Other tracks include "Black Mass," "The Philosopher's Stone," and "ESP." And Garson knew his audience. While the music was experimental, Garson tapped into the occult mainstream of the decade, mixing Satanism, alchemy, magic, and paranormal phenomena into a nightmarish soundtrack. *Ataraxia* followed with songs like "Tarot," "Astral Projection," "I Ching," and "Cabala." Dropping the aura of Lucifer made for a slightly less lurid album, but Garson had mastered the Moog and provided a template for how to use the sound of the future to conjure images of the ancients, ushering it into more popular uses and interests, and poising it for acceptance.

Concurrent with Moog's work were the pioneers of British electronic music, the BBC Radiophonic Workshop, founded by Daphne Oram and Desmond Briscoe in 1958. The Workshop's soundtrack to the BBC television show *Doctor Who* had introduced the mainstream to electronic music in 1963 by way of eerie oscillating thrums that carried the doctor through time and space.

Electronic music was still relegated to commercial use and to the basements of hobbyists, many of whom relied on magazine schematics and shorted-out experiments to build instruments. Electronic music was too obscure, either belonging to the highbrow domain of people like Pierre Schaeffer or to the solitary tinkerer. This reputation made it seem odd, and the fact that it was only popularly heard on soundtracks of science fiction movies made electronic music seem somewhat "weird." Brend notes that one of the first books for electronic music hobbyists, *Electronic Music and Musique Concrète*, was published in 1961 by Neville Armstrong of Neville Spearman Limited. Armstrong released books on a wide range of curious subjects, including UFOs, the paranormal, and fiction by Conan creator Robert E. Howard. (Armstrong is also responsible for the aforementioned *Spear of Destiny*, and in 1978 even tried his hand at an "authentic" version of *The Necronomicon*.) Electronic music, at least in pop culture, echoed the heavenly spheres and the sounds of the untapped realms of human potential. Inner and outer space were locations we wanted to explore simultaneously, but we needed two seemingly incompatible means of propulsion: the arcane sciences to unravel the mysteries of our souls and computers to unravel the mysteries of time and space; electronic music existed comfortably as the soundtrack to both.

A thoughtful, bearded young man in the audience posed a question to the composer and electronic music architect Karlheinz Stockhausen, a young but formidable man himself, his ideas spilling out as he spoke, one after the other, sometimes to the detriment of their meaning. Isn't electronic music dehumanizing? And because it cannot touch on human concerns such as love and sadness, won't it ultimately fall away? Stockhausen, whose life and work was dictated by the possibilities of electronic music, was not the least bit perturbed by the question. "There are other kinds of human beings," he said. It was 1972, and Stockhausen had become enamored of the teachings of the Indian mystic Sri Aurobindo, who taught that the physical evolution of human beings is but one step toward the greater spiritual evolution that is our divine right. Stockhausen's take was a bit more literal. He continued, "We are in a situation where the first so-called human being came out of the non-human kingdom. We are at the threshold of a new terrestrial mutation."

In the 1960s, British and American psychedelic music was selling well in Germany, but young and visionary German musicians without a trend of their own didn't want to simply mimic those bands. Psychedelic music, and the more experimental sounds of the Velvet Underground and Frank Zappa, was a place to start. But they also looked to their own: Stockhausen was one such person.

His students Irmin Schmidt and Holger Czukay would go on to form Can, a band whose proficiency and stellar musicianship was matched only by how far they were willing to push the idea of rock and roll. Their third album, *Tago Mago*, a crucible of avant-garde, jazz, and psychedelic, includes one of the fundamental instances of mixing art and magic. In "Aumgn" an echoing guitar slowly builds into an ambient drone of chanting. The title chant is taken from Aleister Crowley's Creed of the Gnostic Catholic Church, the statement of belief recited by those who wish to join the Ordo Templi Orientis, the magical order whose practices orient around Crowley's teachings. It is a creepy but effective song, and highlights exactly how krautrock bands, as they would come to be known, would differentiate themselves from everything that came before.

Popol Vuh was something of an outlier in the krautrock scene, if such a thing can be said about a group of bands fairly diverse in their overall output. Florian Fricke, its leader, had worked with many of the central people of krautrock, but his vision for music was more religious than any of the other bands. Fricke was a voracious reader of mythology, mysticism, and Eastern philosophy. He was particularly taken by the creation myth of the Mayan people, known as the Popol Vuh, in which the creator, Heart-of-Sky, works to fashion the perfect human being, but ultimately ends up with a creature not unlike a monkey. For Fricke, the myth of Popol Vuh was the subtext for the band's first album, *Affenstunde* (literally "monkey hour"). In a 1996 interview, Fricke, who would pass away five years later, explained that first monkeys had become man, and one day would become "a human being" and "no longer an ape any longer."

Echoing Stockhausen's idea of the suprahuman, Fricke mastered the Moog synthesizer as a way to get to his own subconscious, to unleash his potential. But he would abandon the instrument because, as his widow, Bettina Waldthausen, told the writer Jason Gross, "The electronic sound is against the natural flow of the heartbeat."

Manuel Göttsching was only nineteen years old when he felt the krautrock groundswell. At sixteen he had already been introduced to avant-garde composition through Thomas Kessler, the Swiss composer who was working with electronics as early as 1965. In 1971, Göttsching's band Ash Ra Tempel combined a more blues-based approach, but the group still disrupted rock conventions with long atonal solos, electronics, and abrasive vocals. Their mysticism was often harsh, a struggle against a bad trip with transcendence right on the horizon. A short two years later, Göttsching disbanded Ash Ra Tempel to focus more on solo projects. This would result in the forming of Ashra, an almost entirely electronic soft-rock version of Ash Ra Tempel, with little to recommend it. It wasn't until Göttsching's 1984 solo release *E2-E4* that his vision would change popular music by steering electronic music into the club scene with its influence on techno and house music.

One of krautrock's most important bands, Tangerine Dream, had started as edgy experimenters. Their first album, 1970's *Electronic Meditation*, sounds like an evening at the UFO Club with Pink Floyd—psychedelic-charged investigations of noise using guitars, a typewriter, metal sticks, and organs. Their next trilogy of albums—*Zeit, Alpha Centauri,* and *Atem*—were almost entirely crafted with synthesizers for the sounds of interplanetary excursions, but the band still held to their roots as cutting-edge musicians. By the late 1970s, their music was a mix of heavily produced progressive rock and synthesizer-based symphonies. Live, they played loud, accompanied by complex laser-light shows. In the 1980s, their once-evocative cosmic soundscapes were reduced to New Age balm: the synthesizer had been its applicator.

It's not clear if Robert Moog spoke to the buyers and users of his synthesizers in spiritual terms, but many of them quickly adopted the well-crafted instrument to communicate the selfsame ideas, and he was not shy about sharing these ideas with the friends and the musicians he inspired. At the 2004 Moogfest in New York City, Rick Wakeman of the progressive rock band Yes, and Bernie Worrell, the keyboard virtuoso who was a founding member of Parliament-Funkadelic, stood around Moog, trading stories after the show. Worrell described how playing a Moog synthesizer was like making love. More than once Wakeman said that Moog "changed the face of music." After the conversation expanded into deeper territory, the three men admitted there was also something numinous about the instrument. Wakeman pointed a finger at Moog and said, "It comes from inside this man." Moog, ever humble, waved at the air above him and said, "It comes from out there, it comes through me into the instrument, and then the music comes through you guys and the instrument."

III

At a recent gallery show of his artwork, Roger Dean—best known for his lush and fantastical album covers for Yes in the

1970s—was enjoying the crowd when a man approached him and held out his hand to shake. "Mr. Dean, your work has changed my life," he said. "I have gleaned so many amazing, mystical secrets from looking at your album covers. Can you tell me sort of what you meant by it?" Dean, ever polite, tried to let the man down easily. "I didn't mean anything at all. It was just a good-looking album cover." His superfan, disillusioned, and possibly embarrassed, now turned nemesis. "Well, what do *you* know?" he angrily spat. "You're just the artist!" Despite his pro-testations, Dean might have taken some responsibility for con-tributing to casting a wide mystical net over an entire subgenre of music, known sometimes derogatorily as progressive rock. You are unlikely to find a prog-rocker who refers to their own music in that way, but the term serves as a way to describe a movement in rock, one steering a massive ship away from the siren call of blues-based rock that had so long dominated popu-lar music, toward a more English tradition of what Greg Lake of the supergroup Emerson, Lake and Palmer (ELP) described as "troubadour, medieval storytelling." Rock would inherit this mantle proudly, looking toward the mythology of the past—often heavily informed by occult images—to construct the sound of the future.

Psychedelic rock bands set the course, but in the 1970s, a new wave of bands looked beyond the drugginess of psychedelia to classical music as the true guide. Coupled with the instruments of the future—particularly Moog synthesizers—progressive rock crafted rock suites, with some songs clocking in at twenty min-utes or more. Dean's paintings were otherworldly landscapes of floating islands and boulders, or stone structures rising up like trees. Largely unpopulated, save for the occasional butterfly/ dragon hybrid, there were no aliens, elves, or wizards. His worlds might be long-dead civilizations, like the lifeless plains of Mars haunted by the once-thriving Martian societies in Ray Bradbury's *The Martian Chronicles*, or future lands where people have taken to hibernating in the inexplicable constructions of their cities, endlessly waiting. Dean had perfected the merging of science fiction with mysticism, invoking the imagination of prog-rock listeners who were convinced there was some story or greater truth behind his art, and spent hours listening and poring over the album covers, meant to coexist in an ideological way.

At first, prog-rock musicians were just trying to see how far outside of the accepted structures of rock they could go. The Beatles' *Sgt. Pepper* album had demonstrated that experimentation could prove commercially successful, but as Greg Lake remembers it, his first foray into pushing up against rock norms was a risky proposition. But wouldn't rock fans, more than any others, be willing to try on the new, to accept rebellion within?

By the end of the 1960s, rock had found a healthy balance of maintaining some degree of counterculture aspirations while at the same time being popular enough to be commercially successful. Nevertheless, change was still difficult. Very little in rock history conforms perfectly with being the first, as so much happens in a metaphorical house of mirrors, with influences difficult to unravel. But various people trying slightly different things around the same time may suddenly turn into a kaleidoscopic totality—a hundredth monkey kind of occurrence. One could argue that the first great moment in prog-rock happened at the free Rolling Stones concert held at Hyde Park in London on July 5, 1969.

It was a strange lineup. Supporting acts included the Third Ear Band (an underground act fusing psychedelic rock with world folk music, and some of the most purposefully occult songs of the 1960s) and the British blues guitarist Alexis Korner. When the mostly unknown outfit who called themselves King Crimson took the stage, they launched into an antifolk, antiblues, antipsychedelic song of screeching guitar and angry saxophone, throwing out lyrics like "Cat's foot iron claw / Neuro-surgeons scream for more." The song, "21st Century Schizoid Man," came as a shock to the stoned hippies. Footage shows the crowd looking vaguely scared, possibly worried their beloved and by then easily digestible Rolling Stones had been kidnapped and replaced with fearsome imposters. But King Crimson might, too, have felt like pretenders. Until then, the biggest crowd they had played was fewer than five hundred people. The audience to see the Rolling Stones for free numbered close to five hundred thousand.

Greg Lake, then King Crimson's vocalist, remembers the moment well. The audience had come to expect a certain kind of "head-nodding" rhythm, a "pulsating numbing effect." King Crimson delivered something else entirely, a hostile, but virtuosic, attack. Along with the saxophone, they also employed a flute and a mellotron, instruments not yet typical for a rock band: "And of course it came as a shock. Then they realized that it was a good shock. And then they just stood up. The entire audience stood up. And in one split second, we knew that we had made it."

"21st Century Schizoid Man" is the first track on King

Crimson's debut album, *In the Court of the Crimson King*, a story-book of an album crafting fantasy narratives out of deep human emotion. Lyrics like "The tournament's begun / The purple piper plays his tune" inhabit the same musical landscape as "Confusion will be my epitaph / As I crawl a cracked and broken path."

This would be progressive rock's prototype, lyrical poetry fused with complex and dexterous musicianship transmitting two levels of meaning. Musically there were multiple, sometimes disparate, layers at play. King Crimson became more adept at abruptly shifting gears, playing angular noisy instrumental pieces followed by lyrical ballads. It was made cohesive by the head and heart of King Crimson, Robert Fripp. He had formed the band in 1968 with the drummer Michael Giles (together they had been two parts of the band Giles, Giles, and Fripp), along with Ian McDonald and Greg Lake.

In early King Crimson interviews, Fripp spoke vaguely about an interest in esoteric matters, but when pushed he could spell out a systematic theology. In an interview with *NME* in 1973, Fripp explained that music was a kind of magic, and not in the colloquial sense. Music could actually alter reality: "If you're in front of half a million people and you draw together the energies of that half million and you attract angelic power— which you can also do if you're smart enough—and bind the two together in a cone of power and then direct it, you can make the world spin backwards." Fripp's language here *implies* a deep reading of occult texts, particularly those of the Western tradition by way of the Golden Dawn and Crowley. Fripp explains that the technique—also emphasized by those ceremonial magicians—is the method to express what he calls his "heart and his hips."

The chaotic precision of King Crimson's music was not always welcomed. Critics called it "art rock" as an insult. In a 1969 review of one of their earliest shows in the United States, John Mendelsohn, writing for the *Los Angeles Times*, complimented their proficiency with their instruments, but the praise ended there. "[S]ince when do proficiency and sophistication have much of anything to do with good rock 'n' roll?" Three years later, a reviewer of the same paper called King Crimson a "triumph of the intellect over emotion."

Others seemed to get it. A year later, the *Boston Globe*'s Neal Vitale gushed over the newer incarnation of the band, whose album *Larks' Tongues in Aspic* was released that year to critical acclaim. "The songs are brilliant and dazzling exercises in dynamics and subtle textures," the *Globe* wrote. "The competence of the four musicians is beyond reproach." But this was still missing the point, at least as far as Fripp would see it. Competence was a symptom of something much greater than the band itself, something almost transcendent. As guitarist and Fripp biographer Eric Tamm explains it, by the time of *Larks' Tongues in Aspic*, "Fripp stressed the 'magic' metaphor time and again; for to him, when group improvisation of this sort really clicked, it was nothing short of bona fide white magic."

Fripp described the first year of King Crimson as seemingly beyond what the band was actually capable of: "Amazing things would happen—I mean, telepathy, qualities of energy, things that I had never experienced before with music. My own sense of it was that music reached over and played this group of four uptight young men who didn't really know what they were doing."

Prog-rock bands were particularly adept at presenting themselves as being purveyors of the strange and the paranormal. Emerson, Lake and Palmer's eponymous first album includes "The Three Fates," a suite comprised of "Clotho," "Lachesis," and "Atropos," which sounds like contemporary classical music. The Three Fates, or the Moirai, are of course the three sisters of Greek mythology who wove the destiny of human beings. They would become the model for the three incanting sisters in Shakespeare's *Macbeth*, the witches who toil over their cauldron, cooking up spells and schemes to upend the normal course of things. In every way it was an unconventional thing to find on a rock album, and smacked of intellectualism, the antipathy of rock. But Lake, who left King Crimson to join Keith Emerson and Greg Palmer to form ELP, thinks that despite how big and complex progressive rock could and did become, it was still pop music. By all indications, though, it was pop music that presented itself as something much more arcane.

When production was complete on ELP's 1973 album, *Brain Salad Surgery*, the band agreed that they needed a standout album cover, a design that would reflect the aura of the music, which includes the thirty-minute suite "Karn Evil 9," a science fiction epic about a despotic computer, written in part by Peter Sinfield, the scribe responsible for the lyrics of King Crimson's fantastical early songs. ELP's manager had seen the work of an artist in Zurich and suggested they visit his home. The artist was H. R. Giger, whose techno-fetish paintings had not yet become popularly known. (In 1979, Giger's vision would be seen by millions in the film *Alien*, for which he designed the look of the alien, as well as the fossil-like spaceship where its eggs are lying dormant.)

"It was like a horror museum," Lake recalls, upon visiting the artist's home. "But Giger himself is very sweet, kind, gentle and very sort of softly spoken." The band was led into the dining room where the chairs and table were all carved with black-skull motif: "The whole thing was black. Black chairs, black table, black skulls." Giger showed them some drawings he thought would work well with the music, with metal work and the ELP logo added. Lake insists if one looks carefully, there is a penis in the throat of the figure being "x-rayed."

It is the combination of the music and the cover that, Lake explains, is like a cocktail: "You can put certain elements into a glass and nothing happens. If you put one extra element in, the whole thing becomes effervescent." This is the alchemy of rock and roll, where the songs, lyrics, art, and even the band's logo can become a whole experience that you can hold in your hand when you hold an album.

Prog-rock's roots, being in European music rather than American traditions like the blues, found the genre nudging up against classical forms, which are often thought to be highbrow. But the history of classical music reveals this is not the case. Progressive rock sits more in the tradition of the Romantic composers of the late eighteenth and early nineteenth centuries. Like the Romantic poet and artists, Romantic composers were also excavating a past where they believed a more authentic human spirit dwelled with nature, where the supernatural was a shadow at the edges having never been completely exorcised by Christianity.

Romantic composers wanted music to capture emotion and subjectivity. The composer and pianist Franz Liszt's rapturous performances caused audience members to swoon, and his "flamboyant" style likely influenced the keyboardists of progressive rock, such as Keith Emerson and Rick Wakeman.

Progressive rock also found in the Romantic tradition what had been drawn from British folk music as a method for experimentation. Béla Bartók, one of the last of the Romantic composers, was enamored of the folk music of his native Hungary. As the writer Ivan Hewett explains, "The wild irregular rhythms of Balkan dance encouraged him to think about rhythm in a new way." Bartók would make an appearance on Emerson, Lake and Palmer's first album in the opening track, "The Barbarian," with a folk effect borrowing liberally from Bartók's solo piano work "Allegro Barbaro."

The mythopoeia tradition, popularized by J. R. R. Tolkien through using the term as the title of a poem, later came to describe a modern form of mythology, one that utilizes tropes from ancient mythology to craft contemporary stories. Progressive rock shares in this literary tradition by firing myth in a furnace of modern—sometimes avant-garde—music. The court of the mysterious Crimson King could easily be a location in Middle-earth, but it transcends it through rock's uncanny ability to give even the most fantastical ideas a sense of realness. This is the occult's greatest impact on rock and roll. Over time, by incorporating mystical and magical elements into its music and presentation, rock created a mythos around itself suggesting it was somehow heir to secret wisdom. Sometimes malevolent, sometimes mystical, this special perception of things unseen would drive both its fans and detractors to obsess over possible esoteric meanings.

Like musique concrète and the spirit of music's future it hoped to help shape, listening to rock became a deeply subjective experience. Sometimes it was believed the musicians themselves were just vessels, often unaware they were being used to telegraph designs beyond themselves. The fan at the Roger Dean art opening would not accept that the artist was just grooving off the grand narratives sculpted by his clients: If Dean didn't intend to convey any spiritual riddles, then maybe the bands didn't, either. But this would be shortsighted and obtuse. The only logical conclusion was they were simply conduits, unaware they were being manipulated by the gods. The right formula of mythic world building, extensive use of Moogs, and Roger Dean's artwork could send a band into the stratosphere.

Writing for *Melody Maker* in 1973, the critic Chris Welch called this Yes album the musical equivalent of *Ben-Hur* or *Exodus*. It was said to be the most bloated rock album of all time, the proverbial goliath that would inspire the little rascal named David, otherwise known as punk rock. It was the perihelion of prog-rock, a glorious or pretentious masterpiece, depending on your mood. Yes's *Tales from Topographic Oceans*, released in 1973, is four songs—on four sides—running eighty-three minutes long. The double album was packaged in a Roger Dean painting of a prehistoric alien world, where fish swim on the surface of a desert and in the distance sits a pyramidal structure, a temple where one imagines mysterious beings play ancient synthesizers aeon after aeon.

Bill Bruford describes the genesis of *Tales* as being somewhat prosaic, not the epic creation myth the album begs for. In March 1972, Bruford, his new bride, and assorted friends and acquaintances were in his flat to celebrate his wedding earlier that day. Two of the guests, Jon Anderson of Yes and Jamie Muir—then percussionist for King Crimson—spent much of the night talking about Paramahansa Yogananda, the author of *Autobiography of a Yogi*, which was by then an urtext for spiritual seekers. The conversation would put a "kink in the course of progressive rock." Anderson would use this book as the basis for *Tales from Topographic Oceans*. First published in 1946, the book details the life of Yogananda and his spiritual development meeting saints, magicians, and yogis throughout India. In 1920, Yogananda started the Self-Realization Fellowship. Like the Vedanta movement that brought the teachings of Ramakrishna and Hindu philosophy to the United States at the turn of the twentieth century, the Self-Realization Fellowship divorced yoga and meditation from Hindu culture and religion just enough to make it palpable to anyone, no matter their own religious tradition. Mysticism is immensely egalitarian, which is what has made it so popular, particularly in the 1970s when, despite the sad end to the psychedelic vision of the 1960s, many people were not ready to give up on a non-Christian spiritual identity.

In *Tales*, Anderson took the teachings of Yogananda and attempted to turn them into a narrative, a story told by a techno-minstrel, bigger and grander than the humble, boyish face of Yogananda that stares out from the cover of his autobiography. Anderson was taken by a footnote in the book that describes the *shastras*, the four types of holy literature, and proposed that each of the four album tracks corresponds to one *shastra*. The lyrics of the album are littered with key words and phrases that evoke a vague spiritual quest. This was worrisome to the music journalist David Laing. In a 1974 retrospective of Yes's output up to that time, Laing applauded what Yes had done for progressive rock in particular and popular music in general, but was concerned with the empty mystical gestures that the band was using too liberally. He imagined great success for the band but hoped they would cease mythologizing:

> "Time," "eternity," "Love," "seasons," "millions" are the kind of words which are constants in Jon Anderson's poetic scheme of things. They add up to an attempt to construct a different mythology to our everyday one of historical change and evolution. To anyone who lived through the days of the Underground, this is a familiar project, yet it's one which has very seldom been translated into artistic terms with any degree of success.

The fans ate it up, though. The presentation couldn't have been better to build a rock and roll tower of Babel, a musical effigy that could support any spiritual language the listener spoke. Roger Dean's artwork became an integral part of Yes's mystique and was also abstract enough that it could be the landscape of times past or future or even of another planet or dimension. And Yes's music was remarkably rich and expansive. Anderson didn't need to sing a word to keep the fans coming back. During a review of their 1973 show at the Boston Garden, a reporter all but admits the band's sometimes "lack of cohesion," but it doesn't matter: "'Topographic Oceans' is a marvelous almost symphonically eloquent creation," he writes.

"[H]ow well it relates to the shastras becomes almost inconsequential in light of its aural beauty."

Spiritual excess would define progressive rock just as much as the music. In 1977, Nik Turner—one of the founding members of Hawkwind—journeyed to Egypt, where he would record four hours of playing his flute in the Great Pyramid as part of an attempt to channel cosmic forces that he could transmit back to his fans.

Christian Vander of the influential French band Magma invented a musical language he called Kobaïan and developed an entire mythos based on the planet Kobaïa, the band members' supposedly true homeland. One of the lost treasures of 1970s progressive rock is the group Ramases, whose two albums, *Space Hymns* (with a six-panel gatefold cover by none other than Roger Dean) and *Glass Top Coffin*, are cracked but brilliant artifacts of rock, mythology, and occult belief. The band's leader, Barrington Frost, claimed to have been visited by an Egyptian pharaoh who told Frost to change his name to Ramases and spread the news that a new age was dawning. Despite a lineup of excellent musicians (including the multi-instrumentalist Kevin Godley, who went on to form the strange, sugary pop band, 10cc), the albums failed to garner much attention. While people were eating up spiritually laden progressive rock, they did not heed Ramases' message. The songs feel insular, and Ramases' cryptic lyrics and album notes come across a little cultlike or as just one big inside joke. Frost would abandon his dream of salvific rock and roll and killed himself in 1976.

Robert Fripp saw the signs early on that the behemoth of prog would cease to be able to carry its own weight, both in terms of the hugeness of its ambition and its music. Fripp's own spiritual identity was changing as well. Everything was feeling out of control—Fripp was trying more musical experiments that he didn't often feel he had a hold of. In 1972, Peter Sinfield left the band, having created not only the lyrics that provided King Crimson with their mythopoeic aura, but synthesizer and lighting work as well. The band had already gone through numerous lineups, and there was tension all around. After *Larks' Tongues in Aspic*, King Crimson released *Red* in 1974, which includes the song "Starless," a hallmark of the band's immense output, and what Eric Tamm calls the moment when "the door slams shut . . . on the early era of progressive rock as a whole."

In one of his last interviews from that time, one can begin to see Fripp's shift in wanting to move away from the persona of rock musician to an identity built on merely being a vessel of sound as a spiritual, almost Platonic, idea. In 1974, Fripp told Steve Rosen of *Guitar Player* that music was simply a tool. "I would say that the crux of my life is the creation of harmony, and music you take to be one of the components of that harmony." Personally, though, Fripp was floundering. As much as he wanted music to be an expression of this higher ideal, he felt he had lost the means to do it.

In 1975, Fripp became a student at the International Academy for Continuous Education at Sherborne House in Britain's Cotswold countryside, where the mathematician John G. Bennett attempted to synthesize the opaque and difficult teachings of G. I. Gurdjieff. Gurdjieff is as much of a puzzle as some of his ideas. He was born in Armenia, and in his formative years traveled throughout the East, sitting at the feet of mystics and holy men. During these encounters that he describes in his memoir, *Meetings with Remarkable Men*, Gurdjieff discovered a single stream of esoteric knowledge that he believed could be taught in a systematic way. In 1919, he opened the first of his schools, the Institute for the Harmonious Development of Man, in Russia, with other schools popping up in Paris and the United States a short time after.

Gurdjieff taught that human beings are automatons, asleep to life, less reacting to than being reacted upon by sensations that run through them. Through various physical and mental exercises, such as ritual dance, music, and what he called "dividing one's attention," a process whereby the student is instructed to become aware of both inner and outer states of awareness, man can awake. Gurdjieff himself was mercurial, at one moment the serious teacher, the next a foxlike trickster.

Bennett toned down what Gurdjieff's student Paul Beekman Taylor called the "three-ring circus" of Gurdjieff's personality, in an effort to present the teachings as a practical method of spiritual development. Fripp described his experience at Bennett's school as rigorous, and when he was there, a number of students fled. The house was cold and, according to Fripp, haunted. Students were required to wake early, attend lectures, and spend much of the day in some form of manual craft, such as building walls and metalsmithing. For Fripp, this was an ego-centering experience and taught him that his instincts regarding music had always been correct. Practical application, knowledge of the instrument, and the relationship between it and the body were the only ways to get access to the deeper, spiritual form.

While Fripp was taking his leave of absence from rock, punk

was setting depth charges under progressive rock's massive arena-motivated music. Not quite a return to the blues, punk wanted to strip rock of all its pretensions and return to the force of the three-chord-driven, three-minute (or less) song, powered by guitar and not by synthesizers. Whereas progressive rock gazed in awe at Europe's classical, and sometimes religious, musical heritage, punk had more in common with the Pentecostal Church's immediacy. Punk was the energy of the shout and gospel. Punk's more studious younger sibling, new wave, embraced punk's aesthetic as well as the synthesizer, but replaced safety pins with skinny ties. But neither punk nor new wave could level progressive rock completely. The synth-driven explorations of cosmic and supernal realms would flower in New Age music.

Along with elements of folk, jazz, classical, and Brian Eno's ambient albums, New Age music would become a huge industry led by the Windham Hill and Narada labels. Progressive rock (along with krautrock) is still accused as the primary culprits behind New Age's sterilized sound. Some of those albums that are the crossover moments, however, still merit consideration. Multi-instrumentalist Mike Oldfield's 1973 album, *Tubular Bells*, with its Dalí-like cover of a twisted metal bell, is often considered one of the first true New Age works. It's not nearly as sugary as New Age would become, and there's an argument to be made that what New Age borrowed from it is no fault of Oldfield's. In fact, the sinister flashes of the album inspired the director William Friedkin to use four minutes of *Tubular Bells* for the soundtrack to *The Exorcist*, still considered one of the most frightening movies of all time, and certainly not a film one would associate with New Age philosophy. In a 1975 unpublished *Rolling Stone* interview, Oldfield explained that he wasn't aware that a piece had been turned into a single for the film and, despite how successful it made him, he felt *Tubular Bells* is meant to be heard in its entirety.

Eventually the undemanding sounds of synthesizers, acoustic guitars, and flutes captured an entire spiritual movement that would come to characterize American alternative religion. In the 1980s, except for in the underground, the occult imagination's hold on mainstream rock was becoming neutered, just like the occult itself.

The music writer Paul Stump is even less kind: "New Age is pop music that a superior intelligence from another planet might make, musically adept . . . but utterly missing the point," which is to say that New Age music, like the New Age movement, is filled with potential, but continually softens the impact. Occultism and mysticism were no longer the means of spiritual rebellion; they were simply another choice on the vast menu of available religious symbols and practices.

But their job was already complete. In almost every aspect of rock and popular music, the occult's influence could be felt. Even as more Top 40 acts turned to electronics and the digital studio, the underlying agitation was the same as it had been when young people first tossed a guitar strap over their shoulders. If you make enough noise, no matter your instrument, you can keep the old gods alive forever.

CHAPTER 6

THE GOLDEN DAWN

I

At a small independent bookstore in Cambridge, Massachusetts, Damien Echols gave a reading from his 2012 memoir, *Life After Death*, in which he recounts his torturous eighteen years being on death row for murders he didn't commit, and then constructing a new life for himself when he was released in 2011. It was a brutal and unthinkable crime. In 1993, three eight-year-old boys were killed and mutilated, their bodies found near a muddy drainage ditch. West Memphis, Arkansas—the city where the boys lived and died—is a small metropolis of over twenty-five thousand residents: a town compared with other American urban centers.

The three suspects were easy to come by. They were teenage outsiders, arrested for vandalism and other petty crimes, two of them high school dropouts, and were already pegged as troublemakers. But this was not what damned the suspects to a controversial arrest, trial, and a death sentence for one of them. Echols, Jessie Misskelley Jr., and Jason Baldwin (now known as the West Memphis Three) were called Satanists, and their love of heavy metal music had been said to have soured their minds and corrupted their souls. The district attorney believed the murders were committed as part of a ritual sacrifice to the devil. An article in the *Commercial Appeal*, a daily newspaper of Memphis, Tennessee, reported on a possible explanation for the crime and included this from child psychologist Paul King, who was interviewed for the piece: "Heavy-metal music may sound like irritating noise, but its lyrics 'glorify the power of evil' and the child who sits in his room brooding over the lyrics may display an unhealthy preoccupation."

Much of the prosecution's case pointed to the fact that Echols listened to the band Metallica and copied lyrics from their songs into his journal. The hysteria surrounding the trial of the teenagers in West Memphis, Arkansas, was not merely a local phenomenon, not simply a case of kids who dressed in black and listened to heavy metal stereotyped as delinquents. Their prosecution was only the most dramatic of what had been this ongoing fear of the supposed satanic power of rock and roll.

Echols was thought to be the demonic ringleader of the West Memphis Three, convicted in 1994 for the murder of the three young boys. His interest in pagan religion and heavy metal was what led police to peg him as a suspect. Echols's book admits to an interest in Eastern religion and magic, claiming these ideas helped him get through the dehumanization of prison life and supported him during his subsequent recovery from the trauma of his incarceration.

Henry Rollins—onetime singer of the hardcore punk band Black Flag and counterculture icon—remarked, "I'd find myself up at 3:30 a.m. thinking about Damien. He could have been me. I had those records. I was sullen as a teenager." Alas, the point at which the artist and the surrounding culture meet is often fraught. The necessary ingredients—mysterious and/or theatrical allusions to historically alternative spiritual paths, youth's drive to find its own way, and a good beat—lead to the development and continued growth of rock and roll along the spectrum of sound, signal, and meaning. Even pop music, rock's stepchild, carries the legacy, and continues to inspire exaggerated responses to its associations, intentional or not, to occultism.

II

The video for Jay Z's 2009 single "On to the Next One" is a masterpiece of symbolism. Jay Z stands in the center of the frame, haloed by a circle of dim lights behind him. Throughout the video, frame after frame of flashing images, is a well-dressed man in skull-like makeup reminiscent of the Joker; a white-gowned ninja battling the air with batons; a jewel-studded skull; smoke swirling into Rorschach test patterns; a crucifix; thick red lips dripping blood; and goat skulls with massive horns. Jay Z's raps are fairly standard as far as hip hop goes. It's a self-referential narrative of success, of moving forward, not looking back, embracing his riches, and a warning that his fame and creative output are only going to get greater.

But pay closer attention, as certain fans indicate in the YouTube community, and you might see that some of these gestures and images that make up his persona point to the hidden secret of Jay Z's success. It can't be talent alone—no black man in America could make it as big as Jay Z without help from "the inside." Underlying the truth is that Jay Z sold his soul to the devil—seen clearly in those horns that flash during the video. But this is not any devil. This is Baphomet, believed by some to be the hidden god of the Freemasons revealed during the 33rd degree ritual, who paves the way for the initiate to become part of an even greater fraternity known as the Illuminati. Jay Z raps that he is in control of his own destiny but, studied from another angle, he might be merely a pawn in a sinister game of control.

If you want to find common ground between the extreme far left and the extreme far right, conspiracy theories about the Illuminati will bring even the most hated enemies together. The enemy of my enemy is my friend, as it were. While there may be disagreements over who controls what—and to what degree Jews are involved—there is a basic outline that is generally accepted. But first we have to highlight what conspiracy theorists might see as pesky facts.

A quick look back: In 1776, a Bavarian law professor by the name of Adam Weishaupt gathered together like-minded men to form a society that would attempt to liberalize the spirit of society. Weishaupt had been educated by Jesuits but grew distrustful of a church that constantly seemed to abandon reason for superstition. He called his group the Order of the Illuminati to highlight that they believed in enlightenment—albeit through reason—for humanity. Weishaupt's attack on religion was sure to run afoul of the royalty whose ties to the Catholic

Church were stronger than the abstract ideas of humanism and freedom. Weishaupt made matters worse for himself when he joined the Freemasons and tried to align his idea with theirs. Freemasonry was too heavily invested in its own spiritual symbolism and Rosicrucian-influenced rituals for Weishaupt to make much of an impact, though. His political views were seen as anarchic by the authorities, and he was ordered to disband his order or face the death penalty.

Weishaupt complied, the society dissolved in 1787, and the once-enlightened freethinker died in 1830 a devout Catholic. Weishaupt's criticism of the Church, coupled with his group's relationship to Freemasonry, led Freemasons' critics to contend that the fraternity was in league with the devil. They would declare that Freemasonry purports to believe in God, whom Freemasons call the Great Architect, but this was just for appearance's sake.

Over time, the Illuminati movement has become a blank slate, capable of representing whatever imagined nefarious, occult, or anti-Christian intrigue that needed a label to give it substance. More often, the Illuminati are believed to be the group that controls everything, using smaller organizations like the Freemasons, the Council on Foreign Relations, the Catholic Church, Scientology, and the entertainment industry—especially music— as tentacles of control, touching on every aspect of society.

In 2013, the rapper Professor Griff (best known for his stint with the group Public Enemy, whose 1989 single, "Fight the Power," became the anthem that closed out the 1980s) was interviewed by *Coast to Coast AM*, a syndicated radio show known for its emphasis on topics relating to the paranormal, pseudoscience, and conspiracy theories. Professor Griff (born Richard Griffin) explained how Jay Z, wittingly or unwittingly, is helping the Illuminati use hip hop as a way to infiltrate the black community. Hip hop's original intention, Griff said, was to raise up the dispossessed, but Jay Z and other entertainers are subverting its purpose by using it as a weapon of control. Moreover, the record industry is complicit, allowing the Illuminati to stage rituals as the music is being produced, instilling it with demonic energy.

In interviews, Jay Z is coy, unwilling to admit he is intentionally provocative by his use of symbols in his videos. He front-loads the associations with occultism and secret societies heavily, however. In one video, he wears a sweatshirt emblazoned with Crowley's missive "Do what thou wilt," and at one time his clothing line offered a number of shirts with unambiguous Freemasonry symbols. He does admit, however, that his music is meant to be "provocative." In a 2010 interview with the New York City hip-hop radio station WQHT (Hot 97), Jay Z consciously samples certain images in the same way he might sample a drumbeat: "Great rap should have all kinds of unresolved layers that you don't necessarily figure out the first time you listen to it. Instead it plants dissonance in your head."

Jay Z's use of occult symbols and the public response to that use perfectly encapsulates the locus of the occult in popular culture. For Jay Z, the images work to ignite the imagination, as well as to create rumor and speculation, which can only help to sell albums and increase Internet-video page views. As author Mitch Horowitz explains, Jay Z is a sharp businessman and an even craftier artist: "I think he's a keen observer of everything going on around him. He's a master at using subversive imagery."

At the other end of the spectrum, and whose gaze meets Jay Z in the middle, are the conspiracy theorists for whom music is a potentially dangerous weapon in the arsenal used to control the minds of youth and adults alike. For those who are Christian, the architect behind the hip-hop Illuminati is Satan, who has been using pop music to subliminally convert the masses since Elvis first shimmied his hips. On Judgment Day, people will wake up and see that they have been duped. But it will be too late. They had unwittingly sold their souls during the 666th time they listened to one of Jay Z's songs. This was the kind of thinking that led to the building of a case against the West Memphis Three. The occult imagination had come too far, though. It was too much a part of rock and roll's essence to ever be quieted by fear and delusion. And if a musician is still accused of being in league with some secret occult cabal, all the better. The tools of the magician to mystify are the most powerful of all. If your musical spell has convinced your audience that you are more than you appear to be, you are simply continuing rock's legacy of glamour, of weaving an enchantment that rattles the habitual souls of the masses.

III

The 2012 Super Bowl was one of the most watched television events in U.S. history, with an estimated viewership of 111.3 million people. Three million more watched the halftime show.

Madonna, the headliner for the show, crafted a thirteen-minute-long medley of her songs, a lavish production costing millions. The result was a spectacularly staged performance. The show opens on a stage decorated with Egyptian motifs and similarly costumed dancers as Madonna enters, dressed as the hierophant of an ancient mystery cult, seated in a throne on a chariot being pulled by dozens of "slaves."

The original Hermetic Order of the Golden Dawn would likely have been envious of the attention to detail. Other dancers dressed as armored angels and strange deities spin around Madonna as she sings "Vogue." Tall banners are decorated with a symbol, an *M* cutting into a circle, the two sides of the letter forming what look like massive horns. Madonna's costume is simple, a Roman centurion's skirt, her head adorned by a winged helmet with two pointed appendages rising from the middle.

Madonna's interest in esoteric matters goes way back. Beginning with an awkward conversation with Kurt Loder of MTV in 1997, Madonna tried to explain finding her way to the Kabbalah Centre, where she was taught that, "If you want to have goodness in your life, you have to give it." She also explained that the soul becomes firmly attached to the body at age thirteen (the age of a Bar Mitzvah). In a later 2005 interview with the *Guardian*, having become increasingly devoted to the Kabbalah Centre, Madonna again tries to explain what the teachings mean to her, and defending the controversial center from what the interviewer, Dina Rabinovitch, calls "charlatanism."

The Kabbalah Centre was started in 1969 by the retired rabbi Philip Berg. Berg wanted to divorce the mystical teaching of the Kabbalah from its Jewish context, believing it to have universal spiritual power. While the center uses the Bible and the Jewish Kabbalistic text called the *Zohar* in its teachings, the main thrust of the approach is in the practical application of what the center calls "the world's oldest body of spiritual wisdom." The center contends that Judaism kept the five-thousand-year-old teachings secret until Berg believed that all people should have access. In Judaism, the *Zohar* is considered the primary source of Kabbalistic wisdom. The *Zohar* was written in Aramaic sometime in the thirteenth century, likely drawing from a variety of sources, some old and some contemporary to its own time, and serves as a mystical interpretation of the Torah, the first five books of the Hebrew Bible. The center claims that the power of the *Zohar* is not in what it says, but what it is—an artifact of great power that can alter one's destiny:

> To merely pick up the Zohar, to scan its Aramaic letters and allow in the energy that infuses them, is to experience what kabbalists have experienced for thousands of years: a powerful energy-giving instrument, a life-saving tool imbued with the ability to bring peace, protection, healing and fulfillment to those who possess it.

This occult approach to the Kabbalah has been part of the tradition for centuries, but Berg was the first to give it such wide appeal. He was not the first, however, to extract the occult nuggets.

Renaissance magicians had looked to Jewish Kabbalistic texts as sources of wisdom that could easily conform to their own mystical interpretations of Christianity. Later, occultists followed their lead and found in the Kabbalah a rich mineral vein of esoteric wisdom they could apply to their own systems. For example, in the Golden Dawn, important tools of the student, such as astrology and tarot, had their corresponding Kabbalistic identifier, in particular the *sefirot*, the Kabbalistic tree of life, which became central to Western occultism. Simply put, the *sefirot* refers to the ten aspects of the divine that spring forth from the unknowable Godhead, or *ein sof*. The *sefirot* can be laid out like the geography of the universe. The *sefirot* are a beautifully realized, and in some sense, materialistic view of the universe. Each aspect of creation is delineated by a temperament (judgment, compassion, masculine, feminine), and not only is it easy to show how each individual *sefirah* has a corresponding numerological and astrological meaning, images of the *sefirotic* tree hearken back to the Renaissance alchemical emblems.

For occultists through the ages, Judaism represented the authoritative ancient tradition with enough of its own mystical and legendary magical practice that it offered the perfect complement to an already complex configuration of ideas and practices.

Madonna likely saw her very public interest in an esoteric philosophy as also having artistic potential. The halftime show presents her as a priestess, imbued with divine wisdom, ready and willing to initiate anyone who wishes to enter into her mysteries. Conspiracy theorists had a field day with it. The very next day, the website *The Vigilant Citizen* offered a breakdown of Madonna's show, a paranoid exegesis making note of every element of the performance: Madonna's costume resembles Ishtar, the Sumerian goddess of love, war, and sex; Madonna's throne flanked by sphinxes is a perfect rendition of the chariot in the tarot deck; the first song, "Vogue," ends with a winged sun disc illuminating the stage, a symbol one blogger claims is used by all the major secret societies. Most damning of all, however, is at the end of the show when Madonna disappears in a flash of smoke and the words "World Peace" light the stage, "a PR-friendly slogan used by those pushing for a New World Order lead [*sic*] by a one world government," concluded one blogger.

Given the occult imagination's influence on popular music (and on Madonna herself), it's not a stretch to suggest that Madonna consciously drew from mythology, occultism, and even the symbols of secret societies for her show. On the face of it, it was pure pop spectacle, full of color and drama, signifying Madonna's ego and little more.

This spectacle, whatever its meaning, was only possible because of what came before it. The theater of rock began long ago: in the smoky UFO Club when Arthur Brown wore his flaming helmet, when Hawkwind hypnotized their fans with lights, when Bowie came onstage not as himself but as a crash-landed Ziggy. Madonna's show is simply a later encounter with rock's Dionysian roots, ones that can't be severed. Maybe the conspiracy theorists are right. We are being mesmerized by popular music, and it's an inside job. There is no all-seeing eye in a pyramid scheming with the music industry. It's just who we have always been, a civilization that demands that music shake our spirits.

IV

The first decade of the new millennium proved to be a tumultuous time. The 9/11 attacks, two major wars, economic instability, and an unpredictable future have people scrambling for meaning and stability. What had once been a line in the sand has become a deep gorge between atheists and believers. But many were looking to strike a balance between literalism and symbolism, and art has always provided a perfect vehicle for this kind of exploration.

On July 11, 2012, at the Palace Theatre in Manchester, England, the pop opera *Dr Dee* opened to critical praise. The opera tells the story of the sixteenth-century astrologer, mathematician, and occultist John Dee, a polymath whom Queen Elizabeth I consulted and who created the Enochian alphabet, the supposed grammar of the angels that is still used by occultists today. Dee was the gentleman magician, a lover of wisdom who believed that science and magic were part of the same rational process. But Dee was also a tragic figure. Dee had spent long hours—without much success—staring into his "shew stone," a piece of crystal he believed would reveal to him the secrets of angels and the true nature of the universe. In 1582, Dee was introduced to a man named Edward Kelley, who convinced Dee *he* was the key that would unlock the puzzle that had consumed the counselor to Elizabeth. Kelley would appear to go into trances and prolifically dictated the words of the angels. How much Kelley himself believed or if he was merely using Dee is unclear. At one point he was able to convince the prudish Dee that God wanted them to share their wives. Eventually Dee's interest in the supernatural made enemies in the religious hierarchy and support for him and his work began to dry up. Dee died in poverty.

The creation of *Dr Dee* was the result of a collaboration

between the British theater director Rufus Norris and Damon Albarn, known for his two influential bands, Blur and Gorillaz. Albarn had become friendly with the comic book writer Alan Moore, a self-proclaimed magician who says he worships—in somewhat tongue-in-cheek fashion—a Roman snake god. But what Moore is very serious about is his belief that magic and the creative act are inseparable and that each is a way of conjuring fictions and making them very real. Moore and Albarn wanted to work together, and Moore suggested the magical life of Dee. The two agreed to cowrite the opera, but the huge personalities of both Albarn and Moore came to blows when Moore suddenly dropped out of the project, blaming Albarn for not fulfilling a promise to write for Moore's literary magazine, *Dodgem Logic*. Albarn went ahead alone with the writing.

Albarn believed the opera was an opportunity to bring his occult interests out of the closet. He told the *Telegraph* in 2011, "Doing the research has been the most amazing experience. Everything I've read has led to something else—Christianity to Judaism, Paganism to Nordic mythology, astronomy to Hermetic philosophy—and it just seems to go on and on without end." The opera is an evocative and melancholy narrative of Dr. Dee, with Albarn's vocals skating across music that is part European music, part pop. Other vocalists lend a more classically operatic feel, but the opera is still a rock and roll moment. *Dr Dee* is not rock opera, per se, but it certainly gives a nod to how rock can be used as an operatic form. Albarn's interest in the life of Dr. Dee came at a time when there was what could be called an Occult Revival in rock music and the popular culture. Like the revival of the nineteenth century, this movement is also dominated by musicians and artists who see the occult as full of phenomena ripe for creative speculation and output.

Within the underground music scene there is a permeable sense of pagan ritual, of a serious intent to make magic out of art. The revival of this commingling of hermetic secrets with art led to the formation of two music events in 2009, the Equinox Festival in England and the Musicka Mystica Maxima Festival in New York City, curated by the Ordo Templi Orientis. Both were gatherings of artists and musicians, many of whom also consider themselves occult practitioners.

For the Equinox Festival, the video and graffiti artist Raymond Salvatore Harmon wanted to see if it was possible to construct a literal conference of artists, authors, and esoteric practitioners and to create a platform for people to come together. "It would also be a starting point for future collaborations and projects," Harmon says. "It was an attempt to break down the barriers between different esoteric and creative practices and give them a common ground with which they could push into new territories together." The result was the Equinox Festival, "three days of illumination," that took place in June of 2009. Harmon curated the event—a series of lectures, ritual performances, films, and live music—with a magical intention in an effort to, as he says, "invoke a particular energy." The musical lineup was a who's who of experimental artists, including the saxophonist and avant-garde composer John Zorn; the ambient/drone metal band Aethenor; the industrial electronic outfit Burial Hex; the 1970s progressive folk band Comus; and Peter Christopherson of Throbbing Gristle and Coil, performing one of his last shows before his untimely death in 2010.

Gareth Branwyn, writing for the webzine *Boing Boing*, called the event a mixed success, noting that the highlight was the band Comus, who were able to capture the delightful moment in the 1970s when progressive rock and mysticism came together in an alchemical bath to produce a musical approximation of the philosopher's stone, the key to immortality for rock and roll.

They had the coffin made to fit Scott Conner's size. In his own work as black-metal musician Malefic, Conner would appear to worship darkness, so being nailed into a coffin shouldn't be much of a problem. Stephen O'Malley was putting together *Black One*, the 2005 album for his duo with Greg Anderson that goes by the name Sunn, rendered always as "Sunn O)))." Sunn O))) became infamous as the slowest and loudest of the doom/drone metal subgenre. Their live shows consist of O'Malley and Anderson dressed in black hooded robes, playing sustained chest-vibrating chords at full volume. They offer nothing specific when asked in interviews about their own beliefs except to say they believe music has the power to be transcendent and induce actual physical and mental changes in the audience.

Their presentation, both in the titles of their mostly instrumental songs—such as "A Shaving of the Horn That Speared You" and "Candlewolf of the Golden Chalice"—and their mysterious stage shows, has invited speculation of all sorts regarding their supposed occult proclivities, and they have even been accused of staging a Black Mass on orders from the Church of Satan. O'Malley admits he both loves and hates this kind of publicity, but there is a truth to his interest in esoteric lore and legend. So when his friend Scott Conner asked to sing on their record *Black One*, O'Malley thought, "Let's put him to the test." If in his persona as Malefic he embraces death and isolation, how would he do actually having to sing inside a coffin? The results were better than O'Malley and Anderson could have hoped. Inside the casket Conner felt claustrophobic and anxious, and this came through in the haunted, tortured vocals that the liner notes of the album list as "calls from beyond the grave."

In the 1990s and early 2000s, down-tuned guitars and Cookie Monster vocals would herald in a new heavy metal culture. Doom and death metal, as they are now known, turned up the volume once again on the satanic imagery. A new generation of fans would hear and embrace the siren call of this sinister metal, one embracing decay and darkness as an essential part of the human condition. Sometimes it all went too far. In Sweden during the mid-1990s death metal fans torched churches. Some musicians were quick to distance themselves, but others would embrace the arsons while they touted their own brand of Satanism calling for violence. By the end of the 1990s, heavy metal, in all its permutations—death, dark, doom, to name a few—had dug a direct route to the underworld. It became the soundtrack to our deepest fears, a symphony of horrors for musicians to explore and cultivate.

Rock's essential rebellious spirit is a spiritual rebellion at its core, and this, like all forms of occult and Gnostic practices, is a threat to the establishment, be it religious, political, or social. Religious hierarchies often used fears of witches and demons to

create hysteria in order to control the populace by offering stability in the face of chaos. In contemporary culture, rock from
its beginnings would be demonized. But musicians and fans
would respond by turning their pagan horned gods into devils,
challenging the status quo in a Luciferian wager of who would
ultimately win the souls of youth.

Heavy Metal never let go of its fascination with the devilish
aspects of myth and religion, but groups like Sunn O))) saw
something rich and deeply spiritual in the shock and bombast of
metal's heaviness and bleakness. Drawing from the costumed
and goth-infused death metal found in the icy Netherlands,
doom metal down-tuned all the guitars, drew inspiration from
the drones of Tibetan monks and Hindu ragas, and created a
new mythology of metal, one that embraced decay and darkness as an essential part of the human condition. Bands such as
Sunn O))), Wolves in the Throne Room, and Liturgy have created a new occult mythology born out of the language of rock.
Sleep, the ascended masters of a genre known as "stoner rock,"
play a kind of low, slow metal, simmering with a psychedelic
vibe perfectly matched for a listener whose brain is cooked on
marijuana. (Their masterpiece is the single hour-long song,
"Dopesmoker," a mythical fantasy tale where "Weed-Priests
creedsmen chant the rite."

This kind of knowing and deliberate attempt to instill a
sense of mystery and magic in rock characterizes these new occult music pioneers. Maybe it's because audiences became more
cynical, or maybe it's because there is very little left that is
shocking. In either case, rock musicians have found less reason
to put on airs about their own occult interests or to use esoteric

imagery as a marketing tool. What has evolved is a compelling mix of irony and earnestness that can be found in an entire new generation of rock artists and their music. Today's music represents the fullest culmination of how occult saved rock and created an art form open to every possibility of experimentation and spiritual exploration in the music, the fashion, and even the live performances.

V

Incense smoke wafted over the all-age crowd at the Royale nightclub in Boston as a Gregorian chant filled the room with a deep drone. Three giant faux–stained glass windows formed the backdrop of the stage. The metalheads in the audience were getting antsy, the sonorous voices alerting them that something was beginning. The crowd erupted into shouts and applause when a roadie walked onstage, turned on a small lamp, and adjusted a guitar in its stand. Soon, the lights dimmed lower and the crowd swelled toward the stage, all hands up and throwing horns.

Spotlights cut through the fog that crawled across the stage and five hooded figures walked out, upside-down crosses hung from their necks, faces covered by beaked masks. Their attire was reminiscent of costumes worn by plague doctors during the Middle Ages to protect themselves from contracting the virus. An infectious guitar lick officially announced the proceeding had begun. A tight but fairly poppy heavy metal melody erupted as the audience pushed against the stage. It was then the lead singer emerged, his face painted like Dr. Phibes, his outfit that of a sinister pope, one hand clenched around a staff topped with an upside-down cross, mockery of the pastoral Papal ferula. Papa Emeritus began to sing as if delivering a sermon, calling out a litany of infernal names: "Belial, Behemoth, Beelzebub, Asmodeus, Satanás, Lucifer." His voice wavered between sinister growl and melodically emotive.

The band is Ghost B.C. from Sweden. They are led by Papa Emeritus, who calls his musicians the Nameless Ghouls. They have remained anonymous, preferring instead covert identities as demonic agents. Yet, in interviews, despite being masked or conducted via email, they are remarkably candid. When asked about their interest in Satanism, they do not praise the devil or talk ominously about the destruction of mankind. Instead, they admit to having no "satanic agenda" but draw upon their inspiration from horror movies. One of the Ghouls explained that "in the theater that is Ghost, everything is supposed to feel like it is orthodox devil-worshipping. As an audience member, you can choose to believe whatever you want to. And you can choose to partake, or you can choose not to." Papa Emeritus (whose own identity has changed over time) prefers to play up the role. When asked by the same writer how he worships the devil, the singer replied, "My mere existence is a dishonor for the Church, thus being in favor of 'the old one.'"

It was the new millennium, the Internet a dominant feature of social interactions, people looking anxiously at a possible utopia or dystopia, depending on who was in office at any given time. What were the devils of superstition in the face of a coming global climate disaster? What good was magic when you had a computer in your pocket? The occultism of the New Age movement was reduced to Bikram yoga, sweating your way to enlightenment. And rock and roll is music for nostalgic adults, no good for dancing or taking ecstasy to at all. So it would seem to be the prevailing attitude. But the truth is, people were continuing to explore alternative spirituality; the Internet was a thriving community for Neopagans, Wiccans, and chaos magicians. Social media made it possible to share every kind of spiritual idea in an instant. The occult imagination persisted, but new technology made it possible to create granular subcultures. And musicians could be found exploring in the same ways.

Earlier in 2013, the same year Ghost B.C. haunted Boston, another band was using the occult to stage their own unique ritual. Around 7:00 p.m., very early for a rock concert in any venue, the trio that makes up Om walk through the crowd to a stage set up in the Temple of Dendur in the Metropolitan Museum of Art. Upon entering you meet two pharaonic statues guarding a shallow pool, now littered with the coins of tourists hoping for good luck from whatever ancient Egyptian deities might still be listening. On the other side of the pool stand two massive structures making up the remains of the two-thousand-year-old temple, built in 15 BCE and dedicated to the god Osiris by Augustus Caesar in the Roman province of Egypt. An angled wall of glass comprises an entire side in an effort to remind you that the temple once stood in the stark desert sunlight. Here in the midst of Manhattan in a famous room in a famous museum, a chant begins to fill the hall. As the audience pushes closer to the stage, the chant gets progressively louder. It resonates around the poor acoustics of the room, bouncing off stone and water and glass. The lyrics reference Eastern, Islamic, Jewish, and Christian mysticism, invoking the Kabbalistic feminine attribute Shekinah,

Ezekiel's vision of dreadful angels, astral travel, the Hindu concept of *prana* (breath or spirit), and reincarnation. One song, "Addis," is the complete mantra for the invocation of the Hindu god Shiva. While these religious ideas are fairly disparate, Om brings them together in a way that is more than just fanciful New Age collating. Om weaves their own spiritual mythology, driven by the heavy power of their music. Some might even call it magic, causing change in the audience's consciousness by means of Om's mighty riffage.

Despite the way the concert was a reminder of rock's most awful pretensions and satirical ripeness—such as the mockumentary *This Is Spiñal Tap*'s infamous miniature Stonehenge scene—a moment like Om at the Met shows how rock's spiritual affinity with occultism has never died. But more important, it underscores how the pact rock musicians and audiences made to expand their consciousness and push beyond the restraints of traditional American music and its underlying spiritual identity never ceased. The occult took possession of the imagination of rock musicians and their fans, and redefined popular music and culture even into the new millennium.

BIBLIOGRAPHY AND WORKS CITED

NOTES ON SOURCES

I was wholly dependent on and eternally grateful to Rock's Back Pages, the online library of music magazines. Many of the quotes and factual material came from sources found here, such as *New Music Express* (*NME*), *Sounds*, *Rolling Stone*, *KRLA Beat*, *Beat Instrumental*, *Creem*, and *Kerrang!* Newspapers and other magazines were found in various library databases and other online archives such as *Time*, *Rolling Stone*, and *Playboy*. Magazine name and year are noted in text or in the notes below.

INTRODUCTION: WE ARE ALL INITIATES NOW

Quote by Dan Graham is from his book *Rock/Music Writings* (New York: Primary Information, 2009).

History of Dionysus and the term "god who arrives" are from *Dionysus: Myth and Cult* by Walter F. Otto (Dallas, Texas: Spring Publications, 1991).

CHAPTER 1: (YOU MAKE ME WANNA) SHOUT

Many books were essential for the research of this chapter. Material regarding the beliefs and music of African Americans is from *Slave Religion* by Albert

Raboteau (New York: Oxford University Press, 1978); *The Music of Black Americans* by Eileen Southern (New York: Norton, 1983); *Sinful Tunes and Spirituals* by Dena J. Polacheck Epstein (Urbana: University of Illinois Press, 1977); and *Re-Searching Black Music* by Jon Michael Spencer (Knoxville: University of Tennessee Press, 1996).

Other material on African music and the quote "danced religion" is from *Religion in the New World* by Richard E. Wentz (Minneapolis: Fortress Press, 1990).

Information on the relationship of the blues to African music and religion was found in *Big Road Blues: Tradition and Creativity in the Folk Blues* by David Evans (Berkeley: University of California Press, 1982); *The Devil's Music* by Giles Oakley (Boston: Da Capo Press, 1997); two essential works by Paul Oliver: *Blues Fell this Morning* (London: Cambridge University Press, 1990) and *Savannah Syncopators* (New York: Stein and Day, 1970); and "Yorùbá Influences on Haitian Vodou and New Orleans Voodoo" by Ina J. Fandrich (*Journal of Black Studies*, vol. 375, no. 5, May 2007).

Material on Robert Johnson was informed by *Escaping the Delta* by Elijah Wald (New York: Amistad, 2004).

Lyrics and other useful information were found at the remarkable website Lucky Mojo, a repository of material on voodoo and the blues written and curated by Catherine Yronwode.

Material on the early history of rock was helped by *All Shook Up: How Rock 'n Roll Changed America* by Glenn Altschuler (New York: Oxford University Press, 2003), and *Rock and Roll: A Social History* by Paul Friedlander (Boulder, CO: Westview Press, 1996). Elvis quotes are from *Leaves of Elvis' Garden* by Larry Geller (Bell Rock Publishing, 2008).

Samuel Cardinal Stritch's letter was quoted in "Stritch Calls Rock 'n' Roll Throwback to Tribalism," *Washington Post*, March 2, 1957.

Details on the relationship between the Beat Generation and bebop are from *The Beat Generation* by Christopher Gair (Oxford: Oneworld, 2008).

CHAPTER 2: RELAX AND FLOAT DOWNSTREAM

Two outstanding sources for material from the 1960s are the CD-ROM collections of the complete *San Francisco Oracle* (Berkeley, CA: Regent Press, 2005) and the searchable online archives of the *International Times*. Another essential source for my understanding of the spiritual milieu of the era is *Turn Off Your Mind* by Gary Lachman (New York: Disinformation Press, 2003).

For information on witchcraft and Wicca, I am indebted to three major works: *Drawing Down the Moon* by Margot Adler (New York: Viking, 1979), *The Triumph of the Moon* by Ronald Hutton (New York: Oxford University Press,

2001), and *Real Magic* by Isaac Bonewits (Newburyport, MA: Red Wheel/ Weiser, 1989). Other sources include *Witchcraft Today* by Gerald Gardner (New York: Citadel, 2004) and *God of the Witches* by Margaret Murray (London: Oxford University Press, 1970).

I was deeply educated by *Electric Eden: Unearthing Britain's Visionary Music* by Rob Young (London: Faber and Faber, 2011), a history of folk and British rock's folk roots, particularly in regards to Syd Barrett.

Material on Madame Blavatsky is from *Occult America* by Mitch Horowitz (New York: Bantam, 2010), and *Madame Blavatsky: The Mother of Modern Spirituality* by Gary Lachman (New York: Tarcher, 2012).

The David Thompson quote on Mark Boyle is from an article in *Sound International*, quoted at length at http://www.boylefamily.co.uk/boyle/texts/atlas_notes1.html (accessed May 8, 2014).

Many of the Beatles' press conference quotes were found at www.beatlesinterviews .org and thebeatlesbible.com.

The Paula Scher quote is found in Steven Heller, "Divinyl Inspiration," *Step Inside Design* 20, no. 6 (2004): 58–67.

John Sutherland Bonnell is quoted in "Noted Cleric Criticizes Resurgence of Spiritism," *Los Angeles Times*, February 7, 1968.

June Bolan quote is from http://www.pink-floyd.org/barrett/sydarticle.html (accessed July 1, 2014).

Quote from Wouter J. Hanegraaff is from his useful book *Western Esotericism: A Guide for the Perplexed* (London: Bloomsbury Academic, 2013).

CHAPTER 3: THE DEVIL RIDES OUT

Sources for history of the Rolling Stones came from a variety of magazines and interviews, but two books provided excellent material: *Old Gods Almost Dead: The 40-Year Odyssey of the Rolling Stones* by Stephen Davis (New York: Broadway Books, 2001) and *Up and Down with the Rolling Stones* by Tony Sanchez (London: John Blake Publishing, 2011).

On Led Zeppelin, I am indebted to *Led Zeppelin IV: 33⅓* by Erik Davis (London: Bloomsbury, 2005), *Light and Shade: Conversations with Jimmy Page* by Brad Tolinski (New York: Crown, 2012), *Led Zeppelin 1968–1980* by Keith Shadwick (Milwaukee, WI: Backbeat Books, 2005), and *Hammer of the Gods* by Stephen Davis (New York: Ballantine Books, 1986).

Aubrey Powell spoke to me over the phone about his time with Hipgnosis and working on Led Zeppelin album covers.

Material on Aleister Crowley was easy to come by, but an interview with Rodney Orpheus proved most illuminating along with material from Gary Lachman's

Aleister Crowley: Magick, Rock and Roll, and the Wickedest Man in the World (New York: Tarcher, 2014).

William Yarroll was quoted in "California Probes Rock Music 'Devil,'" *Chicago Tribune*, April 29, 1982.

Material on Anton LaVey and the Church of Satan is from articles referenced in the text as well as a phone interview with Zeena Schreck and the article "Has the Church of Satan Gone to Hell?" by Jack Boulware, *Gnosis* (Winter 1999).

Some material on Ozzy Osbourne is from "Ozzy Osbourne, Off and Rocking," *Washington Post*, April 17, 1986.

Quote about the band Heart comes from "Paying the Price of Sudden Success," *Washington Post*, October 12, 1977.

Some information on the PMRC is from the National Public Radio article "Parental Advisory Labels—The Criteria and The History," October 29, 2010.

Phil Baker quote on Dennis Wheatley is from an article in *Fortean Times* found at http://www.forteantimes.com/features/articles/2623/the_devil_rides_out.html (accessed on July 1, 2014).

CHAPTER 4: THE TREE OF LIFE

A phone interview with Arthur Brown was the source of much of the material on his music and ideas, along with the book *The God of Hellfire* by Polly Marshall (London: S.A.F. Publishing, 2006) and the article "Flame On" by Mike Barnes, *MOJO*, August 2013.

Otto quote is from *Dionysus: Myth and Cult*.

I am grateful to Nicholas Pegg for his outstanding book, *The Complete David Bowie* (London: Titan Books, 2011).

Bowie's quote about Marc Bolan is from *Blood and Glitter* by Mick Rock (London: Vision On, 2004).

Material about *Morning of the Magicians* came directly from *Morning of the Magicians* by Louis Pauwels and Jacques Bergier, trans. by Rollo Myers (New York: Stein and Day, 1964), as well as Lachman, *Turn Off Your Mind*.

Biographical and other information on William Burroughs and Brion Gysin include *William S. Burroughs* by Jennie Skerl (Boston, MA: Twayne Publishers, 1985), *The Beat Hotel: Ginsberg, Burroughs, and Corso in Paris, 1958–1963* by Barry Miles (New York: Grove Press, 2000), *Nothing Is True—Everything Is Permitted: The Life of Brion Gysin* by John Geiger (New York: Disinformation Books, 2005), and a phone interview with Genesis Breyer P-Orridge as well as a 2002 interview done with Richard Metzger, "Annihilating Reality: An Interview with Genesis Breyer P-Orridge."

The interview with P-Orridge is also the source for P-Orridge's quotes, as well as details on Throbbing Gristle and Psychic TV. Other material about the industrial scene (as well as information on goth rock) are from *Rip It Up and Start Again: Postpunk 1978–1984* by Simon Reynolds (New York: Penguin Books, 2006).

Austin Osmon Spare quote on sigils is found in *Stealing Fire from Heaven: The Rise of Modern Western Magic* by Nevill Drury (New York: Oxford University Press, 2011).

Other sources include *The Gothic: A Very Short Introduction* by Nick Groom (New York: Oxford University Press, 2012) for material on goth rock. On magic, art, and Austin Osmon Spare, I consulted *Surrealism and the Occult* by Nadia Choucha (Rochester, VT: Destiny Books, 1992) and *Stealing Fire from Heaven: The Rise of Modern Western Magic* by Nevill Drury (New York: Oxford University Press, 2011).

Some anecdotes about Killing Joke are from a phone interview with the band's bassist, Youth (Martin Glover).

Quote from Cosey Fanni Tutti is from an email interview.

Details on the meeting between David Bowie and William Burroughs were found at http://www.rollingstone.com/music/news/beat-godfather-meets-glitter-main man-19740228 (accessed July 1, 2014).

The quote "nature throwing up," regarding the music of Killing Joke is from http://www.killingjoke.org.uk/aid/articles/1987-1991/torontostar210489.html (accessed July 1, 2014). Other Killing Joke material related to the fanzine interview is from http://www.radcyberzine.com/text/non-rad/kj.81.int.html (accessed July 1, 2014).

CHAPTER 5: SPACE RITUAL

Material on Hawkwind is from *Hawkwind: Sonic Assassins* by Ian Abrahams (London: S.A.F. Publishing, 2005) and the remarkable website The Archive: a history of over thirty years of UK festivals (ukrockfestivals.com) and "Crushed Dreams: The 1970 Isle Of Wight Festival—40 Years On" by Dave Smith, posted on live4ever .uk.com, August 25, 2010 (accessed May 8, 2014).

Some Michael Moorcock information and quotes are from *London Peculiar and Other Nonfiction* by Michael Moorcock (Oakland, CA: PM Press, 2012) and from an email interview with Moorcock.

Quotes by Sun Ra are from "Interview: Sun Ra Pt. 2" by John Sinclair, *Ann Arbor Sun*, April 1967; "Sun Ra: Space Is the Place" by Andy Gill, *NME*, August 7, 1982; and "Sun Ra and His Myth-Science Arkestra" by John Sinclair, *Creem*, November 1972.

I received a complete education on the history of electronic music from *The Sound of Tomorrow: How Electronic Music Was Smuggled into the Mainstream* by Mark Brend (London: Bloomsbury, 2012) and *Electronic and Experimental Music: Technology, Music, and Culture* by Thom Holmes (New York: Scribner's, 1985).

Material on Robert Moog is from the essential 2005 documentary *Moog*, directed by Hans Fjellestad, and a phone interview with Herbert Deutsch.

Stewart Brand quote is from "Making It" by Evgeny Morozov, *The New Yorker*, January 13, 2014. Quotes by Karlheinz Stockausen are from a May 1972 lecture at the Oxford Union found at http://youtu.be/nTeLI5dUzKw.

Interview with Florian Fricke is from a 1996 interview found at http://www .eurock.com/features/florian.aspx.

Quote from Bettina Waldthausen is from an interview with Jason Gross at *Perfect Sound Forever* (www.furious.com), August 2013.

Historical details and other facts on progressive rock are *Mountains Come Out of the Sky: The Illustrated History of Prog Rock* by Will Romano (Milwaukee, WI: Backbeat Books, 2010). Anecdotes and quotes are from phone interviews with Roger Dean and Greg Lake. Some related quotes are from *Progressive Rock Reconsidered* by Kevin Holm-Hudson (New York: Routledge, 2001), *Bill Bruford: The Autobiography* by Bill Bruford (London: Jawbone Press, 2009), and "Yes" by David Laing, *Let It Rock*, February 1974.

Quotes and some information on G. I. Gurdjieff are from *Shadows of Heaven: Gurdjieff and Toomer* by Paul Beekman Taylor (Newburyport, MA: Red Wheel/ Weiser, 1998).

Quotes regarding Pierre Schaeffer from John Mowitt are from his book *Radio: Essays in Bad Reception* (Berkeley: University of California Press, 2011).

CHAPTER 6: THE GOLDEN DAWN

Henry Rollins's quote is from "How Rockers Helped Free the West Memphis Three" by Patrick Doyle, *Rolling Stone*, September 15, 2011.

Mitch Horowitz is quoted in "Jay-Z: A Master of Occult Wisdom?" National Public Radio, September 19, 2009.

Quotes on the contemporary occult scene and music are from an email interview with Raymond Salvatore Harmon and a phone interview with Stephen O'Malley. Some insights into theories around Madonna's Super Bowl appearance are from "'Ye Shall Be as Gods': Madonna's Super Bowl Occult Satanic Ritual" posted at beginningandend.com, February 8, 2012 (accessed May 8, 2014).

Papa Emeritus quotes are from "Show No Mercy: Ghost B.C." by Brandon Stosuy, pitchfork.com, April 12, 2013 (accessed May 8, 2014).

ACKNOWLEDGMENTS

First and foremost, thanks to my editor, Mitch Horowitz, for pushing me to get this just right. I had little more than an idea and he helped turn it into a book. A bigger mensch you will never meet. Of course, I wouldn't even have thought the idea any good if it wasn't for my agent, Matthew Elblonk, who has been a constant support, a kind critic, and a steadfast advocate. Thanks to the brilliant Arik Roper for the cover of my dreams. I was a fan for years, and now am proud to call him a friend.

Thanks to all the folks who contributed their time by way of interviews, suggestions, and support, including Rodney Orpheus, Robert Fripp, Arthur Brown, Greg Lake, Genesis Breyer P-Orridge, Nik Turner, Zeena Schreck, Emil Amos, Aubrey Powell, Roger Dean, Bernie Worrell, Herbert Deutsch, Bill Laswell, Stephen O'Malley, Mark Pilkington, Simon Reynolds, Raymond Salvatore Harmon, Richard Metzger, David Metcalfe, Pam Grossman, Mark Fraunfelder, Chris Bohn, and Cosey Fanni Tutti.

Special thanks to Ethan Gilsdorf, whose fellowship and writerly support were with me all the way. My deepest gratitude to Scott Korb for his rigorous editorial input, spiritual guidance, and unwavering friendship. To my dear friend Joe Gallo, for being there when it all started. And to Ezra Glenn for his loving companionship.

There are too many friends and family to name, but there are some who had a particular impact on the writing of this book, including my

Sunday night D&D group (J. P. Gluting, Michael Marano, Janaka Stucky, et al.), Seth Riskin, Amy Ross, Jim Lopez, Tony Tauber, and Tim Halle.

Thanks to my sisters, Karen Bebergal and Lisa Mead, to my fantastic extended family, Judy Ashworth and the entire Neill clan, with special fondness in my heart for Emily and Sarah. And to the memory of Byron, Ruth, and Eric Bebergal.

Thanks to my buddy and son, Sam, who offered some excellent advice, who kept me laughing, reminding me to take time to play, and who is the light of my life.

But how to thank my wife, Amy? She is my guiding star, my home, and my heart. Her humor, insight, and love kept me afloat. The poets tell of nine muses. But I will lay my flowers only at the feet of Amy.

INDEX

INDEX

INDEX

INDEX

INDEX

ABOUT THE AUTHOR

Peter Bebergal is the author of *The Faith Between Us* (with Scott Korb) and *Too Much to Dream: A Psychedelic American Boyhood*. He writes widely on the speculative and slightly fringe, and recent essays and reviews have appeared in *The Times Literary Supplement*, *Boing Boing*, *The Believer*, and *The Quietus*. He studied religion and culture at Harvard Divinity School. He lives in Cambridge, Massachusetts, with his wife and son.